The H̲ ̲ ̲ ̲ ̲ ̲ ̲ the Bas̲ ̲ ̲ ̲ ̲ ̲ es

A Study Guide

Francis Gilbert

This edition first published in 2015 by FGI publishing:
www.francisgilbert.co.uk;
fgipublishing.com
Copyright © 2015 Francis Gilbert
FGI Publishing, London UK, sir@francisgilbert.co.uk
British Library Cataloguing-in-Publications Data
A catalogue record for this book is available from the British Library.
ISBN-13: 978-1519583079

ISBN-10: 1519583079

Dedication
To Goldie, Sandy, Sindy, Champ & Bat

Acknowledgments
First, huge thanks must go to my wife, Erica Wagner, for always supporting me with my writing and teaching. Second, I'm very grateful to all the students, teachers, lecturers and other lively people who have helped me write this book.
Also by Francis Gilbert:
I'm A Teacher, Get Me Out Of Here (2004)
Teacher On The Run (2005)
Yob Nation (2006)
Parent Power (2007)
Working The System: How To Get The Very State Education For Your Child (2011)
The Last Day Of Term (2012)
Gilbert's Study Guides on: *Frankenstein, Far From The Madding Crowd, The Hound of the Baskervilles, Pride and Prejudice, The Strange Case of Dr Jekyll and Mr Hyde, The Turn of the Screw, Wuthering Heights* (2013)
Dr Jekyll & Mr Hyde: The Study Guide Edition (2014)
Romeo and Juliet: The Study Guide Edition (2014)
Charlotte Brontë's Jane Eyre: The Study Guide Edition (2015)
Austen's Pride and Prejudice: The Study Guide Edition (2015)
Mary Shelley's Frankenstein: The Study Guide Edition (2015)
The Turn of the Screw: The Study Guide Edition (2015)
The Hound of the Baskervilles: The Study Guide Edition

Contents

Introduction

This study guide takes a different approach from most other similar books. It does not seek to tell you about the story and characters in a boring, useless fashion, but attempts to show how it is the author's techniques and interests that inform every single facet of this classic novel. Most study guides simply tell you *what* is going on, and tack on bits at the end which tell you *how* the writer created suspense and drama at certain points in the book, informing you a little about *why* the writer might have done this.

This study guide starts with the *how* and the *why*, showing you right from the start *how* and *why* the writer shaped the key elements of the book.

Definition:

The context of a book is both the *world* the book creates in the reader's mind (contexts of reading), and the *world* it came out from (contexts of writing).

How to use this study guide

This study guide is deliberately interactive; it is full of questions, tasks and links to other sources of information. You will learn about *The Hound of the Baskervilles* much more effectively if you have a go at the questions and tasks set, rather than just copying out notes.

Contexts

Understanding Contexts

In order to fully appreciate a text, you need to appreciate the contexts in which it was written – known as its contexts of writing – and the contexts in which you read the book, or the contexts of reading.

This is potentially a huge area to explore because 'contexts' essentially means the 'worlds' from which the book has arisen. For the best books, these are many and various. The most obvious starting point is the writer's own life: it is worth thinking about how and why the events in a writer's life might have influenced his or her fiction. However, you do have to be careful not to assume too much. For example, Conan Doyle may have based certain elements of Sherlock Holmes upon a very influential figure in his life – the surgeon Joseph Bell -- but you must remember that Sherlock Holmes is a character in her own right in the novel – a vital cog in the narrative wheel, a literary construct and not a real person.

As a result, it is particularly fruitful to explore other contexts of writing. We can look at the broader world from which the story of *The Hound of the Baskerville* arose, the Victorian values that informed it, the details of Conan Doyle's life which shaped its language, and consider carefully how Conan Doyle both adopted and rejected the morals of his time. Other contexts might be the influence of the literary world that Conan Doyle inhabited (what other authors were writing at the time), how religion shaped his views, and so on.

Just as important as the contexts of *writing* are the contexts of *reading*: how we read the novel today. *The Hound of the Baskervilles* remains a hugely influential text; it has been made into numerous films and has been much imitated and parodied. Your own personal context is very important too. You may read this novel very differently if you are a woman or a dog-lover, or dog-hater! In order for you to fully consider the contexts of reading rather than my telling you what to think, I have posed open-ended questions that seem to me to be important when considering this issue.

Questions

What do we mean by context? Why do you need to understand the idea of context in order to write well about *The Hound of the Baskervilles*?

Useful links

This BBC Bitesize webpage refers to poetry, but is relevant for all literature, providing a good visual organizer of the relevant things to think about when talking about context:
http://www.bbc.co.uk/education/guides/z8kyg82/revision

Contexts of Writing: Conan Doyle's Life

Arthur Conan Doyle (ACD) was born in 1859, the third child and elder son of ten, in Edinburgh, Scotland; his father was a chronic alcoholic, but his mother was a lively, brilliant woman who was devoted to her son. Baptized a Catholic, funded by wealthy relatives since his father was very poor, he attended Jesuit schools in the Ribble Valley Lancashire, Hodder and Stonyhurst. Only nine at the time, he hated being sent away from his beloved mother and the repressive atmosphere of these very religious schools. His salvation was in stories – a passion he shared with his mother. Escaping from the brutality of the school in a world of fiction, he became a popular spinner of yarns with his school friends.

In 1875, he passed his London Matriculation Examination at Stonyhurst and studied for a year in a Jesuit college in Austria, following this by becoming a student of medicine at Edinburgh University. He supplemented his studies by becoming a surgeon's clerk to Joseph Bell in Edinburgh. While he was to meet many brilliant characters in Edinburgh such as the writers James Barrie and Robert Louis Stevenson, no one had such an influence on him as Bell, who many critics have come to think was a model for Sherlock Holmes; a man who prided himself on using the scientific method, deduction, rationalism, logic and diagnosis to solve problems.

In addition to working for Bell, he took a number of temporary medical assistantships at Sheffield, Salop and Birmingham and, in 1880, serving as surgeon on a whaling ship; an experience which both terrified and fascinated him, loving as he did the camaraderie on the ship. By now he regularly publishing stories and non-fiction in various journals, including an article on poison in the *British Medical Journal*. He graduated in 1881, and served as a surgeon on a steamer to West Africa, tending to a dying US Minister, who was a black abolitionist leader. Returning to England, he was briefly, more or less swindled by an unscrupulous doctor, he was involved in a failed business venture in Plymouth, but quickly established himself as a successful general practitioner at Southsea. Soon, the break-up of his family distracted him: his father was confined because of alcoholism and epilepsy, while his mother moved to Yorkshire. ACD cared for his young brother, Innes, who was a school boy and surgery page.

In 1885, having attended to John Hawkins who died of cerebral meningitis, ACD married Hawkins' sister, Louisa Hawkins and honeymooned in Ireland. The following year, the first Sherlock Holmes' story, *A Study in Scarlet* was published; his success as a writer began but it did not entirely end his medical career because in 1891 he set himself up as an eye-specialist in just off Harley Street, London. His medical career was not successful; not a single patient entered the surgery. Suffering from a terrible attack of flu, which nearly killed him, ACD emerged to realise that he had to give up his medical career and concentrate entirely upon his writing.

Fuelled by public demand, a flurry of Sherlock Holmes' short stories were written and published in the most popular literary magazines of the day such as *The Strand*. However, ACD became increasingly frustrated by his most famous literary character. In 1893, in order to free himself for 'more serious literary work', he killed off Holmes in 'The Final Problem': Sherlock Holmes and, his arch nemesis, Professor Moriarty plunged to their deaths at The Reichenbach Falls in Switzerland.Settling in Hindhead, Surrey, in an attempt to help his wife's tuberculosis, ACD wrote prolifically trying to find a subject other than Holmes but found himself inexorably drawn back to this money-spinner. In 1899, he and the actor William Gillette, who starred as Holmes for the next thirty three years, wrote a play *Sherlock Holmes*. In 1901, ACD enlisted to fight in the Boer War, to the horror of his family. Suffering from stomach complaints in Africa, he didn't see any action as an out-of-shape 40-year-old but did write a five hundred page blockbuster on the war, *The Great Boer War*, in which he highlighted the shortcomings of the British effort, showing that more soldiers died of typhoid than in battle. Demoralised and ill, he returned to England, trying and failing to establish a political career in Scotland, and then travelling to Dartmoor to research more about the prison there. It was to prove a productive visit; he quickly shaped a story about a ghostly hound, an escaped convict and a creaky manor house. But he realised that the story lacked a central protagonist. "Why should I invent such a character, when I have Sherlock Holmes?" he asked himself. And so it was that Holmes returned to the delight of his fans in serial form in *The Strand* magazine; the novella became a sensation, outselling all previous Holmes stories and selling more copies of the magazine than ever before, whilst provoking more debate about it than any of the other stories.

Yet in many ways, it is not a typical Sherlock Holmes story. Even its authorship is in some doubt. Having met Bertram Fletcher Robinson while returning on the ship *Briton* from South Africa, Doyle went on a short golfing holiday with him a little later. On one Sunday in March 1901, Robinson described an old country legend about a spectral hound; this was to provoke Doyle's trip to Dartmoor. Robinson was later to write: "One of the most interesting weeks that I ever spent was with Doyle on Dartmoor. He made the journey in my company shortly after I had told him, and he had accepted from me, a plot which eventuated in the *Hound of the Baskervilles*. Dartmoor, the great wilderness of bog and rock that cuts Devonshire at this point, appealed to his imagination." Doyle himself was to write to his mother: "Robinson and I are exploring the moor together over our Sherlock Holmes book. I think it will work splendidly – indeed I have already done nearly half of it. Holmes is at his very best, and it is a highly dramatic idea – which I owe to Robinson." Doyle neatly side-stepped the question of Holmes' death by refusing to provide a date, although some critics believe that it is most probably 1889. Others think it is definitely 'post-Reichanbachian' because Holmes is a more human character than in the earlier stories.

In 1906, ACD was grief-stricken by the death of his ailing wife, Louisa, but found solace in marrying Jean Leckie in 1907. Moving to Sussex, ACD became involved in various political causes such as stopping the Belgian oppression in the Congo, changing the divorce laws, forming a local volunteer force when war was declared in 1914 and appealing for mercy for an Irish nationalist who led the Easter Week Rising. Increasingly, he found himself treated suspiciously by the British authorities; his history of *The British Campaign in France and Flanders* was censored for its inflammatory content and implicit criticism of the war.

In 1918, ACD published *The New Revelation* in which he called himself a Spiritualist, claiming that there was a world of spirits beyond the ordinary physical world; this soon became a crusade. Between 1920-30, he toured the world attempting to convert people into believing in the after-life. This didn't stop him publishing stories about the arch-rationalist Sherlock Holmes though, with *The Complete Sherlock Holmes* being published in 1928. He died on 7th July 1930, his epitaph coming from the Sherlock Holmes' story, *The Red Circle*: "Education never ends, Watson. It is a series of lessons with the greatest for the last."

Questions

Why do you think the book might be called *The Hound of the Baskervilles*?

What events, people and ideas in Conan Doyle's life and the wider society may have influenced the writing of the story?

Useful links

The so-called "official" site for Sir Arthur Conan Doyle, which contains much about his life and writing:

http://www.arthurconandoyle.com/

The Wikipedia page is useful, but remember it can be "tampered" with:

https://en.wikipedia.org/wiki/Arthur_Conan_Doyle

The Stanford Sherlock Holmes site contains a wealth of material:

http://sherlockholmes.stanford.edu/biography.html

The Sherlockian Net is basic in layout but full of good links:

http://www.sherlockian.net/acd/

Selected Reading on Conan Doyle's Life

Arthur Conan Doyle (Author), David Stuart Davies (Introduction) *Memories and Adventures: An Autobiography* (Wordsworth Literary Lives, 1997)

Together with this illuminating introduction, this forms perhaps the best introduction to Conan Doyle's life, with the great man himself giving the account.

Hesketh Pearson (Author), Tim Pigott-Smith (Reader) *Arthur Conan Doyle: A Life (Naxos Audio) [Abridged] [Audiobook] (Audio CD)*

In this excellent audiobook biography, Pearson considers how Doyle's life is reflected in his books - including his background as a doctor, and his enduring (and public) belief in spiritualism.

Russell Miller (Author) The Adventures of Arthur Conan Doyle (Harvill Secker 2008)

This entertaining biography is very good on the emergence of Holmes as a literary figure who would dominate Doyle's life

Contexts of Reading

We read this story very differently now than it was read at the time. Some parts of the story still retain their power to shock; the horrific description of the hound and the way it attacks Sir Hugo, Sir Henry and Stapleton still sends shivers down the spine. Perhaps, the dog has become a more menacing symbol than it was then: recent concern about "dangerous dogs" has meant that we don't quite see dogs as very cuddly creatures. Moreover, recent controversies about hunting and its subsequent ban in the UK countryside mean that the hound remains a symbol for the upper classes. Furthermore, the hound is still an emblem for pure savagery, mindless violence, while its piercing cry still scares us. In this sense, the story still carries its full freight of horror.

However, what was considered then to be highly risqué explorations of sex now seem rather tame. Stapleton's dalliance with Laura Lyons and his violent marriage are not as shocking to us as they were then. Nevertheless, Doyle mined a theme which has gained in significance with the passing years: that of men's brutal treatment of women. Throughout the story, women are presented as the victims of male violence: 'Miss Stapleton' is brutally tied up at the end of the story, and Laura Lyons is brutally betrayed not only by her first husband but by her false fiancée.

However, this is a detective story and issues like this are never fully explored and only hinted at. But again, the story has modern pertinence; Holmes' fallibility has a peculiarly modern ring to it. He is not the all-seeing, all-knowing God of the short stories of the previous century. The combination of his absence for much of the story and his fear at the end that he has failed makes the modern reader more sympathetic towards him; there is an Inspector Morse-like quality to him in this story. An atmosphere of mournful regret, of loss – a sense that nothing can be the same again after this adventure.

The story doesn't even have the closure of a Victorian narrative: the story ends with Sir Henry deeply traumatised by the events and possibly unable to recover, and the murderer has mysteriously disappeared into the mire, never heard of but never certainly dead. While solving the mystery of the hound, Doyle leaves much to the readers' imagination. In particular, the character of Stapleton is left more or less unexplained. We learn that he is, in fact, a Baskerville, but his manifest intelligence, his sexual predilections, the mysteries of his marriage and his engagement to Laura Lyons are not entirely 'wrapped up'. He is, without doubt, the most interesting villain to emerge in any of the Sherlock Holmes stories. Unlike Professor Moriaty, Stapleton is not a true psychotic, a pure embodiment of evil; he is presented as revengeful, embittered, troubled in his relationships, but he is also highly educated, charming, inquisitive and very attractive to women.

Questions

It is worth doing some work on contexts before starting the actual book. I would suggest you write a *Hound of the Baskervilles* **learning journal** that records all your thoughts and feelings about the book. Records the truth! After reading the book once, we will then look at academic responses but on the first reading we will really focus upon your thoughts about it.

There are two major questions to consider when thinking about contexts: where is the book coming from and where am I coming from?

The first question is best answered while reading the book; what sorts of values and ideas are enshrined in this book? What is its historical context? What is its literary context? What is its philosophical context? How does the book relate to the life of the author?

It is worth you trying to analyse where you are coming from. Everyone holds a set of assumptions and ideas that profoundly affects how he or she sees the world. Try and answer these questions:

What are your attitudes towards detectives and detective stories? What are your favourite detective/crime stories and why? Who are your favourite detectives and why?

Why are so many detective stories, particularly old fashioned ones, full of men? What is the position of women in these stories?

What are your attitudes towards ghosts? Do you believe they are real?

What are your attitudes towards animals, like hounds?

What does innocence mean to you? Do you think innocent people can be corrupted? If so, how and why? If not, why?

Useful links

You can find links on this Wikipedia page to more information about all the filmed versions of the story:

https://en.wikipedia.org/wiki/The_Hound_of_the_Baskervill es_(disambiguation)

This Wikipedia page is devoted to the modernized version of *The Hound of the Baskervilles* with Benedict Cumberbatch. It's worth looking at how cleverly the story was updated:

https://en.wikipedia.org/wiki/The_Hounds_of_Baskerville

Mark Gatiss's article on how he adapted the story for TV is useful:

http://www.radiotimes.com/news/2012-01-08/mark-gatiss-on-writing-the-hounds-of-baskerville

This BBC website has links to all things Sherlock:

http://www.bbc.co.uk/cult/sherlock/

Now onto the text

What are the vital ingredients of a story? Why is that we are able to believe that a "whole load of words" contain a new world?

Now jot down your expectations about *The Hound of the Baskervilles*. What kind of book do you expect it to be?

Write/sketch/spider-diagram what you think the story will be. Write out how you think it will be structured. What will be the main events of the story? Who will be the main characters and why?

While reading the novel, look back over the notes you have made for this section and constantly ask yourself; how does my context affect the way I read the novel and feel/think about the characters/situations/themes? I have already suggested that you write a learning journal as you read it through, jotting down these thoughts as you go along. Then once you have finished reading, think about the novel's overall effects and how it speaks to you personally.

Why do you think *The Hound of the Baskervilles* is such a popular novel today? Why have so many films/plays/operas etc. been made of it?

Structure and Theme

As with most detective stories, the narrative is structured around the theme of murder. In this case, a possible murder has taken place and another one looks likely to take place. Doyle's story is unusual amongst many of the Sherlock Holmes stories because he has elongated his traditional narrative -- usually a Holmes story was no more than thirty or forty pages. Here, he extends his central theme to embrace and explore other themes often attached to those of murder: deceit, sexual intrigue, inheritance. Moreover, he also develops a theme which is present in some Holmes' stories but never as fully explored as here: that of the supernatural.

Opening: The establishment of the central problem within the London setting; Holmes and Watson learn of Sir Charles Baskerville's suspicious death from Dr Mortimer and believe that Sir Henry Baskerville, fresh off the boat from Canada, is the next candidate.

Complications: Dr Watson, without Holmes at Baskerville Hall, reports back on the possible suspects, learning more about Sir Charles and his death. A cast of suspects is properly developed: Barrymore and his wife, Selden, the psychopath loose on the moor, the botanist Stapleton and his sister, Miss Stapleton, the litigious Mr Frankland and the embittered, poverty-stricken Laura Lyons.

Crisis: Holmes re-appears and informs Watson that Stapleton is married to his supposed sister. Selden is found dead on the moor in Sir Henry's clothing. Laura Lyons learns that Stapleton was married. Holmes pretends to leave for London but returns.

Climax: Holmes, Watson and Lestrade rescue Sir Henry from the hound on the moor. They discover the truth about the supernatural hound and find Mrs Stapleton imprisoned at Merripit House. Stapleton, now discovered to be a Baskerville, disappears into the Grimpen Mire.

Resolution: Holmes explains how and why Stapleton was motivated to murder. Sir Henry attempts to convalesce. There is a deep sense of loss and foreboding at the end of the story.

Useful links to help you get to know the novel better

The following websites are useful because they can give you a strong overview of the novel, but you really do need to think for yourself regarding your opinions of the novel.

http://www.sparknotes.com/lit/hound/summary.html
http://www.shmoop.com/hound-of-the-baskervilles/summary.html
http://www.gradesaver.com/the-hound-of-the-baskervilles/study-guide/summary

The following quizzes are useful to test your knowledge of the story as well:

http://www.gradesaver.com/the-hound-of-the-baskervilles/study-guide/quiz1
http://www.sparknotes.com/lit/hound/quiz.html
http://www.shmoop.com/hound-of-the-baskervilles/quotes-quiz.html

You can find a very simple summary here for struggling readers:

http://www.penguinreaders.com/pdf/downloads/pr/teachers-notes/9781405879934.pdf

Quiz questions here:

http://www.penguinreaders.com/pdf/downloads/pr/activity-worksheets/9781405879934.pdf

Answers are here:

http://penguin.longmanhomeusa.com/content/9781405862486_AK.pdf

There is a help sheet for teachers here, but also useful for anyone looking at the novel:

http://www.pearsonelt.ch/download/media/9780582419292_FS.pdf

Questions/tasks

Once you have read the book, ask yourself this question: to what extent is the novella a successful story? What are its exciting moments and why? Are there moments when the story feels less successful? Give reasons for your answers. Compare one or two filmed versions with the novel; what events/characters/ideas do the film-makers use and what do they leave out, and why?

The Influence of Genre

The emergence of the detective story and the influence of the Gothic

As with many other Sherlock Holmes' stories, the influence of the Gothic is paramount: the setting of creepy Baskerville Hall, the blasted Dartmoor, and the role of the ghostly hound could have been lifted directly from a Gothic novel. These novels, which evolved as very popular potboilers in the eighteen century, followed a set format: a heroine was usually lured by an unscrupulous villain to a haunted castle or old house and terrified out of her wits, only to be rescued, at the end of the narrative, by a handsome hero from the villain's clutches. Invariably, all the ghosts and ghouls she had to suffer at the hands of would turn out to be wicked illusions generated by the villain.

In this sense, Stapleton fits the pattern of the Gothic villain. He is presented as sexually rapacious in the same way as many Gothic antagonists; imprisoning his wife and falsely enticing Laura Lyons into an engagement. His hound is similar to many supernatural elements in Gothic novels: the ghost is revealed at the end as being very real and merely a way for the villain to accomplish murder.

However, it is Doyle's blending of the emerging genre of the detective story with the Gothic which makes this story so interesting. He uses many elements of the Gothic but shoehorns them into the format of a detective story, which as we have seen follows a very set format itself. The blending of the detective story with the Gothic means that Doyle dispenses with many of the excesses of the Gothic: rather than having many ghouls and ghosties, he opts for one and concentrates all his verbal energies in generating a real sense of menace around it. In order for there to be a real sense of threat, he removes Sherlock Holmes from the narrative because he is the one character the reader knows is invulnerable, and uses the voice of Watson, speaking from the lonely crucible of the moor, to bring a genuine atmosphere of fear and danger. While Doyle explores the plight of damsels in distress – a habit of the Gothic – he keeps the hysterics very muted: Laura Lyons' discovery that she has been betrayed by Stapleton is not melodramatic, but pathetic and sad.

In such a way, we see Doyle re-writing the rules of the detective story, which he himself had invented over a decade before; he leaves the certainties of the 'perfect' detective story behind, where all mysteries are solved, and introduces a new type of detective story, a narrative in which investigating psychological issues is more important than solving the case. The trauma that Watson, Sir Henry, Laura Lyons and Stapleton's wife suffer at the hands of the unscrupulous, avaricious Stapleton is more striking than Holmes' bringing the case to a close. The dark, terrifying atmosphere of the moor and the hound infect the resolution of the book: this is a new type of detective story, a narrative laced with the genuine menace of the Gothic and informed by a new 20th century fascination with the psychological.

Questions for Genre

How was Conan Doyle influenced by other writers and genres in the writing of the story? Where did he get his ideas for his characters from?

Useful links

The British Library website on the story is informative:
http://www.bl.uk/romantics-and-victorians/articles/an-introduction-to-the-hound-of-the-baskervilles
These websites are also useful:
http://www.shmoop.com/hound-of-the-baskervilles/genre.html
I thought this Prezi was nicely designed and interesting too:
https://prezi.com/xvmkfjnii_ad/theme-and-setting-in-the-hound-of-the-baskervilles/

Critical Perspectives

Is *The Hound of the Baskervilles* the first modern detective story?

As we have already seen, *The Hound of the Baskervilles* plays around with the genres of the Gothic and the detective story in fascinating ways to create a truly "psychological" detective story, a plot in which it is the psychologies of the villain, the victims and the detectives which plays a leading role. Moreover, there is a deep-rooted pessimism in the story which has led some critics to note that this is the first truly modern detective story in that the detective is not presented as the omniscient being of many Victorian detective stories. Holmes is a haunted, troubled and largely absent figure in the story, plagued by a deep-rooted sense that he has made mistakes and incurred a real cost in uncovering the murderer.

The novel lends itself to a number of other readings. In particular, a feminist reading of the book might examine the way the women are presented in the story. In all cases, they are shown to be the victims of male brutality: even Mrs Barrymore is the victim of her brother Selden's psychosis, inexorably drawn to provide succour for him even though she knows it is wrong. In the case of Laura Lyons and Stapleton's wife we see two intelligent and beautiful women dragged down into the pit of immorality by their need, both psychological and physical, to have men at their sides. In the case of 'Miss Stapleton' we see how Doyle highlights one of the major injustices of the age: the difficulty of women to obtain a divorce from a reluctant husband. A few years later, Doyle would for the divorce laws to be changed.

Related to a feminist reading might be a Marxist interpretation of the novel; in many ways the novel could be read as a parable of the old and new worlds of the ruling classes being at war with one another. Sir Henry, coming as he does could represent the new world order across the Atlantic, with his psychological simplicity, his thirst to possess what he sees as his inheritance, while Stapleton could represent the old order, the 'true' aristocrat: he looks and acts most like his ancestor, the wicked Sir Hugo. But Stapleton for all his brilliance and sophistication of mind is corrupt, immoral, and murderous. He is an embodiment of the dying aristocracy of England, while Sir Henry is a representative of new blood. The new order triumphs and Sir Henry, with the help of Holmes, defeats the old Baskerville line, but at a cost: he is, at the end of the story, nearly broken by the experience. In such a way, we could interpret the story as Doyle's parable of the British aristocracy just before the First World War: a society riven by divisions and psychological problems.

On a deeper, more metaphorical level, the story could be interpreted as a parable about the human mind. The story is full of 'archetypes', symbols which are universal in all cultures: there is the wise man in the form of Holmes, Watson is possibly the fool, Stapleton is a version of the devil and his hound is his agent of evil, the Grimpen Mire and Dartmoor represents the untamed horror of nature, while Baskerville Hall is a version of the threatened, endangered home. On one level, the story is about these archetypal elements going to war with each other. The story is satisfying because it does tap into these archetypal symbols.

There is another interpretation which is that the story is a parable about the process of creativity: in this scenario, Holmes represents the creative artist, constructing his narrative by investigating the world around him but constantly being challenged with new facts, new images, new symbols in the form of the characters and the settings. It is only when he strings them into a coherent narrative at the very end of the story that he manages to provide the solution – which we read in the last chapter. The last chapter in this sense is the first chapter, the chapter that enabled Doyle to start writing the book from the beginning. Once Doyle had found the solution, he could thread together an enjoyable narrative for us to read.

Selected Reading & weblinks on Conan Doyle's writing and *The Hound of the Baskervilles*

Shmoop has a good section on the literary devices used in the story:
http://www.shmoop.com/hound-of-the-baskervilles/literary-devices.html
David C. Humphrey *Sir Hugo's Literary Companion: A Compendium of the Writings of Hugo's Companions*, Chicago On the Subject of Mr. Sherlock Holmes (iUniverse.com 2007)
A compendium of essential essays on Sherlock Holmes, including ones on The Hound of the Baskervilles
Robert F. Fleissner (Author) *Shakespearean and Other Literary Investigations with the Master Sleuth (and Conan Doyle): Homing in on Holmes* (Studies in British Literature) (Edward Mellen Press Ltd 2003) This work presents some major influences on Sir Arthur Conan Doyle (especially Shakespeare), but also deals with the influence of Doyle on others, notably T.S. Eliot. Other essays deal with onomastics, religion, and race.

Questions

What differing views do literary critics have of the novella? Which critics do you most agree with and why? Which ones do you agree with the least and why?

Part 2: Extracts & tasks

How to read and study the novel

What follows are extracts from *The Hound of the Baskervilles* interspersed with commentaries and questions on the text. I have deliberately provided a variety of different question types at the ends of chapters; I have started with "simple" comprehension questions and then moved onto more analytical and creative questions, which not only require you to understand the plot but also arrive at your own personal responses, using evidence from the text to back up your points. The GCSE/A Level questions that follow the comprehension ones are more difficult and don't usually have "right and wrong" answers. The answers to the comprehension questions can be found in the **Answers to the questions** section. The GCSE style questions are the sorts of questions you might typically get in a GCSE exam; the same is true for the A Level questions, which usually invite students to show they have read more and are able to compare and contrast texts in depth. Please interpret the categories of GCSE/A Level in a relaxed fashion: have a go at the exercises which will help you rather than rigidly sticking to the exercises that are "your level". The categories are only rough guidelines. I sometimes ask you to devise a visual organiser to represent ideas/characters/plot-lines in the novel; this means doing a spider-diagram/chart/flow diagram etc. depending upon what you feel is most relevant. To find out more (sometimes known as graphic organisers) look here:

https://www.teachingenglish.org.uk/article/graphic-organisers

Remember if you are uncertain about the plot, you can also refer to the websites listed in the section **'Useful links to help you get to know the story better'**. These websites are good at helping you understand the plot but they won't help you get the higher marks because you really need to think for yourself if you are going to get the top grades.

As I have suggested, you could, while reading the book, put all your answers, notes, creative responses together into a *Hound of the Baskervilles* file or **learning journal**. You could be creative with this file: draw scenes of the important incidents; include spider-diagrams/visual organisers of significant characters and situations; storyboards of the key scenes; copies of articles/literary criticism which you have annotated; creative pieces etc.

Helpful vocabulary to learn before you start reading

While reading the book, **you should keep a vocabulary list**, writing down the difficult words and learning their meanings/spellings, and possibly using the vocabulary in your own writing. The complex vocabulary and sentence structures in the story can be off-putting at first but I feel you should not be put off by the language; embrace it, love it! You will become much better educated when you learn the vocabulary. This is why reading pre-20th century writing is so useful: it makes you more intelligent because you widen your vocabulary and ability to understand difficult passages.

There are some words, I would strongly advise you looking up the meanings of and learning their spellings/meanings before reading; the websites listed below are helpful in this regard.

Weblinks to help you learn difficult vocabulary

The flashcards on Quizlet.com are very helpful in assisting you with learning the difficult vocabulary in the book:

https://quizlet.com/2400874/the-hound-of-the-baskervilles-chapter-1-vocabulary-flash-cards/

There is also a chapter by chapter list of the difficult vocabulary here:

http://www.brighthubeducation.com/homework-help-literature/38980-hound-of-the-baskervilles-vocabulary-and-study-questions/

Verbal Workout has lists too:

http://www.verbalworkout.com/b/b1076.htm

Extracts from *The Hound of the Baskervilles*

By Arthur Conan Doyle

Chapter 1. Mr. Sherlock Holmes

Extract

"Interesting, though elementary," said he as he returned to his favourite corner of the settee. "There are certainly one or two indications upon the stick. It gives us the basis for several deductions."

"Has anything escaped me?" I asked with some self-importance. "I trust that there is nothing of consequence which I have overlooked?"

"I am afraid, my dear Watson, that most of your conclusions were erroneous. When I said that you stimulated me I meant, to be frank, that in noting your fallacies I was occasionally guided towards the truth. Not that you are entirely wrong in this instance. The man is certainly a country practitioner. And he walks a good deal."

"Then I was right."

"To that extent."

"But that was all."

"No, no, my dear Watson, not all—by no means all."

Analysis: As with all the Sherlock Holmes' stories, the great detective stands in strong contrast to his hapless companion, Dr Watson. However, Doyle is careful not to present Watson as a total buffoon as we see in the above extract: Watson is able to deduce what we the reader might be able to from Dr Mortimer's walking stick. Holmes' corrections of Dr Watson's observations serve to remind us of the detective amazing powers of 'deduction'. The modern reader, too familiar with these 'clever-clever' deductions of Holmes may find that Holmes comes across a little too much as a 'know-it-all'; it must be remembered though that the readers, less familiar with what have become well-worn conventions of the detective genre, would have been delighted by them, thrilled by the return of Holmes, who was believed to be dead. Overall, it is a successful opening to the story:

light-hearted, suggestive and, ultimately, symbolic. The walking stick is a symbol for "traversing the moor". The reader is dimly aware that we will be crossing the dark moor of murderous human intent during the story.

Discussion point: To what extent is this a successful opening to the story? What do you think of Doyle's presentation of Holmes?

Extract

"It certainly seems probable."

"Now, you will observe that he could not have been on the staff of the hospital, since only a man well-established in a London practice could hold such a position, and such a one would not drift into the country. What was he, then? If he was in the hospital and yet not on the staff he could only have been a house-surgeon or a house-physician—little more than a senior student. And he left five years ago—the date is on the stick. So your grave, middle-aged family practitioner vanishes into thin air, my dear Watson, and there emerges a young fellow under thirty, amiable, unambitious, absent-minded, and the possessor of a favourite dog, which I should describe roughly as being larger than a terrier and smaller than a mastiff."

Analysis: Doyle's narrative constantly operates by building the reader's expectations with Watson's narrative and having them under-cut by both Holmes' actions and comments, and the events themselves. This is a typical example of this: Watson believes Dr Mortimer to be a "grave" character, but we learn he is actually an "amiable" one from Holmes. Furthermore, this extract shows Doyle's propensity for setting up clues and themes that thread the whole story – a typical convention of the detective genre. Here, it is the theme of 'dogs', which are central to the narrative.

Discussion point: Why are dogs so important in this narrative?

Extract

"Glad to meet you, sir. I have heard your name mentioned in connection with that of your friend. You interest me very much, Mr. Holmes. I had hardly expected so dolichocephalic a skull or such well-marked supra-orbital development. Would you have any objection to my running my finger along your parietal fissure? A cast of your skull, sir, until the original is available, would be an ornament to any anthropological museum. It is not my intention to be fulsome, but I confess that I covet your skull."

Sherlock Holmes waved our strange visitor into a chair. "You are an enthusiast in your line of thought, I perceive, sir, as I am in mine," said he.

"I observe from your forefinger that you make your own cigarettes. Have no hesitation in lighting one."

The man drew out paper and tobacco and twirled the one up in the other with surprising dexterity. He had long, quivering fingers as agile and restless as the antennae of an insect.

Holmes was silent, but his little darting glances showed me the interest which he took in our curious companion. "I presume, sir," said he at last, "that it was not merely for the purpose of examining my skull that you have done me the honour to call here last night and again today?"

"No, sir, no; though I am happy to have had the opportunity of doing that as well. I came to you, Mr. Holmes, because I recognized that I am myself an unpractical man and because I am suddenly confronted with a most serious and extraordinary problem.

Analysis: Mortimer's observation of the shape of Holmes' skull introduces a theme that runs throughout the story: that of using people's appearances to analyse their psychologies. The tone here is dryly comic, pseudo-scientific, and dispassionate. Having established Mortimer as a relatively unemotional, amiable man, Doyle now is able to deliver the lines that are essential for any detective story 'I am suddenly confronted with a most serious and extraordinary problem.' The adjective 'extraordinary' is important here because this is what Holmes' specialises in; the extraordinary, not the mundane. We are leaving the realm of the 'realistic' crime story and entering a different place: a world of swirling mists, of spectral hounds, of ancient curses and ingenious murder.

Discussion point: The belief that criminals and geniuses can now be diagnosed by the shape of their skulls is now utterly discredited. Does this affect our appreciation of the story?

Questions

What do Watson and Holmes believe can be deduced from Dr. Mortimer's walking stick?

How does Watson find out Holmes is right?

How does Holmes know Mortimer is, in fact, visiting?

Why has Mortimer come to Holmes?

What interests Mortimer about Holmes?

GCSE style question: how effective is this as an opening to a detective story?

A Level style question: compare and contrast this opening with the opening with another detective story.

Creative response: plan out a murder mystery, making sure you work out the ending first (this is what most crime writers do), and then work backwards, thinking how you can have a detective slowly discovering the relevant clues. Give it 10 sections/chapters. Reflect upon how good detective stories are structured. You can find more help on planning a

detective   story   here:
**http://www.scholastic.com/teachers/sites/default/files/asset/fil
e/janplanmystery.pdf**

Chapter 2. The Curse of the Baskervilles

Extract

Dr. Mortimer turned the manuscript to the light and read in a high, cracking voice the following curious, old-world narrative:

"Of the origin of the Hound of the Baskervilles there have been many statements, yet as I come in a direct line from Hugo Baskerville, and as I had the story from my father, who also had it from his, I have set it down with all belief that it occurred even as is here set forth. And I would have you believe, my sons, that the same Justice which punishes sin may also most graciously forgive it, and that no ban is so heavy but that by prayer and repentance it may be removed. Learn then from this story not to fear the fruits of the past, but rather be circumspect in the future, that those foul passions whereby our family has suffered so grievously may not again be loosed to our undoing.

"Know then that in the time of the Great Rebellion (the history of which by the learned Lord Clarendon I most earnestly commend to your attention) this Manor of Baskerville was held by Hugo of that name, nor can it be gainsaid that he was a most wild, profane, and godless man. This, in truth, his neighbours might have pardoned, seeing that saints have never flourished in those parts, but there was in him a certain wanton and cruel humour which made his name a by-word through the West. It chanced that this Hugo came to love (if, indeed, so dark a passion may be known under so bright a name) the daughter of a yeoman who held lands near the Baskerville estate. But the young maiden, being discreet and of good repute, would ever avoid him, for she feared his evil name. So it came to pass that one Michaelmas this Hugo, with five or six of his idle and wicked companions, stole down upon the farm and carried off the maiden, her father and brothers being from home, as he well knew. When they had brought her to the Hall the maiden was placed in an upper chamber, while Hugo and his friends sat down to a long carouse, as was their nightly custom. Now, the poor lass upstairs was like to have her wits turned at the singing and shouting and terrible oaths which came up to her from below, for they say that the words used by Hugo Baskerville, when he was in wine, were such as might blast the man who said them. At last in the stress of her fear she did that which might have daunted the bravest or most active man, for by the aid of the growth of ivy which covered (and still covers) the south wall she came down from under the eaves, and so homeward across the moor, there being three leagues betwixt the Hall and her father's farm.

Analysis: The ancient manuscript which recounts the legend of the Baskervilles suggests sexual violence: the maiden is imprisoned in the upper chamber in order to be raped by Hugo Baskerville. Again, we see Doyle setting up a key theme and motif of the story. It is hinted that Stapleton is guilty of such a crime himself. This is typical of the Gothic genre, which the story owes a considerable debt to; the rapacious, sexual libertine. Doyle cleverly evokes the antique nature of the curse through his use of archaic lexis such as 'long carouse' and 'betwixt'. Having Mortimer read the text is another master stroke: this stolid, ordinary doctor believes there is substance in it.

Discussion point: How does the manuscript set up the tone and tenor of the story to come?

Extract

The moon was shining bright upon the clearing, and there in the centre lay the unhappy maid where she had fallen, dead of fear and of fatigue. But it was not the sight of her body, nor yet was it that of the body of Hugo Baskerville lying near her, which raised the hair upon the heads of these three dare-devil roysterers, but it was that, standing over Hugo, and plucking at his throat, there stood a foul thing, a great, black beast, shaped like a hound, yet larger than any hound that ever mortal eye has rested upon. And even as they looked the thing tore the throat out of Hugo Baskerville, on which, as it turned its blazing eyes and dripping jaws upon them, the three shrieked with fear and rode for dear life, still screaming, across the moor. One, it is said, died that very night of what he had seen, and the other twain were but broken men for the rest of their days.

Analysis: There is real horror in the way that the hound 'tore the throat out of Hugo Baskerville', a furious beast of divine retribution it appears. The hound is presented here a punishment for Hugo's crimes.

Discussion point: This description establishes real elements of horror in the story. How and why does Doyle do this?

Extract

"Such is the tale, my sons, of the coming of the hound which is said to have plagued the family so sorely ever since. If I have set it down it is because that which is clearly known hath less terror than that which is but hinted at and guessed. Nor can it be denied that many of the family have been unhappy in their deaths, which have been sudden, bloody, and mysterious. Yet may we shelter ourselves in the infinite goodness of Providence, which would not forever punish the innocent beyond that third or fourth generation which is threatened in Holy Writ. To that Providence, my sons, I hereby commend you, and I counsel you by way of caution to forbear from crossing the moor in those dark hours when the powers of evil are exalted.

"[This from Hugo Baskerville to his sons Rodger and John, with instructions that they say nothing thereof to their sister Elizabeth.]"

When Dr. Mortimer had finished reading this singular narrative he pushed his spectacles up on his forehead and stared across at Mr. Sherlock Holmes. The latter yawned and tossed the end of his cigarette into the fire.
"Well?" said he.
"Do you not find it interesting?"
"To a collector of fairy tales."

Analysis:
Holmes' forthright response is funny and draws a laugh from the reader, but possibly not from the author, who was himself a collector of fairy tales and great believer in the supernatural. His fictional creation's supreme rationalism troubled Doyle and possibly explains the love/hate relationship he had with Holmes; spending most of his writing life unsuccessfully to kill him off. Your own attitudes towards the supernatural will profoundly affect your reading of the story, which, for all its underlying logic, has many mysterious elements.

Discussion point:
Does the modern reader have more sympathy for Holmes' faith in rationalism than readers during Doyle's time?

Extract

"One fact which has not been explained is the statement   of Barrymore that his master's footprints altered their character from the time that he passed the moor-gate, and that he appeared from thence onward to have been walking upon his toes. One Murphy, a gipsy horse-dealer, was on the moor at no great distance at the time, but he appears by his own confession to have been the worse for drink. He declares that he heard cries but is unable to state from what direction they came. No signs of violence were to be discovered upon Sir Charles's person, and though the doctor's evidence pointed to an almost incredible facial distortion—so great that Dr. Mortimer refused at first to believe that it was indeed his friend and patient who lay before him—it was explained that that is a symptom which is not unusual in cases of dyspnoea and death from cardiac exhaustion.   This explanation was borne out by the post-mortem examination, which showed long-standing organic disease, and the coroner's jury returned a verdict in accordance with the medical evidence.

It is well that this is so, for it is obviously of the utmost importance that Sir Charles's heir should settle at the Hall and continue the good work which has been so sadly interrupted. Had the prosaic finding of the coroner not finally put an end to the romantic stories which have been whispered in connection with the affair, it might have been difficult to find a tenant for Baskerville Hall. It is understood that the next of kin is Mr. Henry Baskerville, if he be still alive, the son of Sir Charles Baskerville's younger brother. The young man when last heard of was in America, and inquiries are being instituted with a view to informing him of his good fortune."

Analysis: Here we have the heart of the mystery of the story: the death of Sir Charles' Baskerville. The prevailing atmosphere of Gothic horror and gloom deeply affect our interpretation of his death, which, on first reading, appears to be 'natural'. However, Doyle adept at writing detective stories knows that there is no such thing as a natural death in a Sherlock Holmes' story and whets the reader's appetite to know more by using the phrase 'incredible facial distortion'. We immediately feel that the poor man has died of shock; Doyle builds horror here by not providing us with more details.

Discussion point: How successful is Doyle in creating a real sense of mystery here?

Extract

"Within the last few months it became increasingly plain to me that Sir Charles's nervous system was strained to the breaking point. He had taken this legend which I have read you exceedingly to heart—so much so that, although he would walk in his own grounds, nothing would induce him to go out upon the moor at night. Incredible as it may appear to you, Mr. Holmes, he was honestly convinced that a dreadful fate overhung his family, and certainly the records which he was able to give of his ancestors were not encouraging. The idea of some ghastly presence constantly haunted him, and on more than one occasion he has asked me whether I had on my medical journeys at night ever seen any strange creature or heard the baying of a hound. The latter question he put to me several times, and always with a voice which vibrated with excitement.

"I can well remember driving up to his house in the evening some three weeks before the fatal event. He chanced to be at his hall door. I had descended from my gig and was standing in front of him, when I saw his eyes fix themselves over my shoulder and stare past me with an expression of the most dreadful horror. I whisked round and had just time to catch a glimpse of something which I took to be a large black calf passing at the head of the drive. So excited and alarmed was he that I was compelled to go down to the spot where the animal had been and look around for it. It was gone, however, and the incident appeared to make the worst impression upon his mind.

Analysis: Dr Mortimer's sighting of the hound corroborates for us that the legend has real truth and is not a myth. Notice though how Doyle is careful not to reveal the hound in full at this point; like a magician who saves his best trick until last, Doyle only shows the reader the dog in its full horrific glory at the end of the story.

Discussion point: Why do we only enjoy a glimpse of the dog here?

Extract

"Footprints?"

"Footprints."

"A man's or a woman's?"

Dr. Mortimer looked strangely at us for an instant, and his voice sank almost to a whisper as he answered.

"Mr. Holmes, they were the footprints of a gigantic hound!"

Analysis: Doyle shifts from deploying long chunks of first person narrative to quick-fire questions from Holmes; there is a notable shift in tone in the narrative, moving as it does from substantial, atmosphere explanation to dramatic, urgent interrogation. Holmes' forthrightness could be construed as rudeness and very much the antithesis to the polite Victorian gentleman. The footprints are a detail which appear to contradict the supernatural qualities of the hound.

Discussion point: How does Doyle generate suspense in his use of Holmes' cross-questioning?

Questions

Where does Dr Mortimer live?

What story does the document tell? What does Holmes think of the story? Why does the newspaper story interest Holmes more? Why is Mortimer concerned about the death?

GCSE style question: how does Doyle create a sense of intrigue and mystery with the story of Sir Hugo and the hound?

A Level style question: compare and contrast the story of the hound with other similar supernatural stories.

Creative response: write your own "old" legend about a murderous ghost, setting it in an area where you live.

Chapter 3. The Problem

Extract

"Since the tragedy, Mr. Holmes, there have come to my ears several incidents which are hard to reconcile with the settled order of Nature."

"For example?"

"I find that before the terrible event occurred several people had seen a creature upon the moor which corresponds with this Baskerville demon, and which could not possibly be any animal known to science. They all agreed that it was a huge creature, luminous, ghastly, and spectral. I have cross-examined these men, one of them a hard-headed countryman, one a farrier, and one a moorland farmer, who all tell the same story of this dreadful apparition, exactly corresponding to the hell-hound of the legend. I assure you that there is a reign of terror in the district, and that it is a hardy man who will cross the moor at night."

"And you, a trained man of science, believe it to be supernatural?"

"I do not know what to believe."

Holmes shrugged his shoulders. "I have hitherto confined my investigations to this world," said he. "In a modest way I have combated evil, but to take on the Father of Evil himself would, perhaps, be too ambitious a task. Yet you must admit that the footmark is material."

Analysis: This is a rare moment when Holmes appears to accept that there may be a 'supernatural' realm; a strange moment when he appears to accept that there is not a rational explanation for everything. However, Holmes undercuts his own speculations with some wry irony: "In a modest way I have combated evil, but to take on the Father of Evil himself would, perhaps, be too ambitious a task." Holmes does not rule out the possibility that he could take on the devil but suggests that it might be "too ambitious". The following sentence creates a real sense of antithesis: "Yet you must admit that the footmark is material". From reflecting upon the possibility of battling with Lucifer, Holmes now returns to the small specifics of the case, the "footmark", which seems to indicate there is a real hound.

Discussion point: Doyle revels in creating mystery around the hound here. How and why does he do this?

Extract

"None. The only other kinsman whom we have been able to trace was Rodger Baskerville, the youngest of three brothers of whom poor Sir Charles was the elder. The second brother, who died young, is the father of this lad Henry. The third, Rodger, was the black sheep of the family. He came of the old masterful Baskerville strain and was the very image, they tell me, of the family picture of old Hugo. He made England too hot to hold him, fled to Central America, and died there in 1876 of yellow fever. Henry is the last of the Baskervilles. In one hour and five minutes I meet him at Waterloo Station. I have had a wire that he arrived at Southampton this morning. Now, Mr. Holmes, what would you advise me to do with him?"

"Why should he not go to the home of his fathers?"

"It seems natural, does it not? And yet, consider that every Baskerville who goes there meets with an evil fate. I feel sure that if Sir Charles could have spoken with me before his death he would have warned me against bringing this, the last of the old race, and the heir to great wealth, to that deadly place. And yet it cannot be denied that the prosperity of the whole poor, bleak countryside depends upon his presence. All the good work which has been done by Sir Charles will crash to the ground if there is no tenant of the Hall."

Analysis: As with Agatha Christie, some critics say that Doyle spoils his narratives by not releasing all the crucial clues: here we do not learn that Rodger had a son, which, of course, is vital for the purposes of the narrative. However, this would be to miss the spirit of the Sherlock Holmes' story: the reader's belief in Holmes' genius is an act of faith, a suspension of disbelief throughout. Holmes is, in fact, more in the position of the author, the creator of his own reality, a character who can create his own explanations and truth by revealing them to other characters. We have to accept this is the case otherwise the story becomes absurdly implausible. Perhaps the most interesting element of this narrative is that Holmes is often denied by Doyle full access to the truth until the very end. In other stories, Holmes is smugger; clearly in full possession of the narrative before any of the other characters. Note also how Holmes is the protector of the old aristocratic order of England in this story. As Mortimer says, "it cannot be denied that the prosperity of the whole poor, bleak countryside depends upon his presence".

Discussion point: What do you think of the way Doyle refuses to reveal vital clues until the very end of the story?

Extract

"Mortimer said that the man had walked on tiptoe down that portion of the alley."

"He only repeated what some fool had said at the inquest. Why should a man walk on tiptoe down the alley?"

"What then?"

"He was running, Watson—running desperately, running for his life, running until he burst his heart—and fell dead upon his face."

"Running from what?"

"There lies our problem. There are indications that the man was crazed with fear before ever he began to run."

"How can you say that?"

Analysis: These conversations with Watson are crucial in the story, allowing the reader to have an insight into Holmes' questioning mind. His use of Watson as a foil for his ruminations shows his respect for the good doctor and also enables us to watch the dialectic that enables Holmes to solve the case. Notice how Watson asks all the right questions.

Discussion point: What are the pleasures in eavesdropping upon Holmes' conversations with Watson?

Extract

"You think that he was waiting for someone?"
"The man was elderly and infirm. We can understand his taking an evening stroll, but the ground was damp and the night inclement. Is it natural that he should stand for five or ten minutes, as Dr. Mortimer, with more practical sense than I should have given him credit for, deduced from the cigar ash?"
"But he went out every evening."
"I think it unlikely that he waited at the moor-gate every evening. On the contrary, the evidence is that he avoided the moor. That night he waited there. It was the night before he made his departure for London. The thing takes shape, Watson. It becomes coherent. Might I ask you to hand me my violin, and we will postpone all further thought upon this business until we have had the advantage of meeting Dr. Mortimer and Sir Henry Baskerville in the morning."

Analysis: A typical trope of the Holmes' stories is the detective's tendency to say 'it becomes coherent' or words to that effect and then refuse to tell us what exactly has become clear to him. There is comedy when he immediately asks Watson to hand him the violin. Notice again how Holmes in his most authoritative moods is like the author who is struggling to find the story: "the thing takes shape".

Discussion point: What does Holmes have in common with the author?

Questions

What were the exact circumstances of Sir Charles's death?
What supernatural stories concern Mortimer and the locals?
Why did Mortimer call on Holmes?
What questions does Holmes have about the case?
What do the "tip-toe" footprints in the gravel leading away from the house suggest to Holmes?

What does the cigar ash suggest?

GCSE style question: how does Doyle create a sense of mystery about Sir Charles's death?

A Level style question: compare and contrast the description of Sir Charles's death with another description of a death you have come across in a text of your own choice.

Creative response: write a description of a mysterious death.

Chapter 4. Sir Henry Baskerville

Extract

"Hum! Someone seems to be very deeply interested in your movements." Out of the envelope he took a half-sheet of foolscap paper folded into four. This he opened and spread flat upon the table. Across the middle of it a single sentence had been formed by the expedient of pasting printed words upon it. It ran:

As you value your life or your reason keep away from the moor.

The word "moor" only was printed in ink.

"Now," said Sir Henry Baskerville, "perhaps you will tell me, Mr. Holmes, what in thunder is the meaning of that, and who it is that takes so much interest in my affairs?"

"What do you make of it, Dr. Mortimer? You must allow that there is nothing supernatural about this, at any rate?"

"No, sir, but it might very well come from someone who was convinced that the business is supernatural."

Analysis: The introduction of the warning, constructed as it is, from letters from *the Times* newspaper gave the novel a very contemporary atmosphere at the time, bringing the historic Gothic story of the Baskervilles into the present with a reference to the most popular paper of the day. It is also very sinister and mysterious, ratcheting up the suspense in this London setting, bringing the threat into the city.

Discussion point: Why and how does Doyle generate suspense within the London setting?

Extract

At that instant I was aware of a bushy black beard and a pair of piercing eyes turned upon us through the side window of the cab. Instantly the trapdoor at the top flew up, something was screamed to the driver, and the cab flew madly off down Regent Street. Holmes looked eagerly round for another, but no empty one was in sight. Then he dashed in wild pursuit amid the stream of the traffic, but the start was too great, and already the cab was out of sight.

Analysis: Notice how Doyle makes Sherlock Holmes a man of sharp contrasts; for the first section of the novel he has appeared rather languid, reposing and reflecting in the Baker Street apartment, ruminating upon the facts surrounding the case. Now he springs into action, dashing out of the flat and glimpsing the mysterious man with a bushy beard. As with much of the early part of the story, Doyle is setting up mysteries which will be explored further in the story; we will come across a man with a bushy black beard at Baskerville Hall and believe that he is the man behind the mystery, only to have this confounded too.

Discussion point: What clues does Doyle set up in the London section of the story which are later explored in the Devonshire settings?

Extract

"But what you are really looking for is the centre page of the Times with some holes cut in it with scissors. Here is a copy of the Times. It is this page. You could easily recognize it, could you not?"
"Yes, sir."
"In each case the outside porter will send for the hall porter, to whom also you will give a shilling. Here are twenty-three shillings. You will then learn in possibly twenty cases out of the twenty-three that the waste of the day before has been burned or removed. In the three other cases you will be shown a heap of paper and you will look for this page of the Times among it. The odds are enormously against your finding it. There are ten shillings over in case of emergencies. Let me have a report by wire at Baker Street before evening. And now, Watson, it only remains for us to find out by wire the identity of the cabman, No. 2704, and then we will drop into one of the Bond Street picture galleries and fill in the time until we are due at the hotel."

Analysis: This is a rare example of Holmes actually engaging in some real 'police work', the sort of hunting for clues that real detectives have to do. For much of the time, Holmes relies upon inspired guessing -- or deduction as he calls it -- but here we see him employing a man to track down the newspaper from which the letters on the threatening note were cut out of; a bit of a wild goose chase but nevertheless something that might bear fruit. We also see how Holmes benefits from the burgeoning 'telegram' system of communication; Victorian technology which he relies heavily upon.

Discussion point: Is it a problem for the modern reader that Holmes does so little 'real police work'? Or has Doyle successfully presented a world and a man who clearly has no need for such things? What is the effect here when Doyle does show us Holmes asking a servant to do some 'leg work'?

Questions

What letter does Sir Henry receive at his hotel and why is it disturbing?
What does Holmes deduce about the letter?
What happened to Sir Henry's boots?
What is Sir Henry's response to Mortimer's story about the hound?
Who has been following Holmes/Watson and what happens when Holmes chases him?
Why does Cartwright have to check the bins?
GCSE style question: how does Doyle conjure an atmosphere of mystery and intrigue in this chapter?
A Level style question: compare and contrast this chapter with a text where there are similar mysteries near the beginning of the narrative.
Creative response: write a poem/story called 'The Follower'.

Chapter 5. Three Broken Threads

Extract

As we came round the top of the stairs we had run up against Sir Henry Baskerville himself. His face was flushed with anger, and he held an old and dusty boot in one of his hands. So furious was he that he was hardly articulate, and when he did speak it was in a much broader and more Western dialect than any which we had heard from him in the morning.

"Seems to me they are playing me for a sucker in this hotel," he cried. "They'll find they've started in to monkey with the wrong man unless they are careful. By thunder, if that chap can't find my missing boot there will be trouble. I can take a joke with the best, Mr. Holmes, but they've got a bit over the mark this time."

"Still looking for your boot?"

"Yes, sir, and mean to find it."

"But, surely, you said that it was a new brown boot?"

"So it was, sir. And now it's an old black one."

Analysis: Yet again we find Doyle introducing an apparently trivial mystery which the readers and Holmes know will have vital significance later on. The pleasure comes from working out what the significance will be. Here we see Doyle showing us how the mundane is actually sinister, but leaves us guessing as to why and how it is really sinister. In such a way, we see him deploying a very familiar theme which runs through all his stories; that murderous intent lurks behind apparently mundane mishaps and accidents. Ultimately, Doyle is concerned with appearance and reality; things which appear normal are in fact sinister.

Discussion point: How does Doyle deploy the theme of appearance and reality throughout this story? Would it be true to say that Holmes is the agent who uncovers the hideous reality that hides behind apparently ordinary appearances?

Extract

We had a pleasant luncheon in which little was said of the business which had brought us together. It was in the private sitting-room to which we afterwards repaired that Holmes asked Baskerville what were his intentions.

"To go to Baskerville Hall."

"And when?"

"At the end of the week."

"On the whole," said Holmes, "I think that your decision is a wise one. I have ample evidence that you are being dogged in London, and amid the millions of this great city it is difficult to discover who these people are or what their object can be. If their intentions are evil they might do you a mischief, and we should be powerless to prevent it. You did not know, Dr. Mortimer, that you were followed this morning from my house?"

Dr. Mortimer started violently. "Followed! By whom?"

"That, unfortunately, is what I cannot tell you. Have you among your neighbours or acquaintances on Dartmoor any man with a black, full beard?"

"No—or, let me see—why, yes. Barrymore, Sir Charles's butler, is a man with a full, black beard."

"Ha! Where is Barrymore?"

"He is in charge of the Hall."

Analysis: Doyle has taken his time to set Barrymore as a suspect and this has the effect of making the reader unfamiliar with the conventions of the detective genre think that he is probably the murderer. Of course, those familiar with the genre know that Barrymore is probably a 'red herring', a decoy because he is so obviously implicated here.

Discussion point: Why does Doyle set up Barrymore as a 'red herring'?

Extract

The German was sent for but professed to know nothing of the matter, nor could any inquiry clear it up. Another item had been added to that constant and apparently purposeless series of small mysteries which had succeeded each other so rapidly. Setting aside the whole grim story of Sir Charles's death, we had a line of inexplicable incidents all within the limits of two days, which included the receipt of the printed letter, the black-bearded spy in the hansom, the loss of the new brown boot, the loss of the old black boot, and now the return of the new brown boot. Holmes sat in silence in the cab as we drove back to Baker Street, and I knew from his drawn brows and keen face that his mind, like my own, was busy in endeavouring to frame some scheme into which all these strange and apparently disconnected episodes could be fitted. All afternoon and late into the evening he sat lost in tobacco and thought.

Just before dinner two telegrams were handed in. The first ran:

Have just heard that Barrymore is at the Hall. BASKERVILLE.

The second:

Visited twenty-three hotels as directed, but sorry, to report unable to trace cut sheet of Times. CARTWRIGHT.

"There go two of my threads, Watson. There is nothing more stimulating than a case where everything goes against you. We must cast round for another scent."

"We have still the cabman who drove the spy."

"Exactly. I have wired to get his name and address from the Official Registry. I should not be surprised if this were an answer to my question."

Analysis: The fact that Barrymore has been seen to be at the Hall does not necessarily rule him out, but it seems clear that he is not entirely to be suspected; this is a clever narrative twist created by Doyle, who always keeps us guessing in this story. Notice the metaphor that Holmes uses here, that of 'threads'; there is a sense that he himself is weaving a plot. As we have seen before, on one level we can read these detective stories as analogies of the creative process; Holmes is the creative artist trying to find a clear story amidst the chaos of reality. Once he has solved a case it is as though the story has been finally resolved, finally written.

Discussion point: To what extent do you think the Sherlock Holmes' stories are metaphors for the creative process?

Extract

"He hailed me at half-past nine in Trafalgar Square. He said that he was a detective, and he offered me two guineas if I would do exactly what he wanted all day and ask no questions. I was glad enough to agree. First we drove down to the Northumberland Hotel and waited there until two gentlemen came out and took a cab from the rank. We followed their cab until it pulled up somewhere near here."

"This very door," said Holmes.

"Well, I couldn't be sure of that, but I dare say my fare knew all about it. We pulled up halfway down the street and waited an hour and a half. Then the two gentlemen passed us, walking, and we followed down Baker Street and along—"

"I know," said Holmes.

"Until we got three-quarters down Regent Street. Then my gentleman threw up the trap, and he cried that I should drive right away to Waterloo Station as hard as I could go. I whipped up the mare and we were there under the ten minutes. Then he paid up his two guineas, like a good one, and away he went into the station. Only just as he was leaving he turned round and he said: 'It might interest you to know that you have been driving Mr. Sherlock Holmes.' That's how I come to know the name."

"I see. And you saw no more of him?"

"Not after he went into the station."

"And how would you describe Mr. Sherlock Holmes?"

Analysis: This is a fascinating and comic touch provided by Doyle; the murderer calling himself by the great detective's name. This highlights the fact that there is a moral ambivalence to Holmes; he seems at times as cold-blooded as the villains he pursues and not particularly caring of the victims, who are merely fodder to be interrogated.

Discussion point: What does Holmes have in common with the villains in the stories?

Extract

"Snap goes our third thread, and we end where we began," said he. "The cunning rascal! He knew our number, knew that Sir Henry Baskerville had consulted me, spotted who I was in Regent Street, conjectured that I had got the number of the cab and would lay my hands on the driver, and so sent back this audacious message. I tell you, Watson, this time we have got a foeman who is worthy of our steel. I've been checkmated in London. I can only wish you better luck in Devonshire. But I'm not easy in my mind about it."

"About what?"

"About sending you. It's an ugly business, Watson, an ugly dangerous business, and the more I see of it the less I like it. Yes, my dear fellow, you may laugh, but I give you my word that I shall be very glad to have you back safe and sound in Baker Street once more."

Analysis: Critics have noted that compared with the early stories Holmes is rather more caring; here we see him genuinely worried about Watson's welfare. Nevertheless, he does send his closest friend and companion into danger for all his concern.

Discussion point: Where else do we find Holmes being more caring in this story?

Questions

How does Holmes fool the clerk at the hotel into giving him information about two of the hotel guests?

Why is Sir Henry angry?

Why does Holmes think it is a good idea for Sir Henry to stay at Baskerville Hall?

Who is the only person living on the moor with a black beard? What does Mortimer tell them about Sir Charles's will?

What does Holmes propose should happen?

Where does Sir Henry find his brown boot and why is this confusing?

What two telegrams does Holmes receive that evening and what do they say?

What surprising things does the cab driver tell Holmes?

What are Sherlock Holmes' thoughts that he shares with Watson at this point?

GCSE style question: how does Doyle create a sense of impending menace in this chapter?

A Level style question: compare and contrast the description of the strange man with the bushy beard in this chapter with another description of a menacing person in another text of your choice.

Creative response: write a story/poem called 'The Stalker'.

Chapter 6. Baskerville Hall

Extract

"It was imprudent, all the same," said Holmes, shaking his head and looking very grave. "I beg, Sir Henry, that you will not go about alone. Some great misfortune will befall you if you do. Did you get your other boot?"

"No, sir, it is gone forever."

"Indeed. That is very interesting. Well, good-bye," he added as the train began to glide down the platform. "Bear in mind, Sir Henry, one of the phrases in that queer old legend which Dr. Mortimer has read to us, and avoid the moor in those hours of darkness when the powers of evil are exalted."

Analysis: This chapter marks the end of the first phase of the novel in which the mystery is laid out before us and a cast of suspects is sketched out. Doyle could have opened the story in Dartmoor but decides against this because he is confident enough in the power of his narrative to grip that he can introduce the mystery in a piecemeal fashion in London. This has the effect of creating an urban context in which the mystery is played out, giving us a sense that what happens in the small community of Dartmoor will ripple out into the wide world. Holmes' summary of the suspects and the essential mystery is excellent here and a reminder that the story was written in serial form in which the author couldn't rely on readers remembering various characters from week to week. Notice also that Holmes almost seems to believe in the legend of the Baskerville curse here, giving it extra weight.

Discussion point: Why do you think Doyle sends Watson into Dartmoor without Holmes? Some critics have pointed out that he was bored with Holmes at this point in his career and didn't want to write about him much. Might he have had other purposes?

Extract

"Halloa!" cried Dr. Mortimer, "what is this?"

A steep curve of heath-clad land, an outlying spur of the moor, lay in front of us. On the summit, hard and clear like an equestrian statue upon its pedestal, was a mounted soldier, dark and stern, his rifle poised ready over his forearm. He was watching the road along which we travelled.

"What is this, Perkins?" asked Dr. Mortimer.

Our driver half turned in his seat. "There's a convict escaped from Princetown, sir. He's been out three days now, and the warders watch every road and every station, but they've had no sight of him yet. The farmers about here don't like it, sir, and that's a fact."

"Well, I understand that they get five pounds if they can give information."

"Yes, sir, but the chance of five pounds is but a poor thing compared to the chance of having your throat cut. You see, it isn't like any ordinary convict. This is a man that would stick at nothing."

"Who is he, then?"

"It is Selden, the Notting Hill murderer."

I remembered the case well, for it was one in which Holmes had taken an interest on account of the peculiar ferocity of the crime and the wanton brutality which had marked all the actions of the assassin. The commutation of his death sentence had been due to some doubts as to his complete sanity, so atrocious was his conduct. Our wagonette had topped a rise and in front of us rose the huge expanse of the moor, mottled with gnarled and craggy cairns and tors.

Analysis: Here we see Doyle throw everything into the mystery; not only do we have all the issues explored in the first five chapters, but now we have a homicidal maniac on the loose. We can see here why the story has been much parodied; it almost seems to be parodying itself here with its tales of murderers abounding on the bleak moors.

Discussion point: Do you think Doyle increases the tension with the introduction of Selden?

Extract

We had left the fertile country behind and beneath us. We looked back on it now, the slanting rays of a low sun turning the streams to threads of gold and glowing on the red earth new turned by the plough and the broad tangle of the woodlands. The road in front of us grew bleaker and wilder over huge russet and olive slopes, sprinkled with giant boulders. Now and then we passed a moorland cottage, walled and roofed with stone, with no creeper to break its harsh outline. Suddenly we looked down into a cuplike depression, patched with stunted oaks and firs which had been twisted and bent by the fury of years of storm. Two high, narrow towers rose over the trees. The driver pointed with his whip.

"Baskerville Hall," said he.

Its master had risen and was staring with flushed cheeks and shining eyes. A few minutes later we had reached the lodge-gates, a maze of fantastic tracery in wrought iron, with weather-bitten pillars on either side, blotched with lichens, and surmounted by the boars' heads of the Baskervilles.

Analysis:
Here we have a classic description of a Gothic mansion with its "maze of fantastic tracery" and "boars' heads"; once again we have Doyle relying very heavily on the conventions of the Gothic genre in creating a heady atmosphere. This is why opening the story in London is particularly effective; the story does not lurch into ridiculous parody because this is a novel of contrasts; of the city and the country, of the modern and the Gothic, of the supernatural and the scientific, of the rational and the irrational, of the old and the young, of good and evil, of the clever and the stupid. Here, we can also understand why Doyle has decided to remove Holmes from the story at this point; Watson is a much better character to have alone in such a place. With Holmes we would have felt re-assured that he wasn't under threat and he would not have had to do much detective work. Now part of the tension in the narrative is that we are wondering how well Watson will cope with trying to uncover the mystery; we can feel his fear and anxiety here. There is a real sense he is in jeopardy.

Discussion point:
How effective are Doyle's descriptions of the Dartmoor setting and Baskerville Hall?

Questions

Who does Holmes suspect?
What has Watson brought with him for protection?
What does Sir Henry think of his surroundings and why?
What prisoner has escaped on to the moor?
What does Barrymore tell them?
What is the Hall like and what are Watson and Sir Henry's responses to

it?

What does Watson hear in the middle of the night?

GCSE style question: how does Doyle make the moor and Baskerville Hall such interesting settings for the mystery story?

A Level style question: compare and contrast the descriptions of the Hall/the moor with descriptions of similar places in other texts you have read.

Creative response: write a description of a "creepy" setting; make it as mysterious and menacing as you can!

Chapter 7. The Stapletons of Merripit House

Extract

The fresh beauty of the following morning did something to efface from our minds the grim and gray impression which had been left upon both of us by our first experience of Baskerville Hall. As Sir Henry and I sat at breakfast the sunlight flooded in through the high mullioned windows, throwing watery patches of colour from the coats of arms which covered them. The dark panelling glowed like bronze in the golden rays, and it was hard to realize that this was indeed the chamber which had struck such a gloom into our souls upon the evening before.

"I guess it is ourselves and not the house that we have to blame!" said the baronet. "We were tired with our journey and chilled by our drive, so we took a gray view of the place. Now we are fresh and well, so it is all cheerful once more."

"And yet it was not entirely a question of imagination," I answered. "Did you, for example, happen to hear someone, a woman I think, sobbing in the night?"

"That is curious, for I did when I was half asleep fancy that I heard something of the sort. I waited quite a time, but there was no more of it, so I concluded that it was all a dream."

"I heard it distinctly, and I am sure that it was really the sob of a woman."

"We must ask about this right away."

Analysis: The "sobbing woman" in the night recalls the most famous Gothic narrative of all time: *Jane Eyre*. Doyle enjoys playing with this motif, creating real mystery around it with Barrymore's wife, making us think about Bertha Mason and Grace Poole in Charlotte Bronte's narrative -- a text which would have been very familiar to his readers. However, notice the contrast between the heroes in these two different narratives; Jane Eyre tries to find out about the cries in the night but this is not, at that time, apparently central to the narrative since it is Jane's burgeoning love for Rochester which is focused upon. However, Watson's sole purpose to uncover the mystery, there is, at this point, no deeper emotional layer to the story -- although Doyle will soon introduce one when Henry falls into love with Miss Stapleton.

Discussion point: How effective is the sobbing in the night in creating mystery?

Extract

It seemed hopeless to pursue the inquiry any farther, but it was clear that in spite of Holmes's ruse we had no proof that Barrymore had not been in London all the time. Suppose that it were so—suppose that the same man had been the last who had seen Sir Charles alive, and the first to dog the new heir when he returned to England. What then? Was he the agent of others or had he some sinister design of his own? What interest could he have in persecuting the Baskerville family? I thought of the strange warning clipped out of the leading article of the Times. Was that his work or was it possibly the doing of someone who was bent upon counteracting his schemes? The only conceivable motive was that which had been suggested by Sir Henry, that if the family could be scared away a comfortable and permanent home would be secured for the Barrymores. But surely such an explanation as that would be quite inadequate to account for the deep and subtle scheming which seemed to be weaving an invisible net round the young baronet. Holmes himself had said that no more complex case had come to him in all the long series of his sensational investigations. I prayed, as I walked back along the gray, lonely road, that my friend might soon be freed from his preoccupations and able to come down to take this heavy burden of responsibility from my shoulders.

Suddenly my thoughts were interrupted by the sound of running feet behind me and by a voice which called me by name. I turned, expecting to see Dr. Mortimer, but to my surprise it was a stranger who was pursuing me. He was a small, slim, clean-shaven, prim-faced man, flaxen-haired and leanjawed, between thirty and forty years of age, dressed in a gray suit and wearing a straw hat. A tin box for botanical specimens hung over his shoulder and he carried a green butterfly-net in one of his hands.

"You will, I am sure, excuse my presumption, Dr. Watson," said he as he came panting up to where I stood. "Here on the moor we are homely folk and do not wait for formal introductions. You may possibly have heard my name from our mutual friend, Mortimer. I am Stapleton, of Merripit House."

"Your net and box would have told me as much," said I, "for I knew that Mr. Stapleton was a naturalist. But how did you know me?"

Analysis: Stapleton is an inspired characterisation in the novel; the most complex figure by far. An expert botanist, he appears to have all Holmes' intelligence and a villain's evil intentions and desires. Yet, Doyle is successful in presenting him as a friendly person at this juncture in the story. His equipment, the 'net and box',

is particularly apposite; we learn later he is an obsessively controlling man who locks up his wife and seeks to trap another woman into a false engagement. Over fifty years before John Fowles wrote *The Collector* about a man who collects women like butterflies, he is the collector.

Discussion point: What you think of the way Doyle presents Stapleton at this early stage in the story?

Extract

Something brown was rolling and tossing among the green sedges. Then a long, agonized, writhing neck shot upward and a dreadful cry echoed over the moor. It turned me cold with horror, but my companion's nerves seemed to be stronger than mine.

"It's gone!" said he. "The mire has him. Two in two days, and many more, perhaps, for they get in the way of going there in the dry weather and never know the difference until the mire has them in its clutches. It's a bad place, the great Grimpen Mire."

"And you say you can penetrate it?"

"Yes, there are one or two paths which a very active man can take. I have found them out."

"But why should you wish to go into so horrible a place?"

"Well, you see the hills beyond? They are really islands cut off on all sides by the impassable mire, which has crawled round them in the course of years. That is where the rare plants and the butterflies are, if you have the wit to reach them."

"I shall try my luck some day."

He looked at me with a surprised face. "For God's sake put such an idea out of your mind," said he. "Your blood would be upon my head. I assure you that there would not be the least chance of your coming back alive. It is only by remembering certain complex landmarks that I am able to do it."

"Halloa!" I cried. "What is that?"

Analysis: Here we can feel the author setting up another setting which will become important; we can almost feel the author willing his villain into the depths of the mire. Once again he deepens his characterisation of Stapleton with this characters' intrinsic interest in the mire, his thirst for botanical discovery in its midst. Stapleton is a fascinating characterisation because he is both very controlling and endlessly curious, perhaps more interestingly curious than even Holmes. Whereas the great detective is only intrigued by mysteries and their solutions, there is a suggestion that Stapleton has a more broad-minded imagination, exploring flora and fauna for its own sake, drawn to it inexorably because he is a Baskerville whose land it is. There is a sense here that Stapleton in exploring the mire is exploring himself, traversing his own dark character.

Discussion point: What does the setting of the Grimpen mire add to the novel? What do you make of the characterisation of Stapleton?

Extract

A long, low moan, indescribably sad, swept over the moor. It filled the whole air, and yet it was impossible to say whence it came. From a dull murmur it swelled into a deep roar, and then sank back into a melancholy, throbbing murmur once again. Stapleton looked at me with a curious expression in his face.

"Queer place, the moor!" said he.

"But what is it?"

"The peasants say it is the Hound of the Baskervilles calling for its prey. I've heard it once or twice before, but never quite so loud."

I looked round, with a chill of fear in my heart, at the huge swelling plain, mottled with the green patches of rushes. Nothing stirred over the vast expanse save a pair of ravens, which croaked loudly from a tor behind us.

"You are an educated man. You don't believe such nonsense as that?" said I. "What do you think is the cause of so strange a sound?"

"Bogs make queer noises sometimes. It's the mud settling, or the water rising, or something."

"No, no, that was a living voice."

"Well, perhaps it was. Did you ever hear a bittern booming?"

"No, I never did."

"It's a very rare bird—practically extinct—in England now, but all things are possible upon the moor. Yes, I should not be surprised to learn that what we have heard is the cry of the last of the bitterns."

"It's the weirdest, strangest thing that ever I heard in my life."

Analysis: Of course later on we learn that the legend has some basis in fact; it is the Hound of the Baskervilles, the dog that Stapleton owns and hides on the moor. Notice how Stapleton offers a number of explanations, all of them far fetched but imaginative; his comment that the cry is "the last of the bitterns" is suggestive, a metaphor perhaps for how he feels about being an ignored, disinherited Baskerville.

Discussion point: Sounds play an important part in the story; when and why?

Extract

"Go back!" she said. "Go straight back to London, instantly."

I could only stare at her in stupid surprise. Her eyes blazed at me, and she tapped the ground impatiently with her foot.

"Why should I go back?" I asked.

"I cannot explain." She spoke in a low, eager voice, with a curious lisp in her utterance. "But for God's sake do what I ask you. Go back and never set foot upon the moor again."

"But I have only just come."

"Man, man!" she cried. "Can you not tell when a warning is for your own good? Go back to London! Start tonight! Get away from this place at all costs! Hush, my brother is coming! Not a word of what I have said. Would you mind getting that orchid for me among the mare's-tails yonder? We are very rich in orchids on the moor, though, of course, you are rather late to see the beauties of the place."

Analysis: Perhaps the most poignantly drawn figure in the story is the conflicted, complicit Miss Stapleton, who has to hide her marriage to Stapleton, and who is clearly fearful for the fate of Baskerville. Her covert and mistaken intervention here adds suspense and confusion to the narrative, giving us the sense that not even its main players know fully what is going on. The absence of Holmes adds to the feeling of narrative confusion; Watson is mistaken for Baskerville, the cries over the moors and in the house are unexplained, a sense of menace and foreboding leaks into every crevice. Holmes often stabilises the narrative, bringing to it a sense of order and calm, while Watson is portrayed as rather at a loss -- not as some films have suggested as incompetent -- but puzzled, troubled, bemused.

Discussion point: How does Doyle create a real sense of menace at this point in the narrative?

Extract

A short walk brought us to it, a bleak moorland house, once the farm of some grazier in the old prosperous days, but now put into repair and turned into a modern dwelling. An orchard surrounded it, but the trees, as is usual upon the moor, were stunted and nipped, and the effect of the whole place was mean and melancholy. We were admitted by a strange, wizened, rusty-coated old manservant, who seemed in keeping with the house. Inside, however, there were large rooms furnished with an elegance in which I seemed to recognize the taste of the lady. As I looked from their windows at the interminable granite-flecked moor rolling unbroken to the farthest horizon I could not but marvel at what could have brought this highly educated man and this beautiful woman to live in such a place.

"Queer spot to choose, is it not?" said he as if in answer to my thought. "And yet we manage to make ourselves fairly happy, do we not, Beryl?"

"Quite happy," said she, but there was no ring of conviction in her words.

Analysis: Here the troubled lives of Stapleton are revealed not in the interior of the house, which is wonderfully presented, but in the demeanour of its inhabitants and its location. Notice how Stapleton is almost able to second guess Watson's thoughts, indicating his great intelligence. His rhetorical question to his wife is interesting because, on second reading, one realises it has two layers; on the one hand, Stapleton is requesting that his wife puts on an act for Watson, but, on the other, you realise, insecure, troubled man that he is, he is seeking reassurance.

Discussion point: What does this scene at Merripit House reveal about its inhabitants? How significant do you think the name of 'Merripit' is?

Questions

What does the house seem like during the day? Why does Barrymore provoke suspicion? What does Watson find out from the postmaster?

What is Watson's theory about Barrymore and his wife?

What is Stapleton's theory about Sir Charles's death?

What does Stapleton tell Watson about Grimpen Mire?

What noise do Watson and Stapleton hear and what is Stapleton's thoughts on it?

What does Miss Stapleton tell Watson to do when Stapleton is out of earshot?

How did Stapleton lose his money?

What does Miss Stapleton tell Watson as he is leaving for the Hall?

GCSE style: how does Doyle create a sense of mystery and intrigue in this chapter?

A Level style question: look carefully at the representation of the different social classes in the novel so far; how are the upper, middle and "lower" classes represented?

Creative response: write a poem/story called 'The Servant'.

Chapter 8. First Report of Dr. Watson

Extract

All this, however, is foreign to the mission on which you sent me and will probably be very uninteresting to your severely practical mind. I can still remember your complete indifference as to whether the sun moved round the earth or the earth round the sun. Let me, therefore, return to the facts concerning Sir Henry Baskerville.

If you have not had any report within the last few days it is because up to today there was nothing of importance to relate. Then a very surprising circumstance occurred, which I shall tell you in due course. But, first of all, I must keep you in touch with some of the other factors in the situation.

One of these, concerning which I have said little, is the escaped convict upon the moor.

Analysis: Here we see Doyle using the "pathetic fallacy" to great effect; showing us how the mood of the moor is reflective of the people who live there. Even the upbeat Watson is infected by its depressive qualities, its "grim charm". Already Doyle is managing to give us a claustrophobic picture of life on the moor, a sense of its imprisoning qualities, the frightening obsessions of its inhabitants.

Discussion point: How well does Doyle paint a picture of an isolated society which is in conflict with itself?

Extract

And now, having brought you up to date in the escaped convict, the Stapletons, Dr. Mortimer, and Frankland, of Lafter Hall, let me end on that which is most important and tell you more about the Barrymores, and especially about the surprising development of last night.

First of all about the test telegram, which you sent from London in order to make sure that Barrymore was really here.

Analysis: While Mr Frankland frequently slips in caricature, a comedic grotesque worthy of Dickens, he is an excellent grotesque and very appropriate for our age as much as Doyle's. His miserable litigious nature, his obsessive voyeurism, his appalling self-righteousness are all very entertaining. There is never a sense that he is involved in the murders, although we realise he may know something important.

Discussion point: How successful is the characterisation of Mr Frankland?

Extract

Mrs. Barrymore is of interest to me. She is a heavy, solid person, very limited, intensely respectable, and inclined to be puritanical. You could hardly conceive a less emotional subject. Yet I have told you how, on the first night here, I heard her sobbing bitterly, and since then I have more than once observed traces of tears upon her face. Some deep sorrow gnaws ever at her heart. Sometimes I wonder if she has a guilty memory which haunts her, and sometimes I suspect Barrymore of being a domestic tyrant.

Analysis: Watson's speculations about Mrs Barrymore turn out to be wrong, but they are fascinating nevertheless because a theme of the narrative is the brutality of men against women: we see it in Hugo Baskerville's treatment of the maid before he is chewed up by the infamous hound, we learn about it existing in Stapleton's marriage.

Discussion point: Why does Doyle focus upon men's brutal treatment of women in the story?

Extract

Barrymore was crouching at the window with the candle held against the glass. His profile was half turned towards me, and his face seemed to be rigid with expectation as he stared out into the blackness of the moor. For some minutes he stood watching intently. Then he gave a deep groan and with an impatient gesture he put out the light. Instantly I made my way back to my room, and very shortly came the stealthy steps passing once more upon their return journey. Long afterwards when I had fallen into a light sleep I heard a key turn somewhere in a lock, but I could not tell whence the sound came. What it all means I cannot guess, but there is some secret business going on in this house of gloom which sooner or later we shall get to the bottom of.

Analysis: More mystery about Barrymore; here Doyle manages to reinvigorate our interest in him as a possible suspect, despite the fact that it is clear he wasn't in London when Henry Baskerville was threatened. His role is uncannily similar to that of Grace Poole in *Jane Eyre*: a watcher, a servant, a possible brute.

Discussion point: How successful is Doyle's characterisation of Barrymore?

Questions

What effect does the moor have upon the soul, according to Watson?
   What are Watson's worries for the Stapletons and for Sir Henry?
   What place has Stapleton shown Watson?
   What does Watson learn about Falkland?
   Why is Watson even more suspicious of Barrymore?
   GCSE style question: how does Doyle make the reader feel suspicious of so many characters in this story?
   A Level style question: compare and contrast the representation of Watson with a similar character in another text of your choice.
   Creative response: write a story called 'The Suspicious Father'.

Chapter 9. The Light Upon the Moor (Second Report of Dr. Watson)

Extract

Before breakfast on the morning following my adventure I went down the corridor and examined the room in which Barrymore had been on the night before. The western window through which he had stared so intently has, I noticed, one peculiarity above all other windows in the house—it commands the nearest outlook on to the moor.

> Analysis: The mystery about Barrymore deepens when it becomes clear he is addicted to looking at the moor. Notice here how Watson seems to have recovered from his depression and seems in better spirits as the mystery deepens still further.

> Discussion point: How does Doyle deepen the mystery here?

Extract

Our friend, Sir Henry, and the lady had halted on the path and were standing deeply absorbed in their conversation, when I was suddenly aware that I was not the only witness of their interview. A wisp of green floating in the air caught my eye, and another glance showed me that it was carried on a stick by a man who was moving among the broken ground. It was Stapleton with his butterfly-net. He was very much closer to the pair than I was, and he appeared to be moving in their direction. At this instant Sir Henry suddenly drew Miss Stapleton to his side. His arm was round her, but it seemed to me that she was straining away from him with her face averted. He stooped his head to hers, and she raised one hand as if in protest. Next moment I saw them spring apart and turn hurriedly round. Stapleton was the cause of the interruption. He was running wildly towards them, his absurd net dangling behind him. He gesticulated and almost danced with excitement in front of the lovers. What the scene meant I could not imagine, but it seemed to me that Stapleton was abusing Sir Henry, who offered explanations, which became more angry as the other refused to accept them. The lady stood by in haughty silence. Finally Stapleton turned upon his heel and beckoned in a peremptory way to his sister, who, after an irresolute glance at Sir Henry, walked off by the side of her brother.

Analysis: This passage develops in significance on a second reading. On first reading, it feels like Stapleton is just a rather possessive brother, an odd ball with his botanist's net and quirky questions, but reading the passage again makes us realise that he is genuinely disturbed and jealous, worried by his wife's developing affection for Henry Baskerville and yet unable to fully articulate this.

Discussion point: What do you think of Stapleton's behaviour here?

Extract

"I don't say now that he isn't a crazy man," said Sir Henry; "I can't forget the look in his eyes when he ran at me this morning, but I must allow that no man could make a more handsome apology than he has done."

"Did he give any explanation of his conduct?"

"His sister is everything in his life, he says. That is natural enough, and I am glad that he should understand her value. They have always been together, and according to his account he has been a very lonely man with only her as a companion, so that the thought of losing her was really terrible to him. He had not understood, he said, that I was becoming attached to her, but when he saw with his own eyes that it was really so, and that she might be taken away from him, it gave him such a shock that for a time he was not responsible for what he said or did. He was very sorry for all that had passed, and he recognized how foolish and how selfish it was that he should imagine that he could hold a beautiful woman like his sister to himself for her whole life. If she had to leave him he had rather it was to a neighbour like myself than to anyone else. But in any case it was a blow to him and it would take him some time before he could prepare himself to meet it. He would withdraw all opposition upon his part if I would promise for three months to let the matter rest and to be content with cultivating the lady's friendship during that time without claiming her love. This I promised, and so the matter rests."

Analysis: This explanation has elements of truth in it of course, but we realise, on second reading, that Stapleton's insistence upon Baskerville waiting for three months has a very sinister import because we perceive that he is aiming to kill Baskerville in this time.

Discussion point: What do you think of the characterisation of Stapleton here?

Extract

"Yes, sir, my name was Selden, and he is my younger brother. We humoured him too much when he was a lad and gave him his own way in everything until he came to think that the world was made for his pleasure, and that he could do what he liked in it. Then as he grew older he met wicked companions, and the devil entered into him until he broke my mother's heart and dragged our name in the dirt. From crime to crime he sank lower and lower until it is only the mercy of God which has snatched him from the scaffold; but to me, sir, he was always the little curly-headed boy that I had nursed and played with as an elder sister would. That was why he broke prison, sir. He knew that I was here and that we could not refuse to help him. When he dragged himself here one night, weary and starving, with the warders hard at his heels, what could we do? We took him in and fed him and cared for him. Then you returned, sir, and my brother thought he would be safer on the moor than anywhere else until the hue and cry was over, so he lay in hiding there. But every second night we made sure if he was still there by putting a light in the window, and if there was an answer my husband took out some bread and meat to him. Every day we hoped that he was gone, but as long as he was there we could not desert him.

> **Analysis:** Here the mystery surrounding Barrymore and his wife is more or less cleared up. The story brings up a repeated theme in the story; ordinary people's loyalty to psychopaths. The Barrymores are devoted to Selden because he is a member of their family, Miss Stapleton is devoted to Stapleton for deeper, psycho-sexual reasons.

> **Discussion point:** In what way is the theme of devotion explored in the narrative?

Questions

What is Watson's first guess about why Barrymore is going on to the moor?

What does Watson see when he follows Sir Henry?

What explanation does Sir Henry give for this scene?

What does Stapleton say when he visits the hall later on?

What does Watson learn the connection is with the Barrymores and Selden and what have they been doing for the convict?

What happens when Watson and Sir Henry pursue the convict?

What does Watson see when the lightning strikes?

What does the moor come to symbolize in this chapter?

GCSE style question: What do you think of the representation of Selden in this chapter?

GCSE style question: how does Doyle create a sense of Gothic horror and suspense in this chapter?

A Level style question: compare and contrast the representation of Selden with another criminal figure in a text of your choice.

Creative response: write a story/poem called 'The Escaped Prisoner'.

Chapter 10. Extract from the Diary of Dr. Watson

Extract

"Well, Sir Henry, your uncle had a letter that morning. He had usually a great many letters, for he was a public man and well known for his kind heart, so that everyone who was in trouble was glad to turn to him. But that morning, as it chanced, there was only this one letter, so I took the more notice of it. It was from Coombe Tracey, and it was addressed in a woman's hand."

"Well?"

"Well, sir, I thought no more of the matter, and never would have done had it not been for my wife. Only a few weeks ago she was cleaning out Sir Charles's study—it had never been touched since his death—and she found the ashes of a burned letter in the back of the grate. The greater part of it was charred to pieces, but one little slip, the end of a page, hung together, and the writing could still be read, though it was gray on a black ground. It seemed to us to be a postscript at the end of the letter and it said: 'Please, please, as you are a gentleman, burn this letter, and be at the gate by ten o clock. Beneath it were signed the initials L. L."

Analysis: Doyle now introduces sexual intrigue into the scenario involving Sir Charles Baskerville's death with the introduction of the burnt letter, and the mysterious initials, 'L.L'. The begging tone of the letter, 'please, as you are a gentleman' suggests that Sir Charles knew something compromising about the lady, or had compromised her. In such a way, we see Doyle increasingly shaping his narrative around sexual intrigue; there is increasingly a sense that this case is not about greed or ambition, but motivated by disturbed sexual, buried desires.

Discussion point: Why and how does sexual intrigue slip into the narrative?

Extract

"How does she live?"

"I fancy old Frankland allows her a pittance, but it cannot be more, for his own affairs are considerably involved. Whatever she may have deserved one could not allow her to go hopelessly to the bad. Her story got about, and several of the people here did something to enable her to earn an honest living. Stapleton did for one, and Sir Charles for another. I gave a trifle myself. It was to set her up in a typewriting business."

Analysis: Here again, Doyle the feminist comes to the fore; Laura Lyons is painted a pathetic, sad creature, the victim of masculine cruelty and neglect, but temporarily assisted by Stapleton and Sir Charles. Notice how Doyle is cleverly providing clues as to why she is now again in trouble. His presentation of her is overwhelming of being a victim; there are echoes of the narrative in her story. She is like the helpless maiden who Hugo Baskerville dragged to the hall, she is as mysterious as Mrs Barrymore, she is a prisoner of poverty and the moor.

Discussion point: What do you think of Doyle's presentation of Laura Lyons?

Extract

"But what is it that alarms you?"

"Look at Sir Charles's death! That was bad enough, for all that the coroner said. Look at the noises on the moor at night. There's not a man would cross it after sundown if he was paid for it. Look at this stranger hiding out yonder, and watching and waiting! What's he waiting for? What does it mean? It means no good to anyone of the name of Baskerville, and very glad I shall be to be quit of it all on the day that Sir Henry's new servants are ready to take over the Hall."

"But about this stranger," said I. "Can you tell me anything about him? What did Selden say? Did he find out where he hid, or what he was doing?"

"He saw him once or twice, but he is a deep one and gives nothing away. At first he thought that he was the police, but soon he found that he had some lay of his own. A kind of gentleman he was, as far as he could see, but what he was doing he could not make out."

"And where did he say that he lived?"

"Among the old houses on the hillside—the stone huts where the old folk used to live."

Analysis: Never content with one mystery where several more will do, Doyle introduces the mysterious stranger, building up a great deal of suspense about his intentions and purposes. The absence of Holmes is vital here since the stranger is Holmes; also we gain a sense of Watson's floundering detective work in the context of so much going on.

Discussion point: How is Selden presented at this point?

Questions

What makes Watson almost believe in the hound?
Why is Barrymore upset?
What secret does Barrymore reveal about Sir Charles?

Why did Barrymore not reveal this information?

What does Mortimer tell Watson about the initials L.L.?

Who, according to Barrymore, has also seen the mysterious figure on the moor?

GCSE style question: looking back over the novel as a whole so far, how does Doyle make the moor such an enigmatic place?

A Level style question: how does Doyle explore the theme of secrecy in this novel?

Creative response: write a story/poem called 'The Secret'.

Chapter 11. The Man on the Tor

Extract

"I have the pleasure," said I, "of knowing your father."

It was a clumsy introduction, and the lady made me feel it. "There is nothing in common between my father and me," she said. "I owe him nothing, and his friends are not mine. If it were not for the late Sir Charles Baskerville and some other kind hearts I might have starved for all that my father cared."

"It was about the late Sir Charles Baskerville that I have come here to see you."

The freckles started out on the lady's face.

"What can I tell you about him?" she asked, and her fingers played nervously over the stops of her typewriter.

"You knew him, did you not?"

"I have already said that I owe a great deal to his kindness. If I am able to support myself it is largely due to the interest which he took in my unhappy situation."

"Did you correspond with him?"

The lady looked quickly up with an angry gleam in her hazel eyes.

"What is the object of these questions?" she asked sharply.

"The object is to avoid a public scandal. It is better that I should ask them here than that the matter should pass outside our control."

She was silent and her face was still very pale.

Analysis: The beauty of Laura Lyons is a shock and forms an interesting comparison with Miss Stapleton, who is also beautiful. Notice how Doyle characterises her as having "*something subtly wrong with the face, some coarseness of expression, some hardness, perhaps, of eye, some looseness of lip which marred its perfect beauty.*" There is a sense in this description of the face that she lacks discipline, lacks strength in resisting the men who wish to conquer her beauty, which indeed proves to be the case. The dialogue grows in significance on second reading; it is ironic that Watson in trying to avoid a public scandal with Lyons may well be provoking one.

Discussion point: How important are Doyle's description of faces in the novel in telling us about the characters' personas?

Extract

The woman's story hung coherently together, and all my questions were unable to shake it. I could only check it by finding if she had, indeed, instituted divorce proceedings against her husband at or about the time of the tragedy.

It was unlikely that she would dare to say that she had not been to Baskerville Hall if she really had been, for a trap would be necessary to take her there, and could not have returned to Coombe Tracey until the early hours of the morning. Such an excursion could not be kept secret. The probability was, therefore, that she was telling the truth, or, at least, a part of the truth. I came away baffled and disheartened.

Analysis: This is one of the best "interview scenes" in any Sherlock Holmes' story because it is obvious that Lyons is telling the truth, and yet we, along with Watson, are "baffled". Unlike him we are not "disheartened" but intrigued because the mystery feels like it has so many loose ends that we wonder how the writer will tie them together. The Basil Rathbone film, the best filmed version of the novel, leaves out the sub-plot of Laura Lyons altogether, and yet, I think it is very important in crystallising the essential theme of the story which is really about "oppression"; oppression of women by men, oppression of the present by the past, oppression of man by nature, the oppression of desire, the oppression of family. The interview is so powerful because we clearly gain a sense of Laura's oppression at the hands of her husband, but she remains mysterious to us amidst her misery.

Discussion point: In what way is "oppression" a key theme in the story?

Extract

"They have treated me shamefully—shamefully. When the facts come out in Frankland v. Regina I venture to think that a thrill of indignation will run through the country. Nothing would induce me to help the police in any way. For all they cared it might have been me, instead of my effigy, which these rascals burned at the stake. Surely you are not going! You will help me to empty the decanter in honour of this great occasion!"

But I resisted all his solicitations and succeeded in dissuading him from his announced intention of walking home with me. I kept the road as long as his eye was on me, and then I struck off across the moor and made for the stony hill over which the boy had disappeared.

Analysis: Many of the scenes in the novel are about people being watched, observed, scrutinised, puzzled over. Here, Watson's pursuit of the "urchin" makes us feel that finally he will begin to uncover some mysteries.

Discussion point: What do you think of Doyle's characterisation of Frankland? What are his essential motives?

Extract

Outside the sun was sinking low and the west was blazing with scarlet and gold. Its reflection was shot back in ruddy patches by the distant pools which lay amid the great Grimpen Mire. There were the two towers of Baskerville Hall, and there a distant blur of smoke which marked the village of Grimpen. Between the two, behind the hill, was the house of the Stapletons. All was sweet and mellow and peaceful in the golden evening light, and yet as I looked at them my soul shared none of the peace of Nature but quivered at the vagueness and the terror of that interview which every instant was bringing nearer. With tingling nerves but a fixed purpose, I sat in the dark recess of the hut and waited with sombre patience for the coming of its tenant.

And then at last I heard him. Far away came the sharp clink of a boot striking upon a stone. Then another and yet another, coming nearer and nearer. I shrank back into the darkest corner and cocked the pistol in my pocket, determined not to discover myself until I had an opportunity of seeing something of the stranger. There was a long pause which showed that he had stopped. Then once more the footsteps approached and a shadow fell across the opening of the hut.

"It is a lovely evening, my dear Watson," said a well-known voice. "I really think that you will be more comfortable outside than in."

Analysis: It is one of the most famous "re-appearances" in all literature, and an inspired narrative twist on Doyle's part -- much imitated by thriller writers since the story was written. Once again, we see how Doyle specialises in the "red herring"; making us believe that the second stranger on the moor must be involved in some way in the murder.

Discussion point: Why does Doyle return Holmes back to the narrative at this point?

Questions

Who does Watson visit and what does he learn about her?
What does Laura Lyons say are the reasons why she wrote to Sir Charles and why does she say she didn't see him?

Why is Watson troubled by her?

Who does Falkland believe the mysterious figure is on the moor?

What does Watson realise when he enters the hut of the mysterious dweller on the moor and why?

Why is he surprised when the figure enters?

GCSE style question: how does Doyle spring surprises upon the reader in this novel?

A Level style question: compare and contrast the narrative surprises in this novel with another relevant text.

Creative response: write a story called 'The Tramp' in which the tramp figure turns out be a surprising person.

Chapter 12. Death on the Moor

Extract

"But why keep me in the dark?"

"For you to know could not have helped us and might possibly have led to my discovery. You would have wished to tell me something, or in your kindness you would have brought me out some comfort or other, and so an unnecessary risk would be run. I brought Cartwright down with me—you remember the little chap at the express office—and he has seen after my simple wants: a loaf of bread and a clean collar. What does man want more? He has given me an extra pair of eyes upon a very active pair of feet, and both have been invaluable."

"Then my reports have all been wasted!"—My voice trembled as I recalled the pains and the pride with which I had composed them.

Holmes took a bundle of papers from his pocket.

"Here are your reports, my dear fellow, and very well thumbed, I assure you. I made excellent arrangements, and they are only delayed one day upon their way. I must compliment you exceedingly upon the zeal and the intelligence which you have shown over an extraordinarily difficult case."

Analysis: Here Watson's frustration and anger with Holmes is quite poignant.' Then my reports have all been wasted!' – My voice trembled as I recalled the pains and the pride with which I had composed them. Whereas Watson has seemed somewhat buffoonish before, now he comes across as a fully rounded character who is hurt by Holmes' implicit lack of trust in him.

Discussion point: Is Watson presented as a complex figure in the story or merely an ineffectual clown who blunders upon mystery after mystery?

Extract

"Sir Henry's falling in love could do no harm to anyone except Sir Henry.

He took particular care that Sir Henry did not make love to her, as you have yourself observed. I repeat that the lady is his wife and not his sister."

"But why this elaborate deception?"

"Because he foresaw that she would be very much more useful to him in the character of a free woman."

All my unspoken instincts, my vague suspicions, suddenly took shape and centred upon the naturalist. In that impassive colourless man, with his straw hat and his butterfly-net, I seemed to see something terrible—a creature of infinite patience and craft, with a smiling face and a murderous heart.

"It is he, then, who is our enemy—it is he who dogged us in London?"

"So I read the riddle."

"And the warning—it must have come from her!"

"Exactly."

The shape of some monstrous villainy, half seen, half guessed, loomed through the darkness which had girt me so long.

Analysis: Here Doyle introduces some vital information about Stapleton which more or less tells us that it is Stapleton who is the murderer. Making Miss Stapleton his wife is an inspired choice on Doyle's part, making the character a sexual being who is willing to use his wife as bait for Sir Henry.

Discussion point: In what ways does the information that Stapleton is married to Miss Stapleton change our perception of him?

Extract

Again the agonized cry swept through the silent night, louder and much nearer than ever. And a new sound mingled with it, a deep, muttered rumble, musical and yet menacing, rising and falling like the low, constant murmur of the sea.

"The hound!" cried Holmes. "Come, Watson, come! Great heavens, if we are too late!"

He had started running swiftly over the moor, and I had followed at his heels. But now from somewhere among the broken ground immediately in front of us there came one last despairing yell, and then a dull, heavy thud. We halted and listened. Not another sound broke the heavy silence of the windless night.

I saw Holmes put his hand to his forehead like a man distracted. He stamped his feet upon the ground.

"He has beaten us, Watson. We are too late."

"No, no, surely not!"

"Fool that I was to hold my hand. And you, Watson, see what comes of abandoning your charge! But, by Heaven, if the worst has happened we'll avenge him!"

Blindly we ran through the gloom, blundering against boulders, forcing our way through gorse bushes, panting up hills and rushing down slopes, heading always in the direction whence those dreadful sounds had come. At every rise Holmes looked eagerly round him, but the shadows were thick upon the moor, and nothing moved upon its dreary face.

"Can you see anything?"

"Nothing."

"But, hark, what is that?"

A low moan had fallen upon our ears. There it was again upon our left!

Analysis: Holmes's defeatism almost amounts to depression in this story; he has disappeared for much of the narrative and now feels that he is beaten. Real suspense is now generated because we feel there is a genuine chance that Holmes will "lose". Holmes' subdued, alienated mood is a match for the new century that the story was written in; we can feel the optimism of the Victorian era fading and being replaced by a darker pessimism that things could go wrong.

Discussion point: What effect does Holmes' pessimism have on the reader?

Extract

"He shall. I will see to that. Uncle and nephew have been murdered—the one frightened to death by the very sight of a beast which he thought to be supernatural, the other driven to his end in his wild flight to escape from it. But now we have to prove the connection between the man and the beast. Save from what we heard, we cannot even swear to the existence of the latter, since Sir Henry has evidently died from the fall. But, by heavens, cunning as he is, the fellow shall be in my power before another day is past!"

Analysis: Here we see Holmes becoming aware of the fallibility of his methods; his quest for a "well rounded and complete" case means that he could have "thrown away the life" of Baskerville. Holmes is aware that there is a cold-blooded quality to what he does; that he lacks humanity in his quest for perfection.

Discussion point: To what extent are Holmes' methods presented as being fallible in this story?

Extract

"A beard! A beard! The man has a beard!"

"A beard?"

"It is not the baronet—it is—why, it is my neighbour, the convict!"

With feverish haste we had turned the body over, and that dripping beard was pointing up to the cold, clear moon. There could be no doubt about the beetling forehead, the sunken animal eyes. It was indeed the same face which had glared upon me in the light of the candle from over the rock—the face of Selden, the criminal.

Then in an instant it was all clear to me. I remembered how the baronet had told me that he had handed his old wardrobe to Barrymore. Barrymore had passed it on in order to help Selden in his escape. Boots, shirt, cap—it was all Sir Henry's.

Analysis: More twists and turns! Here Doyle's plays with the readers expectations and snobberies. Because Selden is a murderous psychopath, we are not so sorry that he is dead and feel relief that Sir Henry is still alive and Holmes' pride is intact.

Discussion point: What is the effect of the discovery of Selden's body?

Extract

"What do you mean, then?"

"Oh, you know the stories that the peasants tell about a phantom hound, and so on. It is said to be heard at night upon the moor. I was wondering if there were any evidence of such a sound tonight."

"We heard nothing of the kind," said I.

"And what is your theory of this poor fellow's death?"

"I have no doubt that anxiety and exposure have driven him off his head. He has rushed about the moor in a crazy state and eventually fallen over here and broken his neck."

"That seems the most reasonable theory," said Stapleton, and he gave a sigh which I took to indicate his relief. "What do you think about it, Mr. Sherlock Holmes?"

My friend bowed his compliments. "You are quick at identification," said he.

Analysis: The appearance of Stapleton is full of dramatic irony -- we are aware that Holmes and Watson know about him and he yet is not. The presentation of Stapleton as calm and rational is very important here: he is almost Holmes-like in the way he spots Holmes immediately. Notice here how Watson is presented as being quite quick witted in his explanation of how Selden died, not revealing how they suspect Stapleton as being involved.

Discussion point: What is the effect of Stapleton's appearance here?

Questions

Why is Watson offended? Who does Holmes suspect and why?

Who do Holmes and Watson believe the hound has first killed and why? Who has the hound really killed?

Why does Stapleton say he had come out?

GCSE style question: how does Doyle make the death of Selden such a thrilling and unexpected moment?

A Level style question: compare and contrast the death of Selden with another "killing" scene in a text of your choice.

Creative response: write a story/poem called 'The Wrong Man', in which the wrong person is killed.

Chapter 13. Fixing the Nets

Extract

"Is it like anyone you know?"

"There is something of Sir Henry about the jaw."

"Just a suggestion, perhaps. But wait an instant!" He stood upon a chair, and, holding up the light in his left hand, he curved his right arm over the broad hat and round the long ringlets.

"Good heavens!" I cried in amazement.

The face of Stapleton had sprung out of the canvas.

"Ha, you see it now. My eyes have been trained to examine faces and not their trimmings. It is the first quality of a criminal investigator that he should see through a disguise."

"But this is marvellous. It might be his portrait."

"Yes, it is an interesting instance of a throwback, which appears to be both physical and spiritual. A study of family portraits is enough to convert a man to the doctrine of reincarnation. The fellow is a Baskerville—that is evident."

"With designs upon the succession."

"Exactly. This chance of the picture has supplied us with one of our most obvious missing links. We have him, Watson, we have him, and I dare swear that before tomorrow night he will be fluttering in our net as helpless as one of his own butterflies. A pin, a cork, and a card, and we add him to the Baker Street collection!"

Analysis: Throughout the story there is a repeated emphasis upon the importance of faces: that their shapes and aspects reveal the hidden personality underneath. Here this theme comes to fruition with Holmes' analysis of the family portrait of Sir Hugo; he recognises Stapleton.

Discussion point: Why does Doyle's narrative focus upon the importance of faces?

Extract

The boy returned with a telegram, which Holmes handed to me. It ran:
Wire received. Coming down with unsigned warrant. Arrive five-forty. Lestrade.

"That is in answer to mine of this morning. He is the best of the professionals, I think, and we may need his assistance. Now, Watson, I think that we cannot employ our time better than by calling upon your acquaintance, Mrs. Laura Lyons."

His plan of campaign was beginning to be evident. He would use the baronet in order to convince the Stapletons that we were really gone, while we should actually return at the instant when we were likely to be needed.

Analysis: Here the narrative is beginning to make sense as Holmes' plans become evident. As we have seen before, Holmes is instrumental in shaping the narrative, even when he is absent; he is the creator of action, the structure of action.

Discussion point: How much of the story is provided by Holmes' actions?

Extract

"You have confessed that you asked Sir Charles to be at the gate at ten o'clock. We know that that was the place and hour of his death. You have withheld what the connection is between these events."

"There is no connection."

"In that case the coincidence must indeed be an extraordinary one. But I think that we shall succeed in establishing a connection, after all. I wish to be perfectly frank with you, Mrs. Lyons. We regard this case as one of murder, and the evidence may implicate not only your friend Mr. Stapleton but his wife as well."

The lady sprang from her chair.

"His wife!" she cried.

"The fact is no longer a secret. The person who has passed for his sister is really his wife."

Mrs. Lyons had resumed her seat. Her hands were grasping the arms of her chair, and I saw that the pink nails had turned white with the pressure of her grip.

"His wife!" she said again. "His wife! He is not a married man."

Sherlock Holmes shrugged his shoulders.

"Prove it to me! Prove it to me! And if you can do so—!"

The fierce flash of her eyes said more than any words.

"I have come prepared to do so," said Holmes, drawing several papers from his pocket.

Analysis: Here we see the power of Stapleton's attraction. Laura Lyons is clearly distraught when she realises that she has been led into a false engagement with Stapleton; we learn implicitly that Stapleton was obviously very attractive to her. Here, Doyle hints at the underlying sexual tension in the story by writing *"The fierce flash of her eyes said more than any words."*

Discussion point: Laura Lyons has a small but very important role in the narrative. What is that role?

Extract

The London express came roaring into the station, and a small, wiry bulldog of a man had sprung from a first-class carriage. We all three shook hands, and I saw at once from the reverential way in which Lestrade gazed at my companion that he had learned a good deal since the days when they had first worked together. I could well remember the scorn which the theories of the reasoner used then to excite in the practical man.

"Anything good?" he asked.

"The biggest thing for years," said Holmes. "We have two hours before we need think of starting. I think we might employ it in getting some dinner and then, Lestrade, we will take the London fog out of your throat by giving you a breath of the pure night air of Dartmoor. Never been there? Ah, well, I don't suppose you will forget your first visit."

Analysis: The re-appearance of Lestrade is interesting because Holmes treats him so nicely. In the earlier stories, he was treated as a buffoon by Holmes but here he is greeted warmly. Quite why he is in the story, we never really learn because Holmes could have completed the case easily without him. However, we gain a sense that Doyle is trying to move with the times here: the era of the enlightened amateur detective is drawing the close -- even Holmes needs the moral and logistical support of the police.

Discussion point: What is the role of the police in the story?

Questions

Why does Holmes say that they can't arrest Stapleton?

What does Holmes deduce from looking at the portrait of Sir Hugo?

What does Holmes instruct Sir Henry to do the next morning?

What is Holmes' plan? Who will arrive later that day with an unsigned warrant?

What do Holmes and Watson learn from Laura Lyons?

What is Holmes planning to do next?

GCSE style question: How does Doyle represent women in this chapter and generally in the novel?

A Level style question: compare and contrast the representation of women in this novel with another text or texts of your choice.

Creative response: write a story/poem called 'The Victim'.

Chapter 14. The Hound of the Baskervilles

Extract

With long bounds the huge black creature was leaping down the track, following hard upon the footsteps of our friend. So paralyzed were we by the apparition that we allowed him to pass before we had recovered our nerve. Then Holmes and I both fired together, and the creature gave a hideous howl, which showed that one at least had hit him. He did not pause, however, but bounded onward. Far away on the path we saw Sir Henry looking back, his face white in the moonlight, his hands raised in horror, glaring helplessly at the frightful thing which was hunting him down. But that cry of pain from the hound had blown all our fears to the winds. If he was vulnerable he was mortal, and if we could wound him we could kill him. Never have I seen a man run as Holmes ran that night. I am reckoned fleet of foot, but he outpaced me as much as I outpaced the little professional. In front of us as we flew up the track we heard scream after scream from Sir Henry and the deep roar of the hound. I was in time to see the beast spring upon its victim, hurl him to the ground, and worry at his throat. But the next instant Holmes had emptied five barrels of his revolver into the creature's flank. With a last howl of agony and a vicious snap in the air, it rolled upon its back, four feet pawing furiously, and then fell limp upon its side. I stooped, panting, and pressed my pistol to the dreadful, shimmering head, but it was useless to press the trigger. The giant hound was dead.

Sir Henry lay insensible where he had fallen. We tore away his collar, and Holmes breathed a prayer of gratitude when we saw that there was no sign of a wound and that the rescue had been in time. Already our friend's eyelids shivered and he made a feeble effort to move. Lestrade thrust his brandy-flask between the baronet's teeth, and two frightened eyes were looking up at us.

"My God!" he whispered. "What was it? What, in heaven's name, was it?"

"It's dead, whatever it is," said Holmes. "We've laid the family ghost once and forever."

In mere size and strength it was a terrible creature which was lying stretched before us. It was not a pure bloodhound and it was not a pure mastiff; but it appeared to be a combination of the two—gaunt, savage, and as large as a small lioness. Even now in the stillness of death, the huge jaws seemed to be dripping with a bluish flame and the small, deep-set, cruel eyes were ringed with fire. I placed my hand upon the glowing muzzle, and

as I held them up my own fingers smouldered and gleamed in the darkness.
"Phosphorus," I said.
"A cunning preparation of it," said Holmes, sniffing at the dead animal.

Analysis: Doyle saves his best for last. This fabulous, expressive description of the hound and its phosphorus coating is full of verbal energy and menace, providing a fitting climax for the story. In many ways, the hound represents the "unconscious", the savage heart of nature, a pure manifestation of desire. He is "gaunt", clearly "starved" in order to make him even more murderous.

Discussion point: What do you think of the presentation of the hound here?

Extract

The room had been fashioned into a small museum, and the walls were lined by a number of glass-topped cases full of that collection of butterflies and moths the formation of which had been the relaxation of this complex and dangerous man. In the centre of this room there was an upright beam, which had been placed at some period as a support for the old worm-eaten baulk of timber which spanned the roof. To this post a figure was tied, so swathed and muffled in the sheets which had been used to secure it that one could not for the moment tell whether it was that of a man or a woman. One towel passed round the throat and was secured at the back of the pillar. Another covered the lower part of the face, and over it two dark eyes—eyes full of grief and shame and a dreadful questioning—stared back at us. In a minute we had torn off the gag, unswathed the bonds, and Mrs. Stapleton sank upon the floor in front of us. As her beautiful head fell upon her chest I saw the clear red weal of a whiplash across her neck.
"The brute!" cried Holmes. "Here, Lestrade, your brandy-bottle! Put her in the chair! She has fainted from ill-usage and exhaustion."
She opened her eyes again.
"Is he safe?" she asked. "Has he escaped?"
"He cannot escape us, madam."
"No, no, I did not mean my husband. Sir Henry? Is he safe?"
"Yes."
"And the hound?"
"It is dead."
She gave a long sigh of satisfaction.
"Thank God! Thank God! Oh, this villain! See how he has treated me!"

Analysis: What's fascinating in the story is the contradiction between the Stapleton who we encounter in conversations -- the erudite, rational, questioning, quick-witted man -- and his actions. We have seen the way he has trained the hound to be so murderous, and now we find the way he has imprisoned his wife like one of the butterflies in his museum, bounded and trussed to the pillar. Doyle hints at the man's sexual savagery here.

Discussion point: What is the effect of Doyle's description of Mrs Stapleton's imprisonment here?

Extract

"It is worth a mud bath," said he. "It is our friend Sir Henry's missing boot."

"Thrown there by Stapleton in his flight."

"Exactly. He retained it in his hand after using it to set the hound upon the track. He fled when he knew the game was up, still clutching it. And he hurled it away at this point of his flight. We know at least that he came so far in safety."

But more than that we were never destined to know, though there was much which we might surmise. There was no chance of finding footsteps in the mire, for the rising mud oozed swiftly in upon them, but as we at last reached firmer ground beyond the morass we all looked eagerly for them. But no slightest sign of them ever met our eyes. If the earth told a true story, then Stapleton never reached that island of refuge towards which he struggled through the fog upon that last night. Somewhere in the heart of the great Grimpen Mire, down in the foul slime of the huge morass which had sucked him in, this cold and cruel-hearted man is forever buried.

Analysis: Stapleton's death in the mire is a fitting end for him; disappearing into the murky heart of Dartmoor, swallowed by the land itself, the land which claimed so much of him.

Discussion point: What do you think of this death scene? Why does Doyle leave it unclear as to whether Stapleton has died in it?

Questions

What do Holmes, Watson and Lestrade see inside Stapleton's house?
What upsets Holmes and why?
What shocks the men and what is Holmes's response to this threat?
What are the circumstances of Holmes's rescuing of Sir Henry?
What do they discover about the hound?
What do they find when they return to Stapleton's house?
What does Miss Stapleton tell them?
Why do they not search for Stapleton that night?
What happens to Sir Henry the next morning?
How long does it take for Sir Henry to recover?
What do they think has happened to Stapleton and why?
What is Holmes's view of Stapleton?

GCSE style question: how effective is this chapter as an exciting climax to the story?

A Level style question: compare and contrast this climax with another climactic ending in a text of your choice.

Creative response: write a story/poem called 'The Rescue'.

Chapter 15. A Retrospection

Extract

"My inquiries show beyond all question that the family portrait did not lie, and that this fellow was indeed a Baskerville. He was a son of that Rodger Baskerville, the younger brother of Sir Charles, who fled with a sinister reputation to South America, where he was said to have died unmarried. He did, as a matter of fact, marry, and had one child, this fellow, whose real name is the same as his father's. He married Beryl Garcia, one of the beauties of Costa Rica, and, having purloined a considerable sum of public money, he changed his name to Vandeleur and fled to England, where he established a school in the east of Yorkshire. His reason for attempting this special line of business was that he had struck up an acquaintance with a consumptive tutor upon the voyage home, and that he had used this man's ability to make the undertaking a success. Fraser, the tutor, died however, and the school which had begun well sank from disrepute into infamy. The Vandeleurs found it convenient to change their name to Stapleton, and he brought the remains of his fortune, his schemes for the future, and his taste for entomology to the south of England.

Analysis: Here Holmes becomes the master of the narrative, summarising the key points of it here, explaining the history of Stapleton; notice how Stapleton is actually presented as being from an exotic heritage, and his wife in particular, recalling shades of Bertha Mason in *Jane Eyre*. The important thing here is that Doyle offers us closure with Holmes' summary of the events and causes. All loose ends are tied up. In such an ambiguous drama as this, Holmes' summary has the effect of comforting the reader that all is right with the world, that everything is under control.

Discussion point: At this point, is Holmes' summary of events comforting at the end of this story?

Extract

"No doubt. There only remains one difficulty. If Stapleton came into the succession, how could he explain the fact that he, the heir, had been living unannounced under another name so close to the property? How could he claim it without causing suspicion and inquiry?"

"It is a formidable difficulty, and I fear that you ask too much when you expect me to solve it. The past and the present are within the field of my inquiry, but what a man may do in the future is a hard question to answer. Mrs. Stapleton has heard her husband discuss the problem on several occasions. There were three possible courses. He might claim the property from South America, establish his identity before the British authorities there and so obtain the fortune without ever coming to England at all, or he might adopt an elaborate disguise during the short time that he need be in London; or, again, he might furnish an accomplice with the proofs and papers, putting him in as heir, and retaining a claim upon some proportion of his income. We cannot doubt from what we know of him that he would have found some way out of the difficulty. And now, my dear Watson, we have had some weeks of severe work, and for one evening, I think, we may turn our thoughts into more pleasant channels. I have a box for 'Les Huguenots.' Have you heard the De Reszkes? Might I trouble you then to be ready in half an hour, and we can stop at Marcini's for a little dinner on the way?"

Analysis: The story closes on a dark note: "the terrible and paralyzing spectacle which the beast presented" and "the fog", and perhaps even more pertinently, Holmes' "reproach" to his "management" of the case. The mood is sombre. Even the closing line of Holmes' invitation "for a little dinner" can't alleviate the sense that things very nearly ran out of control, that the case has weakened Holmes and possibly destroyed Sir Henry, who we learn has to be treated for his nervous reaction to the events. There is a sense of shock. The new century looms, the Victorian era is drawing to a close. The certainties of the old Sherlock Holmes' stories have been replaced by the uncertainties of this one. Holmes is now living in a world where "proof" before a jury is required, where brilliant detection is not enough. Entrapment is what is required.

Discussion point: Why does Doyle end on this gloomy note?

Questions

What do we learn about Stapleton in this chapter?

Why did Holmes have to put Sir Henry's life in danger in order to capture Stapleton?

Why do Holmes and Watson believe Sir Henry was so ill after the hound's attack?

What do they think will improve Sir Henry's condition?

How do they think Stapleton might have claimed the estate without raising suspicion?

GCSE style question: how successful is this resolution to the story?

A Level style question: compare and contrast the resolution to this story with another story that has a similar type of resolution.

Creative response: write a story/poem called 'The Truth' in which the truth about a person is revealed publicly.

Answers to the questions

IMPORTANT NOTE: the answers to these questions are deliberately very brief; many of them could be much longer.

Chapter 1. Mr. Sherlock Holmes

What do Watson and Holmes believe can be deduced from Dr. Mortimer's walking stick? Watson believes that he is an elderly, well-respected doctor who lives in the country, and received the stick as a gift from a hunting club. Holmes believes the stick was a present from a hospital, and that Mortimer was a student at the hospital, and has now taken a country practice. He believes Mortimer is forgetful, friendly and owns a dog.

How does Watson find out Holmes is right? By looking in his Medical Dictionary.

How does Holmes know Mortimer is, in fact, visiting? Because he sees a dog at his window.

Why has Mortimer come to Holmes? Because he has heard of his ability to solve problems.

What interests Mortimer about Holmes? The shape of his skull, which could be an "ornament in an anthropological museum".

Chapter 2. The Curse of the Baskervilles

Where does Dr Mortimer live? Who gave him the manuscript he has in his pocket and what has happened to this person? He lives out on a moor in Devonshire. He was given the manuscript by Sir Charles Baskerville who died three months ago.

What story does the document tell? It tells the story of Sir Hugo Baskerville who owned the Baskerville estate during the time of the Great Rebellion (mid-1600s). He trapped a woman in the upper chambers of his house because she refused to sleep with him. One night she escaped and Sir Hugo and his men pursued her on horses. Sir Hugo was attacked by a hound and killed by having his throat torn out, while the other men who saw the incident remained traumatized for the rest of their lives. It is believed that the hound has haunted the Baskervilles ever since, seeking revenge for their past crimes.

What does Holmes think of the story? He is bored by it; he thinks it is only interesting to a collector of fairytales.

Why does the newspaper story interest Holmes more and why? It explains that Sir Charles Baskerville died mysteriously on his estate while out of a walk one night; it was presumed he had a heart attack. His only heir, Sir Henry Baskerville, is arriving from America shortly.

Why is Mortimer concerned about the death? Because Sir Charles became obsessed by the legend of the hound shortly before his death. Seeing something like a hound cross his path one night, Sir Charles, acting on the advice of Mortimer, decided to escape to London but died the night before he was due to leave. When investigating the death, Mortimer found the footprints of a huge animal near the dead body. He did not tell the press.

Chapter 3. The Problem

What were the exact circumstances of Sir Charles's death? What were the surroundings like where he died and why is this important? Sir Charles died in a gravel alleyway, surrounded by hedges, with three gates, one of which leads to a summer house, one to the main house, and one to the moor. The footprints of the animal were found 20 yards from Sir Charles.

What supernatural stories concern Mortimer and the locals? That the hound has been seen again both before and after Sir Charles died.

Why did Mortimer call on Holmes? Because he is worried about Sir Henry who is arriving in London.

What questions does Holmes have about the case? Question 1: has a crime been committed at all? Question 2: what is the crime and how was it committed?

What do the "tip-toe" footprints in the gravel leading away from the house suggest to Holmes? That Sir Charles was running away, terrified out of his wits.

What does the cigar ash suggest? That Sir Charles was waiting for someone.

Chapter 4. Sir Henry Baskerville

What letter does Sir Henry receive at his hotel and why is it disturbing? Sir Henry receives a note telling him to stay away from the moor; it's upsetting because no one is supposed to know he is staying at the hotel.

What does Holmes deduce about the letter? That it is written by an educated man pretending to be poorly educated; that it was written in a hurry; that possibly the person knows Sir Henry because he didn't use his own handwriting.

What happened to Sir Henry's boots? One has gone missing after he left them to be polished at the hotel.

What is Sir Henry's response to Mortimer's story about the hound? That nothing will stop him returning to the home of his ancestors and that he has heard the legend of the hound.

Who has been following Holmes/Watson and what happens when Holmes chases him? A man with a bushy black beard and piercing blue eyes was following them from a cab and escapes in it when Holmes tries to hail a cab.

Why does Cartwright have to check the bins? He needs to find the newspapers from which the note was cut out from.

Chapter 5. Three Broken Threads

How does Holmes fool the clerk at the hotel into giving him information about two of the hotel guests? By pretending to know them.

Why is Sir Henry angry? Because another one of his boots is missing.

Why does Holmes think it is a good idea for Sir Henry to stay at Baskerville Hall? Because it will enable him to catch the person who is responsible for the note and possibly Sir Charles's death.

Who is the only person living on the moor with a black beard? Barrymore, Baskerville Hall's butler.

What does Mortimer tell them about Sir Charles's will? That he left Barrymore and his wife some money, as well as several other people, including himself. Sir Henry inherited the estate, but in the event of Sir Henry's death, because he has no heirs, the estate will go to distant relatives the Desmonds.

What does Holmes propose should happen? Watson should go with Sir Henry for protection and Holmes will arrive on Saturday.

Where does Sir Henry find his brown boot and why is this confusing? In the hotel cabinet; it's confusing because Mortimer had searched it thoroughly. The waiter knows nothing about it.

What two telegrams does Holmes receive that evening and what do they say? He receives a telegram that Barrymore has been at the hall, and that Cartwright has found nothing in the hotel bins.

What surprising things does the cab driver tell Holmes? That the man with the bushy beard called himself Mr Sherlock Holmes and had told him to say nothing to anyone.

What are Sherlock Holmes' thoughts that he shares with Watson at this point? That their enemy is "worthy of our steel" and that this will be an ugly business.

Chapter 6. Baskerville Hall

Who does Holmes suspect? Barrymore and his wife; a groom at the Hall; two farmers on the moor; Mortimer; Mortimer's wife; Stapleton the naturalist; Mr Frankland.

What has Watson brought with him for protection? A gun.

What does Sir Henry think of his surroundings and why? He is impressed, having never seen them before.

What prisoner has escaped on to the moor? Selden, the Notting Hill Murderer, a brutal psychopath.

What does Barrymore tell them? That he plans to leave his employment as a butler and travel, using the money Sir Charles bequeathed him.

What is the Hall like and what are Watson and Sir Henry's responses to it? The Hall is gloomy and both men find it a troubling place.

What does Watson hear in the middle of the night? He hears a woman's sob.

Chapter 7. The Stapletons of Merripit House

What does the house seem like during the day? More cheerful than it was the night before.

Why does Barrymore provoke suspicion? He says that his wife couldn't have been the one sobbing, but Watson believes it is obvious she has been crying when he meets her.

What does Watson find out from the postmaster? That it was Barrymore's wife and not Barrymore who took the telegram asking him about his whereabouts.

What is Watson's theory about Barrymore and his wife? That they wanted to scare Sir Henry so that they could have the house to themselves.

What is Stapleton's theory about Sir Charles's death? That he was scared to death by the appearance of a random dog which he believed was the hound.

What does Stapleton tell Watson about Grimpen Mire? That is very dangerous because it is like quick-sand and that he knows the two safe paths through it.

What noise do Watson and Stapleton hear and what is Stapleton's thoughts on it? They hear a roar like a large animal is crying out; Stapleton says the locals believe it is the hound, but he thinks it has a natural cause.

What does Miss Stapleton tell Watson to do when Stapleton is out of earshot? To go back to London.

How did Stapleton lose his money? He managed a school which closed down after an epidemic killed off three students.

What does Miss Stapleton tell Watson as he is leaving for the Hall? That she should ignore his previous warning, but that she is worried for Sir Henry. She believes her brother wants Sir Henry to stay because the locals benefit from the Baskerville charity.

Chapter 8. The First Report of Dr. Watson

What effect does the moor have upon the soul, according to Watson? It makes you feel like you are with prehistoric man.

What are Watson's worries for the Stapletons and for Sir Henry? He is worried that the Stapletons live in a very remote area when Selden is on the loose, and that Stapleton won't be happy if he discovers that Sir Henry is attracted to Beth Stapleton, the sister.

What place has Stapleton shown Watson? Where Sir Hugo was supposed to have been killed by the hound.

What does Watson learn about Falkland? That he has spent much of his money on pointless lawsuits and that he is an astronomer.

Why is Watson even more suspicious of Barrymore? He continues to see that Mrs Barrymore has been crying and worries that Barrymore is abusive. He also saw a figure who looked like Barrymore hurrying across the moor towards the house, saw him enter an unused part of the house, look through a window and groan, and then go to his room, and heard a lock turning.

Chapter 9. The Light upon the Moor [Second Report of Dr. Watson]

What is Watson's first guess about why Barrymore is going on to the moor? To see his lover.

What does Watson see when he follows Sir Henry? He sees Sir Henry meet Miss Stapleton; they argued and then when Sir Henry tries to kiss Miss Stapleton, her brother stepped out and began arguing too.

What explanation does Sir Henry give for this scene? Miss Stapleton had begged Sir Henry to leave the moor, but he said he wouldn't unless she came with him; when he tried to kiss her Stapleton appeared and interrupted them, clearly resentful about their relationship.

What does Stapleton say when he visits the hall later on? That he will approve of the marriage to his sister if Sir Henry waits three months.

What does Watson learn the connection is with the Barrymores and Selden and what have they been doing for the convict? That Selden is Mrs Barrymore's sister and that they have been helping him by giving him food every night.

What happens when Watson and Sir Henry pursue the convict? They hear a cry which sounds like the Hound of the Baskervilles, and Selden escapes from them by throwing a rock at them.

What does Watson see when the lightning strikes? A silhouetted figure.

What does the moor come to symbolize in this chapter? Irrationality, the "old ways" of mankind, prehistoric thinking.

What do you think of the representation of Selden in this chapter? He is represented as someone who is incorrigibly criminal; he has an "evil yellow face" and is a "crafty and savage animal".

Chapter 10. Extract from the Diary of Dr. Watson

What makes Watson almost believe in the hound? The gloomy and the terrible noises he heard twice on the moor.

Why is Barrymore upset? Sir Henry and Watson had promised not to try and capture Selden but had, in fact, pursued him. Barrymore said Selden would find a new life in South America and not trouble anyone after that.

What secret does Barrymore reveal about Sir Charles? That he was going to meet a woman in the alleyway the night he died with the initials L.L., who had sent a letter from Combe Tracey.

Why did Barrymore not reveal this information? Because he feared it would harm Sir Charles's reputation.

What does Mortimer tell Watson about the initials L.L.? They are the initials of Laura Lyons, the daughter of Frankland; she married a poor artist who left her, was rejected by her father and lives in Combe Tracey.

Who, according to Barrymore, has also seen the mysterious figure on the moor? Selden, who had believed him to be living in a deserted house on the moor, and was receiving food from Combe Tracey.

Chapter 11. The Man on the Tor

Who does Watson visit and what does he learn about her? He visits Laura Lyons; she is very beautiful.

What does Laura Lyons say are the reasons why she wrote to Sir Charles and why does she say she didn't see him? She said she asked for money so that she would not have to move back with her husband but then received the money and so did not visit Sir Charles.

Why is Watson troubled by her? She seemed very anxious and pale.

Who does Falkland believe the mysterious figure is on the moor? Selden.

What does Watson realise when he enters the hut of the mysterious dweller on the moor and why? He sees a piece of paper with his name on, and realizes that he is the one being pursued, not Sir Henry.

Why is he surprised when the figure enters? It is Sherlock Holmes!

Chapter 12. Death on the Moor

Why is Watson offended? Because Holmes did not inform him of what he was doing, he believes his reports were useless, and he was used as a pawn in Holmes's investigation.

Who does Holmes suspect and why? Stapleton; there is evidence he has a relationship with Laura Lyons. Miss Stapleton is actually Stapleton's wife, not his sister. Stapleton changed his name after his school venture failed, and was the man with the beard in London. It was his wife who tried to warn them.

Who do Holmes and Watson believe the hound has first killed and why? Sir Henry because he is wearing Sir Henry's clothes on him.

Who has the hound really killed? Selden, who was dressed in Sir Henry's clothes.

Why does Stapleton say he had come out? He heard the sounds of the hound.

Chapter 13. Fixing the Nets

Why does Holmes say that they can't arrest Stapleton? They do not have enough evidence and the hound has not been seen.

What does Holmes deduce from looking at the portrait of Sir Hugo? That his facial shape is the same as Stapleton's, and that Stapleton is therefore a Baskerville.

What does Holmes instruct Sir Henry to do the next morning? To accept Stapleton's invitation to dinner and go there alone.

What is Holmes' plan? To make Stapleton think that Holmes and Watson have left for London and that Sir Henry is alone, thus making Stapleton think he is free to murder Sir Henry using the hound.

Who will arrive later that day with an unsigned warrant? Inspector Lestrade.

What do Holmes and Watson learn from Laura Lyons? That Stapleton had promised to marry her; that she should not go to Sir Charles because he would give her the money she needed and that if she said anything, she would be found guilty of Sir Charles's death.

What is Holmes planning to do next? To fetch Lestrade from the station, and then head towards Dartmoor, where Baskerville Manor is.

How does Doyle represent women in this chapter and generally in the novel? They are portrayed as victims, and less intelligent than the men.

Chapter 14. The Hound of the Baskervilles

What do Holmes, Watson and Lestrade see inside Stapleton's house? Stapleton and Sir Henry are drinking, but Miss Stapleton is not there.

What upsets Holmes and why? The fog because they can't see much; it means that they can't see Sir Henry as he is walking home.

What shocks the men and what is Holmes's response to this threat? The hound suddenly appears, luminous and terrifying; Holmes cries out and he tries to shoot the animal.

What are the circumstances of Holmes's rescuing of Sir Henry? Holmes and Watson shoot at the dog, Holmes runs after the hound, and shoots at it five times until it is dead; it was just about to tear Sir Henry's throat out.

What do they discover about the hound? That it is a cross-breed between a mastiff and a bloodhound. Phosphorus has been placed around its muzzle which is the reason why it looks like it is breathing fire, and it is covered in a glittery, glowing substance.

What do they find when they return to Stapleton's house? They find Miss Stapleton who is tied up and gagged in a room full of collected butterflies and moths.

What does Miss Stapleton tell them? That she realizes now she was Stapleton's pawn, and that he is probably hiding out on Grimpen moor where he keeps the hound.

Why do they not search for Stapleton that night? Because it is too dangerous to cross the moor.

What happens to Sir Henry the next morning? He is very ill with fever.

How long does it take for Sir Henry to recover? A year.

What do they think has happened to Stapleton and why? He has fallen into the bog on the moor and died. They find his boot near the bog.

What is Holmes's view of Stapleton? That he is the most dangerous man he has ever investigated.

Chapter 15. A Retrospection

What do we learn about Stapleton in this chapter? That he was the son of Sir Rodger Baskerville, the younger brother of Sir Charles. When Sir Rodger died in South America, Stapleton stole some money and fled to England. He set up a school which failed, and then learnt about Sir Charles. He moved down to Devonshire and hatched his plan about the hound when he discovered that Sir Charles was superstitious about it. He cultivated a friendship with Laura Lyons so that she would arrange to meet Sir Charles to the alleyway. He then persuaded Laura not to go, and set the hound on Sir Charles, who died of fright. Both Stapleton's wife and his sister suspected him of murder but were too much under his influence to do anything. Stapleton stole Sir Henry's boot to give the hound his scent; however, the boot was too new to have a strong scent and Stapleton had to steal another one to give the hound a proper scent. His wife sent a warning note to Sir Henry because she suspected what he was up to.

Why did Holmes have to put Sir Henry's life in danger in order to capture Stapleton? Because he did not have enough evidence against him.

Why do Holmes and Watson believe Sir Henry was so ill after the hound's attack? He was broken-hearted when he realized Mrs Stapleton's complicity.

What do they think will improve Sir Henry's condition? World travel and the knowledge that Mrs Stapleton did try and stop the murder that night; this was the reason why Stapleton tied her up.

How do they think Stapleton might have claimed the estate without raising suspicion? Holmes does not really know, but he thinks Stapleton might have returned to South America and made the claim there, or disguised himself in London, or used someone else to make the claim.

Speaking and Listening Exercises

Work in a group and devise a **chatshow** based on the novel. Make sure that you have an interviewer (chat-show host) who questions the main characters in the novel about their thoughts and feelings regarding what has happened to them. The aim is that students need to show that they understand the storyline and characters by talking in role about the events in the novel. You can include dead characters such as Stapleton, Selden and Sir Charles if you wish to do so. You could also invite

You could put Stapleton on **trial**, accused of causing the death of Sir Charles, Selden and the attempted murder of Sir Henry. Set things up so that you have a prosecuting lawyer who is accusing Stapleton of the crimes of murder, blackmail (Laura Lyons) and imprisonment (his wife). Have a defence lawyer who argues that there is evidence that he should be treated leniently. Call witnesses for the prosecution and defence who are characters from the novel such as Watson, Holmes, Sir Henry, Laura Lyons, Mrs Stapleton, Falkland, Barrymore and his wife etc; or the author; or "made-up" characters such as a psychiatrist who has assessed Laura Lyons/Beth Stapleton. Use the trial to explore different views on the novel. Then possibly write it up as a script or review what you have learnt from doing it.

Put the main characters in **therapy:** Stapleton, Sir Henry, Beth Stapleton, Laura Lyons are the most obvious ones, but you could possibly put Holmes in therapy as well. Have them visit a therapist to discuss their problems with him/her. You could do this so that they go into therapy at various stages during the story. Write a review of what you have learnt from doing this afterwards.

Work in a group and devise a **radio drama** of the major parts of the novel. Different groups could work on different sections of the book; e.g. the opening with Holmes questioning Mortimer, learning about the legend of the hound etc; the scenes at Baskerville Hall and on the moor; the climax on the moor; the resolution with the explanation about Stapleton. Make the drama short and punchy. This exercise will help you get to know the text in much more depth: the editing of the novel will help you summarise key points.

How to write top grade essays on the novel

In order to write a good essay about *The Hound of the Baskervilles*, you need to understand it. You will need to know what the difficult vocabulary means and be aware of how the text is the product of the world it comes from: late nineteenth century England. You will also need to be aware of what the examiners for your particular question are looking for. For GCSE, it appears that most questions are, at the time of writing this guide, "extract based"; you will be given a small extract and asked to consider how the author builds suspense or drama in the extract, or presents the characters or key themes in a particular way. In order to achieve highly, you will need to answer the question carefully and not simply re-tell the extract; this is something that I have seen many good students do. The A Level questions are much more like the ones posed in the **essay question section** of this study guide and the A Level style questions posed at the end of the chapter questions. Sometimes, you might be asked to compare the novel with other literary texts, depending upon the nature of the task and/or exam board. For A Level, you need to be aware of other literary critics' views on the novel.

You should consider a few key questions with extract questions:

For extract questions, consider how has the author **built up** to this particular moment? Think carefully about what the reader already knows before they have read the extract. You will need to know the story well in order to do this.

What literary devices does the author use to make the passage interesting or to reveal a particular character in a certain light? Think very carefully about the author's use of language: Doyle's use of descriptions to create a certain atmosphere or paint a sketch of a character/event; his use of dialogue to reveal character and create drama/tension; his use of imagery (metaphors/similes/personification). You will need to pack your essay full of the relevant terminology if you want to aim for higher marks as it appears in many mark schemes as a key requirement.

You need to be aware of a number of different interpretations of the novel. The weblinks below should help you with this.

Finally, you need to provide evidence and analysis to back up your points. As a cornerstone of your essay writing technique, you should be aware of the **PEEL** method of analysing texts: making a Point, providing Evidence, Explaining how your evidence endorses your point, and Linking to a new point.

Writing about the story/narrative

I would strongly advise you to read my section on the **structure and themes of the novel here** before writing about the effects the narrative structure of the book creates. There are many, many things to say about the story of the book, but you should think about your own personal response as well: what did you find the most engaging parts of the novel and why? Look back over the notes you have made while you read the novel and use them to shape an original response. You need to avoid just re-telling the story, which is very easy to do in highly pressurised situations and you're not thinking straight!

Writing about the characterisations

There are many websites which can help you with writing about the characters in the novel, already listed earlier on in this book. What most of them don't say is a very important thing I've already mentioned; Doyle's characters are *not* real people, they are literary creations and we become interested in them because of their similarities and differences. A central technique of Doyle's is to make the reader think about how and why characters are similar and different; we are constantly being invited to compare and contrast characters in our minds. This is a central way that Doyle generates suspense and drama in the novel; the novel is full striking comparisons and contrasts. Where Holmes is clever, secretive, and powerful, Watson is less intelligent, more open and often lack in power at key points in the novel. Doyle reveals the suspects to be similar and different: Stapleton shares an unbalanced strange nature with Falkland (and Holmes), but his interest in nature makes him different; both Laura Lyons and Miss Stapleton appear to be victims of Stapleton's web of intrigue, but Miss Stapleton seems to be less desperate then Laura, who is presented as an almost desperate woman. We never quite know what the intentions of many of the characters are; why did Beth Stapleton and Laura Lyons not report Stapleton? Why are Barrymore and his wife really sheltering Selden? It is the ambivalence of the characters – never quite knowing whether they are telling the truth or not – which creates much of the suspense in the novel.

Task

Look at some character studies online and devise a chart or **visual organiser** which illustrates the similarities and differences between the major characters, exploring the effects that these similarities and differences have upon the reader.

Writing about the settings

Doyle is an interesting writer because he avoids describing the physical surroundings in huge depth in the way that a writer like, say, Thomas Hardy might; instead we gain more of a sense of the place from vividly drawn details and through the dialogue of the characters. Nevertheless, certain settings play a very important part in the book: Holmes's Baker Street apartment, the London hotel where Sir Henry is staying, Baskerville Hall, Stapleton's house, the alleyway where Sir Charles died and, of course, the moor.

You can find more information about settings here:

Task

Look carefully at the use of settings in the novel; what purpose do they serve? Why does Doyle set particular scenes in particular settings? Think also about the time of day/night he sets his scenes; how does the time of day/night create certain effects?

Suspicion

A central technique of Doyle is to make the reader feel suspicious about the characters' motives and actions. Once you begin to appreciate the role of suspicion in the novel and understand how Doyle generates suspense from Watson and Holmes's suspicions, you will be able to analyse how he makes the narrative dramatic. The central point is that we never quite know who is guilty until three quarters of the way through the book. There are plenty of "red herrings" (people who look suspicious but are not): Barrymore and his wife, Selden, Falkland, Laura Lyons. However, Doyle continues the suspense even when we know Stapleton is the prime suspect because we are suspicious about what might happen to Sir Henry at Stapleton's hands.

Task

Look back over the novel, and work out when and where the governess is suspicious and what clues both back up her suspicions and undermine them. Devise a visual organiser which charts the suspicious moments so that you can see clearly on one page where such moments occur, and think about the effect they have upon the reader. Why does Doyle have so many "red herrings"?

Use of language

Above all, you need to analyse the effects of Doyle's language upon the reader; exploring what the language makes the reader think, feel and see.

Task

Devise a chart/visual organiser/notes on the different types of language Doyle uses in the novel, providing quotes and examples for the following types of language:

Descriptive language: language which describes people, places and situations

Imagery: language which makes comparisons

Important dialogue: important quotes that people say that make the plot move on.

Useful links

These websites contain some incisive analysis on the use of language:

http://www.shmoop.com/hound-of-the-baskervilles/literary-devices.html

http://www.enotes.com/topics/hound-baskervilles/in-depth

https://quizlet.com/12633758/literary-terms-found-in-hound-of-the-baskervilles-flash-cards/

http://thebestnotes.com/booknotes/Hound_Baskervilles/Hound_Baskerviles01.html

Possible essay titles

To what extent is *The Hound of the Baskervilles* a conventional detective novel?

To what extent does *The Hound of the Baskervilles* deploy the conventions of a Gothic novel?

To what extent is the characterization of Stapleton convincing?

Why is Sherlock Holmes actually not present for much of the novel?

To what extent is the novel about the conflict between rationality and superstition?

Compare and contrast the novel with another text which explores the theme of murderous desire.

To what extent is *The Hound of the Baskervilles* a sexist narrative?

Why does *The Hound of the Baskervilles* use a number of different literary forms, such as letters to old legends, in its unfolding narrative?

Glossary

Characterisation -- a literary term which encapsulates why and how an author presents a character through the use of dialogue, description, contrast to other characters

Dolichocephalic -- long-headed

Dyspnoea -- laboured breathing due to inadequate action of the heart.

Genre -- type of text

Imagery -- the poetical devices a writer uses such as metaphors, similes, personification

Litigious -- prone to settle matters in the law courts

Metaphor -- A comparison which does not use 'like' or 'as'

Narrative -- A story

Presentation -- a literary term which encapsulates the way an author presents a character, issue, idea, or image

Supra-orbital development – a disproportionate amount of skull about the eye

Symbol -- An object or thing which represents a larger concept or idea

Rapacious – grasping, greedy

Theme -- a dominant idea in a text

About the Author

Francis Gilbert is a Lecturer in Education at Goldsmiths, University of London, teaching on the PGCE Secondary English programme and the MA in Children's Literature with Professor Michael Rosen. Previously, he worked for a quarter of a century in various English state schools teaching English and Media Studies to 11-18 year olds. He has also moonlighted as a journalist, novelist and social commentator both in the UK and international media. He is the author of *Teacher On The Run, Yob Nation, Parent Power, Working The System -- How To Get The Very Best State Education for Your Child*, and a novel about school, *The Last Day Of Term*. His first book, *I'm A Teacher, Get Me Out Of Here* was a big hit, becoming a bestseller and being serialised on Radio 4. In his role as an English teacher, he has taught many classic texts over the years and has developed a great many resources to assist readers with understanding, appreciating and responding to them both analytically and creatively. This led him to set up his own small publishing company FGI Publishing (fgipublishing.com) which has published his study guides as well as a number of books by other authors, including Roger Titcombe's *Learning Matters* and Tim Cadman's *The Changes*.

He is the co-founder, with Melissa Benn and Fiona Millar, of The Local Schools Network, **www.localschoolsnetwork.org.uk**, a blog that celebrates non-selective state schools, and also has his own website, **www.francisgilbert.co.uk** and a Mumsnet blog, **www.talesbehindtheclassroomdoor.co.uk**.

He has appeared numerous times on radio and TV, including Newsnight, the Today Programme, Woman's Hour and the Russell Brand Show. In June 2015, he was awarded a PhD in Creative Writing and Education by the University of London.

29280688R00051

Printed in Great Britain
by Amazon

Codeword

RED SHAMROCK

Best Wishes
W. K. Mead
Nov 2012

by

William K. Meade

This book is a work of fiction. Any resemblance to any
person living or dead is purely coincidental.

Printed in Victoria, BC, Canada

Note for Librarians: a cataloguing record for this book that includes Dewey Decimal Classification and
US Library of Congress numbers is available from the Library and Archives of Canada. The complete
cataloguing record can be obtained from their online database at:
www.collectionscanada.ca/amicus/index-e.html
ISBN 1-4120-4068-X

TRAFFORD

This book was published *on-demand* in cooperation with Trafford Publishing. On-demand publishing is
a unique process and service of making a book available for retail sale to the public taking advantage of
on-demand manufacturing and Internet marketing. On-demand publishing includes promotions, retail sales,
manufacturing, order fulfilment, accounting and collecting royalties on behalf of the author.

Offices in Canada, USA, UK, Ireland, and Spain
book sales for North America and international:
Trafford Publishing, 6E-2333 Government St.
Victoria, BC V8T 4P4 CANADA
phone 250 383 6864   toll-free 1 888 232 4444
fax 250 383 6804   email to orders@trafford.com

book sales in Europe:
Trafford Publishing (UK) Ltd., Enterprise House, Wistaston Road Business Centre
Crewe, Cheshire CW2 7RP UNITED KINGDOM
phone 01270 251 396   local rate 0845 230 9601
facsimile 01270 254 983   orders.uk@trafford.com

order online at:
www.trafford.com/robots/04-1875.html

10   9   8   7   6   5   4   3

Quote

Democracy is the most inefficient form of government, but consider the alternatives

Winston Churchill.

CHAPTER 1

Joe Kearns opened his eyes to the buzz of the alarm clock on the small table beside his bed. It was six thirty on the morning of the fifteenth of January 1986. A cutting wind from the Northeast had frozen the city of Dublin in its icy grip. After the night the room was cold. Just then he heard the hot water start to circulate in the radiator under the window. Moving one hand from underneath the warm cover he turned on the cassette radio beside his bed. The announcer was reading the first news of the day.

In Belfast a policeman had been shot dead. The Irish Freedom Army had claimed responsibility.

Two people had been killed in a road accident.

A machine tool factory in Limerick was to close with the loss of eighty jobs, management said it was due to failure to reach agreement with staff over new work practices.

A bus and train strike was to start on Monday.

There was to be a March and demonstration against British occupation in Northern Ireland this afternoon, finishing with a meeting at the General Post Office in O'Connell Street.

This was followed by a weather forecast.

In the darkness he slipped a tape into the machine and pressed play. The sound of Mozart's Magic Flute overture filled the room.

Listening to the music he drifted into that somnolent feeling where the mind absorbs the sound while the body tries to sleep. As the music played his mind went back to yesterday at the newspaper. His editor had applauded his investigation into the cattle smuggling in the border areas. It would be published in the Sunday edition. Joe smiled as he recalled the Irish Customs Officer's words.

"Sure the cattle come back and forward up here so quickly they're dizzy and there's nothing we can do about it, so much for the common market. They bring them out to collect the subsidies and back by an unapproved road then tomorrow repeat the performance. We can even recognise some of the bloody animals."

He had continued,

"There's a lot of money being made by some people up here including our Subversive friends. They use the money to finance what they call their 'armed struggle I'd say they finance themselves as well."

That some of those people resented Joe's interest in their affairs had become evident early in the investigation. At first it was the odd hint when he was talking to some of the locals in the pub. Then there were the phone calls to his room at the hotel in the small hours of the morning. When he lifted the receiver there was no one there. He had chosen to ignore these warnings and continued. The night he was driving back to Dublin a very large cattle truck tried to run him off the road. It was sheer luck that the car fetched up against a small tree which prevented it from tumbling into the river about twenty feet below. He had managed to get it back on the road with nothing more than a damaged front wing and continue his journey home.

When he opened his eyes again the room was bright. The tape had switched itself off. Throwing off the covers he went into the bathroom and showered and shaved. A mop of dark blonde hair topped the face looking out from the mirror. The features were pleasant, giving some account of their owner's strong willed character. The nose was slightly bent to one side, the result of an encounter on the rugby field during his student days.

Aged twenty-eight, he was a man who did not suffer fools gladly. His bachelor flat, which he rented from the widow downstairs was crammed with books and a collection of classical music tapes and records with which he entertained himself. He was not a man who socialised, in a strict sense of the word. Yes he had lots of friends, some of whom were married to a wife and a mortgage, some even had a couple of children.

For him it had been different. He had some girl friends during his university days, none of which lasted more than a few weeks. Then shortly after he had started work at his present newspaper the reporter with whom he was working invited him to an after wedding party. Joe was sipping a glass of wine when he saw her. Copper coloured hair, cut short, blue eyes in an oval face and a trim figure, she was talking to a tall bearded man of about fifty. Joe felt he had never seen such a beautiful girl. Something like an electric shock went through him and he found himself moving across the room towards her and in a voice not his own asking her if she would like to dance. With an amused smile she agreed. From that moment on they were inseparable.

The only girl in a family of four boys, Mary Boyle was full of the joys of life. She was a teacher in a kindergarten school, loved music, the theatre and travelling, all together they seemed ideally suited to each other. After two years of each other's company they were engaged and the wedding was planned for the Spring. The future looked extremely rosy for the young lovers. Then something happened which was to change Joe's life forever.

Mary's pride and joy was a ten year old Austin Mini. She had driven into Dublin to meet Joe. After a meal they had gone to a show. When they came out the city was blanketed in patchy fog. Joe had kissed her goodnight and watched the Mini's taillights disappear into the gloom.

At around midnight on the road to Sutton Mary's Mini was in collision with a stolen Volvo driven by a sixteen-year-old youth high on drugs. She had no chance and was killed instantly. The youth was flung clear, uninjured.

The next few days were hell on earth for Joe. Nothing made sense. His whole world was gone. He woke up at night, thinking, its all a nightmare, she's not dead, but then the reality would come and the terrible pain. The funeral was just a blur.

He absorbed himself in his work, devoting all of his time to chasing stories for his paper. The tougher they were the harder he worked, building a reputation as a dedicated and astute reporter. Shunning friends and family he moved into his present flat after seeing it advertised in his own paper. It was an ideal set-up. He rented the top floor from Mrs Black who occupied the ground floor with her two cats. With only her and himself in the house the arrangement worked very well as she also acted as his cleaning lady and took care of his laundry.

He dressed casually in jeans, shirt and sweater. A noise below announced Mrs.Black's arrival from morning Mass. Soon she would call him to join her in a cup of tea or coffee. She, for her part had taken an instant liking to her lodger and had more or less adopted him for the son she never had. At times he resented her interference, when she would ask him if he had eaten, or did he want anything done. Still there had developed a bond of sorts between them. He had never told her about the tragedy in his life but with a woman's logic she had sensed the deep hurt that was there.

"Joe, are you up? Tea's made, or would you like coffee"?

He came downstairs into the tiny kitchen.

"Morning Molly, tea will do fine thanks".

He sat down and she poured tea into a blue cup, at the same time pushing a plate of toast across the table. The ginger cat glared at him from its perch on the corner of the draining board. He poured in milk and sugar and buttered a piece of toast. Mrs. Black sat down opposite and looked at him.

"You were in late last night Joe?"

This was a question rather than a statement. It was a sad fact that the only disadvantage to the arrangement was that to get upstairs he had to use the same hall door as Mrs. Black. She slept in a bedroom off the hall and each time he came in late he tried his hardest not to make much noise. He sometimes wondered if she ever slept as she usually remarked on his entry whenever he saw her next day.

"Sorry about that Molly, I had to stay late to finish my story, I hope I didn't disturb you".

She shook her head.

"No Joe I wasn't asleep, tell me are you going to take a few days off and have a rest? You look very tired, you can't keep on working, working, working, you really should have a bit of a holiday you know."

Here we go again, he thought, what do I say to her? She really means well.

"It's nice to know somebody cares about me, thanks Molly, you know I might just do that one of these days, I do feel like a few days doing nothing."

He sipped his tea as she looked at him.

8

"You know Joe, I never see you going anywhere, if you're not working you're up there listening to your music, one thing's for sure you're the best lodger I've ever had here, not a bit of trouble, but I worry about you I really do"

She was looking at him with real concern.

"All right Molly, I promise I will take a few days off and have a rest."

She filled a saucer of milk and placed it on the drainer in front of the cat, which stood up and lazily started to lap. Joe finished his tea.

"Thanks Molly, I'll be off now, I've got to make arrangements about the car and go into town afterwards, I'll see you later."

He drove out of the side street and over the humpbacked Canal Bridge on to the main road. At that hour on a Saturday morning there was little traffic. A blue Transit van appeared in his mirror and followed him until he turned at a sign pointing to Rathmines. After about half a mile he turned into a narrow lane. At the bottom was a large yard with a building which had once been the stables of an elegant house of Dublin 'Gentry'. Now it housed a workshop for repairing crashed cars. Inside the open door a figure in overalls and mask was busy spraying the wing of a Fiat. The man looked up as Joe approached and raised a gloved hand. Kearns waited at the car until he had finished. The man took off his mask and goggles and came outside.

"Joe, how are you? You must be in trouble to be round here, what happened to the wagon?"

Paddy McKenna shook Joe's hand and examined the damaged wing of the Volkswagen.

"That's a nice bit of a clatter you got Joe, yours or theirs?"

Kearns gave him a grin.

"Theirs Paddy, tried to run me off the road. I'm afraid I came off second best on that one, didn't even get a number, lucky to survive, can you do the job for me?"

McKenna nodded,

"I'll take it on Monday, its going to take a couple of days Joe and its also going to need a new wing."

"Right Paddy, I'll drop it round early, I won't need it next week, I'm taking a few days holiday, I'll see you then."

McKenna gazed at a point somewhere beyond Joe's head.

"One of these days you're going to find yourself either dead or badly injured, will you for God's sake watch yourself."

Joe acknowledged with a nod and got back into the car. He drove into the city centre and parked in one of the side streets off O'Connell Street. Going into a bookshop he browsed around the shelves without finding anything that interested him. A music shop was his next stop where after a while he bought a couple of tapes of the Berlin Philharmonic playing Grieg and Tchaikovsky. Coming out of the shop he walked towards the river Liffy. It was nice to be able to stroll around without having to look over his shoulder, Yet he had an uneasy feeling that he was being watched. Once he glanced around and failed to see anything suspicious. The feeling persisted however. Perhaps some of those gentlemen from up around the border were after him, well, tough, it was too late to stop the story now. Tomorrow it would be front-page news.

He reached the junction of O'Connell Bridge and Bachelor's Walk. Standing there he watched the crowds hurrying about their Saturday shopping. Making a sudden decision he crossed the junction and started walking in the direction of the street, where he had parked the car. Once again he glanced behind and thought he saw a man in a blue anorak looking at him. Two hundred yards further on he looked again. The man was still there. At the next junction he was almost beside him. Joe glanced at him. The man's eyes met his and he turned away. Kearns was now sure, he must be a tail, were there any more? At the next crossing the man came alongside, this was it. The man reached out a hand. Joe drew back, the hair starting to rise on his neck. The man spoke.

"Any chance of the price of a cup of tea man? I haven't eaten since yesterday."

Joe let out his breath in a gasp. He reached into his pocket and took out a couple of one pound note's and thrust them at the man who muttered a thanks and disappeared into the crowds. Relief surged through Joe as he made his way to the car. On the other hand he realised just what the last job had taken out of him, his nerves were certainly not the best. Now he was even imagining he was been followed. He smiled wryly at the thought.

If he could have seen the man in the anorak he would have had more cause to ponder. He was standing in a doorway talking into a two-way radio. Folding down the aerial he stuck the radio inside his jacket and got into a car with a driver which was parked at the kerb.

By the time Joe got back to his flat his mind had settled somewhat. Odd that fellow asking him for a few bob. He had been sure he was going to have a go at him. Joe laughed to himself. Come on Kearns you're really slipping, you do need a holiday, when was it you took some time for yourself, not since, the old memory came back, he shook his head. Molly is right, you do need a break, but where would you go in January in Ireland. He was no great lover of the sun so Spain or Portugal did not appeal to him.

Maybe he would go down to his sister in Kerry. He had not seen her for two years. The farm, which she and her husband ran, was out in the country where he could get lost every day. Maybe even take a few photos, he had not done that for quite a while. That was it! On Monday he would leave the car with McKenna and take the train to Kerry, As he opened the door his phone started to ring. He picked it up and the voice of Ken McGuiness, the sub editor, greeted him.

"Joe? The Boss would like to know if you're doing anything this afternoon?"

"What's it this time Ken?"

Joe felt just a little bit wary.

"This demo. In O'Connell Street today, will you have a look at it? He knows it's not your usual but there's no one else available."

"I suppose we had better keep him happy, Okay. I'll do it, what's the deadline Ken?"

"Thanks Joe, Try to get your report in here before seven, see you later."

The phone went dead.

The march started from St.Stephen's Green at two thirty led by a pipe band. About five hundred people, young, old and children, some carrying banners and a Tricolour, walked behind. It wound its way through Westmoreland St, and across O'Connell Bridge. At the General Post Office it halted. One side of the street was now completely blocked and Gardai routed traffic around the obstruction.

A small platform had been erected and a figure stepped forward to address the crowd. Joe, moving in close recognised him as prominent Left Wing politician from Belfast. The crowd gave a cheer. He held up his hand and began to speak. He soon had the crowd shouting at the injustices perpetrated on their fellow countrymen in Northern Ireland. As he went on speaking the mood of the crowd got uglier. The speaker was skilfully working on the emotions of the people and turning the crowd into a mob. The good-humoured crowd was vanishing. Joe watched as some young men, most of them sporting beards and with their heads covered in anorak hoods, who had been standing near the platform began moving out into the crowd now swollen by some more spectators from among the Saturday shoppers. At times some of these individuals would interrupt the speaker to highlight some more incidents of attacks on the nationalist population in the North by the British Army and the R.U.C. The mood of the crowd got uglier still.

Shouts of "Down with Britain," "Army Out" and other slogans were now being shouted. Joe began to think that this was beginning to look as if some people wanted to start a riot. The man on the platform appealed for calm. The young men shouted for action now. They were now taking control. Some Gardai started to move out to the edge of the crowd. None of them wore riot gear. A shout went up from one of the young men.

"Come on we'll march to the British Embassy."

The crowd roared its approval.

A Garda Inspector with a loud hailer climbed on to the platform and addressed the crowd telling them they would not be allowed to march anywhere and to please disperse. Watching from behind one of the huge pillars. Joe became aware of a man in a grey raincoat moving towards the platform. Taking a brick from under his coat, he took careful aim and threw it at the Inspector. It hit him squarely on the forehead and he pitched forward into the crowd. As if at a signal all hell broke loose. People started to run in all directions. Missiles came from nowhere. There was screaming, shouting and cursing. The Gardai drew their batons and charged the crowd. More Gardai in riot gear streamed out of a side street opposite. A bottle hit the pillar beside him and he ducked as glass showered all around. A flash of panic ran quickly through him. All around people were dashing here and there trying to get away from the madness. A man in an anorak lunged at him with a club. Joe stepped sideways and stuck out his foot, tripping him and he went down screaming curses. Two Gardai pounced on him and dragged him away. In the midst of the confusion he saw a small girl of about five or six clutching a lollipop running wildly with the rest. Suddenly she stumbled and fell in the gutter. Three or four steps and he had snatched her up. Her nose was bleeding and she had a cut on the side of her face. He struggled through the fleeing figures around the corner into Henry Street. Joe could feel a cold anger surge through him. The child was whimpering like a kicked puppy. What idiot brought a child to a thing like this?

In the nearest doorway he tried to calm her, cleaning her face with his handkerchief. Things were quieter here although struggles were still going on in front of the Post Office. A first aid man arrived and had a look. He told Joe to take her to a nearby shop, where a post had been set up. There a nurse put some sticking plaster on her cheek and cleaned up her face, her nose had stopped bleeding. She patted her on the head.

"Now your dad can take you home Miss."

Joe suddenly realised he had better try to find the child's parents. He took her hand and went up to the corner where two Gardai were standing. Joe explained about the child showing them his press card. One of them suggested that he take her to the police station in College Street.

They started to walk in that direction, the child sobbing a little. Joe talked softly to her asking her name. She made no reply. After a little while he gave up and they moved slowly through the crowd. There were groups of people standing around aimlessly watching the proceedings.

Joe broke through the edge of the crowd and started to move slowly towards O'Connell Bridge and College Street. After they had gone about a hundred yards there was a shout behind them. Joe turned. A girl was running towards them waving frantically. Her coat was torn and her face and hair grimy. She swept the child into her arms, tears running down her cheeks.

"Joanna, thank God your safe, I've been searching for you everywhere, are you all right?"

She looked to Joe for the answer.

For a moment he did not reply, looking into her eyes, which he noted were grey with a tinge of green. She certainly is pretty he thought. So this is the child's mother. She must be mad bringing a kid to a meeting like that. There was anger in his voice as he answered her.

"The little girl is all right, a small scratch on her cheek, that's all, no thanks to you, this was no place to bring a child."

The girl looked at him, her face flushing.

"We were not at that meeting, we were just passing by when the trouble started and we got separated. Thanks for helping her, I don't know what I would have done if anything had happened to her."

She hugged the child to her. Joe, feeling rather foolish and suitably chastened said,

"All right, I'm sorry, I shouldn't have said that. It really isn't any business of mine, I'm glad she's all right and that you found us, now, are we quits?"

She looked at him for a moment. Then with a smile said,

"Yes, we're quits, now I suppose I had better get this young lady home."

There was the sound of breaking glass behind them. Joe looked around. Scuffles were still going on between Gardai and some of the crowd. He turned to the girl who was wiping the child's face oblivious to the scene around them.

"I think we had better move away from here, you never know what might happen if we stay."

As the girl looked around there was another crash of breaking glass. Gardai in full riot gear started to pour out of one of the streets and line up to charge the remains of the crowd. The girl looked at Joe, fear in her eyes. She caught the child's hand tighter. Joe started to move them down away from the trouble.

"Have you got a car?"

He asked her. She shook her head.

"Where do you live? I have a one, it's parked in that side street over there we can get to it down this way."

14

He steered them into an alleyway, which led them towards the parked Volkswagen. The girl told him that she lived in Sandymount on Sea Road. The child had taken his hand and walked between them. The girl started to brush her coat down as if ashamed of her appearance. Joe could not help smiling, she really looks the worst for wear he thought. She glanced at him and her face grimaced.

"So well you might laugh, I must look a sight."

She gathered her torn coat around her. Passers by were looking at them curiously. Joe looked at her again, she really is very pretty. It was so long since he had even spoken to a girl like her he found himself somewhat tongue-tied. He tried to tell her she looked all right.

"Oh, it's not that bad, when you get home you will be able to clean up, and you Joanna."

He ruffled the child's hair. She responded by asking him with a child's curiosity,

"What's your name?"

The girl shook her hand.

"That's not a nice thing to ask Joanna."

Joe laughed and said,

"Oh the child's all right, my name's Joe, Joanna."

The girl flashed him a look.

"You're not to call him Joe, Joanna, you call him Mister?"

She looked at him appealingly but some devil in him made him just smile into her eyes. She flushed and looked away. They had reached the car. As Joe unlocked it, she kept her eyes averted. The child kept up a conversation with him. They sat in the back seat and Joe drove out towards Sandymount. They had gone a short distance when the girl spoke.

"I'm sorry, you've been so good to us, only for you God knows what would have happened to Joanna back there, please tell me your name Mister...?"

Her voice trailed off.

Joe glanced in the mirror,

"Only if you promise to call me Joe, Is it a deal?"

She nodded.

"Okay. It's Kearns, Joe to you, now you haven't told me yours,"

Like a flash young Joanna piped in.

"It's Jean Joe, Jean's her name, Jean McKay."

They both laughed.

He said in mock seriousness,

"Delighted to meet you Jean McKay and you Joanna."

Young Joanna seems to have recovered quickly he thought. The rest of the journey was taken up by the child's incessant questions, punctuated by Jean telling her to leave him alone. When they reached Sea Road Jean gave him directions and they turned into the gates of a large detached house standing in its own grounds.

As they drove up an older woman, whom Joe guessed was Jean's mother was waiting anxiously on the steps.

"Jean, Joanna, are you all right? I heard about the trouble on the radio. I was so worried. Knowing you were in O'Connell Street, my God, look at your clothes and Joanna! What's wrong with her face?"

She put her hand to her mouth. Jean took the child up the steps saying,

"We're all right mother, its only a scratch, thanks to this gentleman here, we're okay."

Her mother turned to Joe.

"Thank you very much for bringing them home, please come inside Mr.?"

"Kearns"

Joe told her and declined the invitation, saying he had to get back to the paper. She was persistent however and tried to persuade him further saying,

"Please come in, just for a moment, I'm sure Jean would like to say thank you herself, she's just gone to tidy up."

He shook his head and gave her a smile,

"Thanks very much Mrs.McKay, but there's no need. I'm glad I was able to help, I really must go now, I have work to do."

At that moment Jean came down the steps. She had changed her clothes and removed the grime, her blond hair had been brushed.

"You're not leaving already Joe, I haven't even thanked you properly yet, at least come in, and have a cup of tea,"

He followed them into the house, his eyes on the girl.

They chatted about trivial things, while he had tea and biscuits. The girl thanked him again and Joanna came into the room with a large teddy bear. She came over to Joe and said solemnly,

"Thank you for saving me Mr.Kearns."

Joe gave her a smile.

"That's all right Joanna, maybe I'll see you again sometime."

He stood up.

"Thank you all very much but I do have to go, this report won't wait and the editor will be crying for it."

The child clung to his hand as they walked to the door. They stood on the steps and waved as he drove away towards the city. In the office he started to write up his report.

CHAPTER 2

On that same Saturday morning in Moscow there were few people to be seen on the snow-covered streets of the Capitol. The few cars that mingled with the buses and trams were mostly military. In the Kremlin itself preparations were going ahead for a meeting of the Politburo whose thirteen members were the most powerful men in the Soviet Union. All decisions regarding events both inside and outside the country were discussed and passed or rejected by these men. It was here that espionage reports from the free world were finally discussed and the go ahead given for further action. The fate of many countries had been decided at these meetings. Now it was to be the turn of another small country. Just one more step in the push towards world domination. This was what the coming meeting was about. Several members were already breakfasting in the plush dining room. This section of the Kremlin resembled a top class hotel like those found only in the decadent west. There was no shortage of luxury. The state certainly looked after its most important citizens.

Speculation was rife as to what the meeting was about. There had been no agenda issued, just the time and the place. Reason decreed that it was something big. No one was forecasting anything specific. Every member there was suspicious of his neighbour. It was always wise not to say too much, after all this was the home of the KGB and one never knew what small talk got back to the President. Woe betide any member who happened to displease the Head of State. He could suddenly find himself reduced in stature and quite possibly lose his ministerial position. It was better to wait and see. One could, indeed was expected, to discuss and examine every facet of the business in hand. Many arguments took place at the conference table but the President always had the final say.

The Minister of the Interior finished his coffee and turned another page of the report he had brought with him. He was quite sure that it would not be required at this particular meeting because Gregor Ichinskey was almost certain that his son in law Colonel Ivan Gudenuv was going to be here to day. When speaking with him some days previous the Colonel had hinted to him that he had applied to the President for approval of his proposals for the project he had been working on for the past couple of years.

Ichinisky was proud of his son in law. Indeed he regarded Gudenuv as a son. When his daughter first introduced the tall army officer he was impressed with his good manners and easy grace. His wife had agreed and did much to encourage the match. When he had a security check done on the young Gudenuv he passed with flying colours. At that time he was in the intelligence section of the army. When Olga and he married the President himself had called Ichinisky aside to say how highly he thought of the young man. Shortly afterwards Gudenuv was promoted to full Colonel, the youngest in that particular branch. Ichinisky had never sought any favours for his son in law. All promotions were in recognition of his total dedication to his work. With his fluent knowledge of English he had even made several trips to England and America to check on agents in place.

In New York he had been introduced to an American Senator as a refugee of Jewish extraction who had escaped from the Soviet Union. The man took him under his wing and the amount of information he picked up when travelling with the Senator was staggering. They even visited the Kennedy Space Centre where he was given a rundown on the latest methods of tracking satellites. He even managed a few photographs with his special camera disguised as a cigarette lighter. It was different in England however. Here he found he could not penetrate the reserve of officials. However he did make contact with a number of moles in very high positions. They had been recruited many years previously and were native English. Some of them were in the higher echelons of the civil service, some more were even in M.I.5 itself, others prominent in trade unions. It was no wonder he was treated with such respect by all that knew him in the Kremlin.

An acknowledged expert on subversion of all kinds he had even learned to fly. He often took over from his personal pilot when things allowed. Ichinisky hoped that Gudenuv's plan would get the go ahead this morning. He deserved it. For the last six months Gudenuv had almost vanished. Olga had spent most of her time with her parents since the Colonel was seldom home any more except for an occasional visit every other weekend and that for just one day. Once Ichinisky had taken himself over to the special complex East of Moscow where he talked to Gudenuv about Olga. The Colonel had explained that he was working against time to finalise the operation he was then working on. More he would not tell him except to say that if it worked it would place the Soviet Union in a position never before thought possible. When Ichinsky tried to question him further he would only smile. Gently he took his arm and guided him toward the door.

"Father, go home please, I have tried to explain to Olga and I'm sure she understands, it's hard on her I know, It's also hard on myself but I'll make it up to her I promise. I appreciate your concern but I must do this job. Time is running out now. This operation, must start in the next few weeks if we're to achieve our objective."

He opened the door of the Minister's car. In silence Ichinisky shook his hand. Gudenuv saluted him as he drove away. Since then he had not seen or heard from the Colonel until his phone call last week. From Olga he had learned that the Colonel had been home a lot more in recent days. At least his meeting had achieved something. He looked at his watch, half an hour to go. At his signal a waiter brought him a glass of vodka. It was a little early in the day but he felt he needed it.

At that particular time the subject of his thoughts was sitting in the back seat of a black Zil car with military plates which had just entered the Kremlin complex through one of the four gates in its fifty-foot walls. Taking a left turn the driver entered a large courtyard where a number of black limousines were already neatly drawn up, each roof wearing a mantle of snow. Stopping his vehicle as close to the entrance as possible. The driver got out and opened the rear door, springing to attention as he did so.

Colonel Ivan Gudenuv picked up his briefcase and map roll and stepped from the car. He was tingling with suppressed excitement. This morning he was going to address the President and members of the Politburo of the Soviet Union. The mere fact that he had been granted the privilege was acclaim in itself. He had sent his request to the President with a resume of his plans and almost by return he had a phone call from the Great Man's secretary granting the meeting. Now he was here. If he succeeded who knew what promotion would follow. The time was certainly right. He had kept his finger on the pulse for the last few years. The plan had been formulated and carefully matured to a fixed timetable. It only required a yes from these men to set it in motion.

For the past five years he had been in charge of the special espionage school situated in heavily wooded country about twenty miles east of Moscow. Here Communist sympathisers and agents from around the world came to learn the deadly trades of subversion and terrorism. How to use modern weapons bomb making, political assassinations, these were all part of the course. The more subtle ways of breaking a country were also on the agenda. Infiltration of trade unions and other local organisations were high on the list. By the use of strikes and riots a country's economy could be destroyed and a socialist take over effected.

Gudenuv entered the building after going through a security check. He turned a corner, almost colliding with a small bearded man of about sixty with watery eyes and a small moustache. He was carrying a large file and a bulging briefcase. This was Anatol Kirof, personal secretary to the President. Gudenuv had met him several times before and liked the little man whom he always found helpful.

"Good morning Ivan, so you're here to present your plan, are you nervous?"

"Morning Anatol, yes, to tell the truth I feel like a soldier about to face his first real battle, what kind of humour is He in this morning?"

Kirof looked straight ahead,

"Ivan I think your plan will be accepted, He likes it, but make sure nothing goes wrong. He hates been made to look foolish. His men will watch you every step of the way. He knows and appreciates your work but that will not save you if anything goes wrong."

They entered the meeting hall together. Most of the Ministers were already seated at the long mahogany table over which a huge portrait of Lenin looked down. Heads turned as the two entered. Gudenuv moved to the far end and sat down. The hum of conversation, stilled at their entry, now resumed as the rest of the Members filed in and took their seats. A few moments later the door at the side of the room opened and Dimitri Gagarin, the President of the Soviet Union took his seat at the head of the table.

Aged sixty-five Dimitri Gagarin was heavily built with a craggy face with deep-set eyes which missed nothing. There was an air of cunning about the man, which boded ill for anyone who incurred his wrath. He looked around the Assembly and spoke.

"Comrades, this special meeting has been called at the request of Colonel Gudenuv to ask for our approval for the final phase of an operation which has been ongoing for a number of years now. The Colonel himself has been working on this for the last two years and feels that the time is now ripe for the completion of the plan. Some of you already know some of the details. I must emphasise that everything here today is to be regarded as top secret. Hence you will have noticed that we have no secretaries. No notes will be taken. Now I call on Colonel Gudenuv to give you the full outline of his plan, Colonel if you please."

Gudenuv looked around the table at the sea of expectant faces and began.

"Comrades, as you already know we have always looked for a way of gaining military advantage over the Western Capitalists without resorting to outright war. So far we have not succeeded very well in the Western Bloc Countries. I have here the final phase of an operation which give us complete control of the Western approaches to Europe. It will also give us a missile base against the Eastern seaboard of the United States of America."

A murmur went around the room. The Colonel resumed,

"This will be accomplished with the minimum involvement by us except for a number of agents strategically placed and a supply of arms. For many years now we have been helping our Comrades in Ireland who wish to establish a thirty-two county Socialist Republic. The position now is that our Comrades in the North of Ireland are politically well supported in certain areas. In the South the economy is in a state of near collapse. Our agents, who by organising strikes and making excessive wage demands have succeeded in closing numerous factories and slowing industry to almost a stop, have brought this about. Some others have infiltrated the higher reaches of the civil service and encouraged the implementation of large tax demands on the population. This also has led to a fall in living standards and more unemployment, dissent is widespread."

"Now what I propose is the take-over of Ireland over a three day period between the first and third of April. It will then be declared a Socialist

22

Republic. On the first of April the Irish Government meets at a special location for a weekend summit. At this meeting the whole government will be present. There our Irish Comrades will arrest them. They will later be charged with crimes against the state. The new Government is already selected and will declare itself immediately. The heads of the Army and Police will be summoned and made to swear loyalty to the new state. The new leader will call on the nation to remain calm. All known anti Soviets, of whom we have lists prepared will be arrested. The new Government will then request help from us, as we will be the first nation to recognise the new Republic. We can then land a certain number of troops who will have been waiting on ships stationed around the Irish Coast. Our embassy in Dublin will be fully manned and will monitor all operations. All heads of our Irish sections in Ireland have been notified to be ready for action. They will only get the exact date and times about a week before hand. This should ensure total secrecy. In the meantime we have been letting rumours of a coup circulate for over a year now, The authorities are so used to this that they have grown complacent and treat then with contempt. I think that the same will happen with the real coup. No one will be expecting it when it does happen. This I believe, is the opportunity for us to consolidate our position over the Americans and at the same time cover the whole of the Western approaches to Europe, it is within our grasp. I think we should avail of it."

Here Gudenuv paused and looked around the table at the faces of the thirteen. They were all watching him closely. Some doodled with pen or pencil but all showed interest. He continued,

"At the same time and for a few weeks beforehand in England our Comrades have been instructed to start a series of strikes and riots and create general public disorder. This will have the effect of having the police and army fully engaged. They may even have to withdraw troops from Northern Ireland. Our Irish friends will be instructed not to cause any incidents in Northern Ireland from about the end of January."

They will declare that they are members of a thirty two county Republic on the same day as the new Dublin Government and appeal to them for help A volunteer army will be despatched to help them. Britain will be so busy with her own problems she will be taken completely by surprise."

"Then Comrades, following a call for help from the new State we will land about two thousand troops. By the third of April we will be in command of Ireland North and South and have complete control of the Western approaches to Europe. After that we can perhaps look to a Socialist take over of England, that Comrades is my plan, it now awaits your approval."

Gudenuv laid down his papers and looked around at the most powerful men in the Soviet Union. There was silence for a moment. Then Igor Berior the Minister of the Interior spoke.

"Comrades the plan is ingenious and will surely give us a distinct advantage, but if we gain Ireland do you not think that Britain and America will do their utmost to stop us, remember what happened in Cuba with Kennedy."

Gudenuv spoke again,

"Comrades America and Britain will not interfere because we will not be directly involved. We will have just responded to a call for help from a friendly state. America and Britain are not aggressive and would not dare invade a small country like Ireland. They will probably protest to the United Nations, you all know how things can be delayed there. We have three days to do this job with the help of our Irish friends. Contry to popular belief the Irish people are not given to fighting. Most people are happy to accept any conditions and obey instructions from any authority. They have no access to weapons and are afraid of the Republicans. With a quick take-over of Government we'll have no trouble with the local population."

The Defence Minister looked around the table and spoke,

"Comrades this plan has been developed over a number of years and Colonel Gudenuv has spent a lot of time on it, I'm sure nothing has been left to chance, we should say yes."

There was no sound from the rest of the meeting. The President shifted in his seat.

"Good, any one against? No, Colonel Gudenuv you will proceed with the plan as you see fit, please keep me informed of progress, by the way have you chosen a codeword for the operation?"

Gudenuv looked directly at the President,

"Yes Comrade, the code-word is 'Red Shamrock.'"

The President gave a wry smile,

"And very appropriate too, Comrades this meeting is at an end."

People started to leave. The Colonel was putting his papers into his briefcase when Ichinskey came over to him.

"Congratulations Ivan, I had no idea of the magnitude of the plan you were working on. I wish you the best of luck, It's a mammoth task but if it succeeds will be a great victory for the Soviet Union. If you need any help from me I am always available."

Gudenuv shook his hand in silence. Just then the President's secretary, Kirof, came over and called the Colonel aside.

"Ivan, a word in your ear, watch out for spies in your camp from the Defence Minister, if you succeed he will try and take the credit, if you fail, he will see to it that you are disgraced, his men will be watching as well as the President's."

He shook the Colonel's hand and walked off. Gudenuv settled himself into the back seat of the car. As the driver headed back to the complex Kirov's words rang in his ears. By now the snow had deepened and the driver was finding it hard to keep in a straight line, despite the snow tyres. Surely there was nothing that could go wrong. He had checked and double-checked all the information. All the agents were in place and had been for a long time now. Long enough to be accurate in their assessments of the local situation. No one but himself knew the final timetable and the dates. The three Irishmen back at the complex would not be informed of the full details even when he briefed them tomorrow morning. No, it would work, yet he had a faint flicker of doubt. A shiver went through him, he well knew the penalty for failure. At the very least it would mean exile to some remote outpost in Siberia. The wheels had started to turn and that monster called fate had taken him into its grip. Tomorrow he would dispatch the three Irishmen on their journey with their shipload of arms. The car drew up at the door of his quarters. Inside he gave orders for the Irishmen to be in his office at eight a.m. next morning.

CHAPTER 3

The three men concerned were sitting in the recreation room. Two of them were drinking Russian beer. The third sipped thoughtfully at a glass of Vodka. They were all aged between twenty-five and thirty. Their leader was the man with the vodka. He had been in Moscow for the past three years after making an escape from police in Dublin. The others had joined him about eighteen months ago. They had just been informed of Gudenuv's orders. Now they sat and wondered what was to happen. John O'Shea the youngest of them took a sip of his beer and gave an opinion.

"Maybe its back to Ireland for us, I'm sick of this bloody place anyway, we can go nowhere without an escort, the Winter's so bloody cold and we're cooped up her like chickens in a pen."

Fergus Doyle poured beer into his glass, swallowed, and grimacing put it down.

"Can't be too soon for me, even the bloody beer is useless, what do you think is on George?"

George Reilly looked at the two across the table. Apathy stared back at him. Hell, he thought what's the difference, they might as well know now. Gudenuv will explain to them in the morning anyway. He himself knew they were going to take a shipment of arms home. Gudenuv must be starting them off tomorrow or the next day. He had hinted to George last week that the time was near.

"Don't get too excited lads, there's something big in the wind, we're going back, you'll be told more in the morning, I don't even know the full details myself yet, In the meantime keep your mouths shut."

John O'Shea stopped himself halfway through a loud, 'Whoopee'.

Fergus Doyle grinned and slapped him hard on the back.

All three shook hands across the table.

One of the young men seated at a table across from them glanced around at the commotion and smiled. George Reilly smiled back, noting the young man's hand, which was just a stump with a thumb. Someone had told him he was from Bolivia and that he had lost his hand in a premature explosion of a home-made bomb. That it had damaged his eardrum was evident from the hearing aid he wore in his left ear. George turned to the others.

"Come on boys, time we packed and turned in, we may be leaving here in a hurry in the morning."

He spoke softly. They rose and wandered slowly back to their quarters. Reilly left them at their room and entered his. He lay down on the iron-framed cot with its thin mattress. Putting his hands under his head he stared up at the ceiling. Having spent the last three years working with Gudenuv on the plan he still did not know all the details. The Russian certainly played his cards close to his chest. The two next door were untried. They had come to Moscow as rather soft members of the Brotherhood. He had watched as their training progressed and seen the changes. They had toughened, yet he wondered how they would behave in a given situation.

George Reilly was twenty-nine years old and from county Tipperary. As a fifteen-year-old youth he had been a member of the local football team and youth club. Then he was recruited into the junior section of the Subversive movement.

At first it was a bit of fun to wile away the winter nights. Gradually he learned the more serious side of the business of the ongoing fight to make the six counties of Northern Ireland part of a thirty-two county Republic. To an impressionable youngster this sounded very heroic. At the end of the year he had taken the Oath and became a full member. It was all very secret and around the area there were only about twenty full members.

Sources of Subversive's funds were obtained mostly from Bank and Post Office robberies. George took part in his first one at eighteen. Three of them held up the bank in Cahir taking twenty thousand pounds. Afterwards he had been thrilled with the excitement of it all. Then there were nights when they were trained in using weapons and made go on training exercises. Arms would occasionally come along the line in small quantities. As time passed he was given command of his own three-man team. A born leader he led them on many successful raids. A hit here, lie low for a couple of weeks, then another hit. He planned with meticulous detail. His team-mates joked that as they were so successful they should go into business for themselves and become millionaires. Then three years ago it happened.

Their target was the Bank of Hibernia in the Main Street of Roscrea. One of the team, Paul Short, had gone by train to Dublin and returned with a stolen Ford Sierra. It was a dark metallic red with a small dent in the left-hand wing. This was their getaway vehicle. A few miles outside the town, a lane way led to a long abandoned quarry. Here the number plates of the Sierra were changed. Then a false floor was fitted in an old Toyota High Ace van. This was where the money would be hidden and driven through the inevitable roadblocks by George himself. The others would use a small Fiat belonging to the other team member Mickey O'Keefe. The guns would be hidden and recovered later The cars and van were hidden in the derelict buildings, everything was ready.

The evening before the raid they made their way to the quarry. It was one of those balmy summer evenings, George was to recall later. Mickey O'Keefe suggested they go into the town for a last check and a meal. Paul Short elected to stay, telling the others to bring back some burgers and chips. George and O'Keefe took the Sierra and drove into Roscrea. They parked in the local supermarket car park, which connected to the main street by a passageway. After walking by the bank and checking their escape route they went into a cafe and ordered a meal.

Garda Tom Miles pushed the laden food trolley towards the supermarket checkout. His wife Eileen and their two boys of eight and ten trailed behind. It was the last day of his five-day break. He reached the checkout and started to unload the groceries. The two boys went to the other end and reloaded the trolley. Outside they started to argue about which would push it to the car. Tom scolded them, telling them to take it easy. Both boys released their grip. The trolley started to move fast down the incline, gathering speed as it went. Tom took off after it at a run. It was heading for a dark red Ford Sierra parked on its own at the bottom of the slope. He managed to get his hand to it just before it reached the Sierra. Breathless, he hung on until he regained his breath, noting that there was already a dent in the front wing of the car. Pushing the trolley towards his own car he thought dark thoughts about what he would do to the boys later. Cleaning and tidying up around the garden for the next few days might put some manners on them. Eileen took one look at his face and wisely decided to say nothing. She ordered the boys into the car. They drove home in silence.

Tom Miles checked into the Garda station at ten minutes to eight next morning, to the good-humoured banter of some of his colleagues. He was detailed for patrol car duty with a young recruit just out of the training centre at Templemore. As they drove out of the yard he ran his eye down the list of stolen vehicles which all Garda cars carry and which is updated daily. Midway down he came on a metallic red Ford Sierra stolen in Dublin three days previous, distinguishing mark, slight damage to left front wing. Into his mind flashed a picture of last night's episode with the trolley. That car had been a red Sierra with a dent in the left wing. Was it the same car? if so what was it doing in Roscrea? He talked to the station requesting more information and asking for engine and chassis numbers. As a matter of course the report then went to the local Special Branch men.

At nine thirty, some three miles on the Dublin side of Roscrea, Tom spotted the car in a line of traffic heading into the town.

"Turn around Sean."

He told the young driver,

"Unless I'm losing my marbles this has all the hallmarks of a bank robbery."

He radioed the station as the car turned in pursuit and told the young driver.

"Don't get too close Sean, there's five banks in the town, let's try and find out which one they're after."

He kept the radio open reporting their progress. Station said they had an armed response unit standing by. The patrol car was travelling behind a car towing a caravan. Through the rear window of the caravan they could just see the Sierra some three cars ahead. They were now at the town outskirts and approaching a junction when the traffic lights stopped the car and caravan. A large truck joined the line effectively blocking the view. They moved off on the green, Tom muttering curses and drove to the end of the street. The red car had vanished.

"Back Sean, Go back."

As they passed the Bank of Hibernia, the red Sierra turned out of a side street and pulled into the kerb in line with the main door of the bank. The call over the radio alerted the station to the target bank. Tom directed the young driver to turn into another side street, which led to the supermarket car park. Jumping out, the two men ran towards the passageway leading to the main street.

Lenny McIntyre will remember that Friday for the rest of his life. As bank porter his morning duty was to unlock the doors at precisely ten-o clock. The old clock on the wall started to chime the hour. Lenny inserted the keys, turned them and grasping the handle opened the door. He was suddenly thrown backwards as the door came in at him. Two men rushed in and pointed hand guns at him and the staff.

One slammed the door shut. The other vaulted the long mahogany counter and ordered the staff to lie on the floor. He scooped up piles of notes into a canvas bag.

Outside Paul Short sat at the wheel of the Sierra. The engine was running. He felt the butt of the Colt revolver stuck inside his jacket. A woman with a pushcart and a small child by the hand was walking towards the car. Further on two men who looked like farmers were standing talking. A battered grey Toyota with two men in it pulled in to the opposite kerb. In the mirror he saw a squad car approaching slowly down the street. Further down and blocking it completely a large truck had pulled across at an angle. Paul Short began to feel uneasy. If that truck did not move their escape route was blocked. He glanced around. The squad car had stopped about three cars back, double-parked. He felt as if they were watching him and the car.

The bank doors burst open and Reilly and O'Keefe rushed towards the car. Two uniformed figures ran towards them shouting for them to stop. Mickey O'Keefe fired at them the gun bucking in his hand. Tom Miles felt a thump in his left side, which flung him into the woman and child, all collapsing in a heap on the pavement. The two men had jumped out of the Toyota and using it for cover, loosed some shots at the tyres of the Sierra, shredding them like paper. The other called on the men to surrender. Mickey O'Keefe fired a couple of shots at them before a burst of Uzi fire caught him in the neck and hurled the almost head-less corpse back across the bank steps. Paul Short sat petrified behind the wheel of the now useless Sierra watching the carnage around him. George Reilly had flung the bag of money into the car and climbed in after it. As he scrambled back out a half spent bullet caught him in the right leg and he fell to the ground. They were surrounded by armed detectives and uniformed Gardai. Someone threw a coat over the body on the steps and a doctor and an ambulance arrived. Paul Short still sat in the Sierra. It was now eight minutes past ten. Tom Miles and George Reilly travelled in the same ambulance to hospital.

Three months later the trial of George Reilly and Paul Short began in the Special Criminal Court in Dublin. Armed troops and Gardai sealed off the courthouse and surrounding streets. Everyone and every vehicle entering the area was searched and checked. All persons entering the courthouse were subjected to a search before being allowed in.

Each morning the prisoners were brought from Portlaois prison to Dublin in a convoy of armed soldiers and Garda vans. They would arrive with sirens blaring just before eleven a.m. It was during the third day that Reilly found the message. Some time during the morning he had reached into his jacket, more out of boredom than anything else. His fingers found a piece of rolled up paper. Slowly he withdrew his hand. Unrolling the paper he put his hand to his mouth as if stifling a yawn. On the tiny piece of paper he read the words, 'Be Ready'. He could feel the excitement, they were going to try a rescue attempt. Dropping his hand he rubbed the paper between his fingers until it disintegrated.

When the court broke for lunch the prisoners were locked in cells in the basement. Here they would be served a meal supplied by a local hotel. At two p.m. the court would resume and the prisoners brought back to the courtroom. They had just started to climb the stairs when there was a flash and a bang and shouts of fire. Thick black smoke started to envelop the area. The Special Branch man leading them shoved them back towards the cells, shouting at them to stay down. He then ran up through the smoke into the courthouse and locked the door. The other man ushered them along in front of his Uzi. The smoke was getting thicker now and they were all coughing. It was hard to see. At the open door of the cell the Branch man lowered his weapon and stepped to one side. Reilly seized his chance. He swung round and pushed Short and the man into the cell. The Uzi clattering on the floor. Slamming the door shut he turned the key in the lock. His foot kicked against the gun. Picking it up he tried to find his way out.

With the wall for guidance and coughing and choking in the smoke he made his way back the way they had come. He found another passageway opposite the stairs. The smoke seemed to be less here and he felt a faint breeze on his face. He found a wide door, which opened, into a large room. Groping for a light switch he flicked it on. It was piled high with turf, which was used as fuel to feed the furnace of the heating system. He made his way to the darkest corner and burrowed into the turf. He then broke the bulb by firing a sod of turf at it. Then he lay down and covered himself with sods of turf until he felt he was well hidden.

After a while the commotion seemed to be dying and he knew they would be searching for him. Footsteps and voices sounded in the corridor outside and the door slowly opened. Two young soldiers peered into the room their F.N. rifles at the ready. Reilly held his breath. A Garda shone a powerful torch around the room.

"Nothing here lads,"

They moved on down the passageway, he settled down to wait for night.

It was pleasantly warm in the room Soon he dozed off. When he awoke some hours later all was quiet. He lay there for a while in the darkness. Above his head he could see a glint of light. Climbing up the mound of turf he found it was coming from a circular steel cover used as an opening for the delivery of the fuel. He eased his shoulder under it and pushed it gently off its rim. Easing the cover to one side he let his eyes come level with the roadway. He could not believe his luck. He had surfaced under a parked lorry in a side street. The wall of the courthouse was about three yards away. On the corner under a street lamp a couple of soldiers, their rifles held casually stood talking. Crawling out he lay on the wet roadway and gently slid the cover back in position. It slipped into place with a slight clang. One of the soldiers glanced casually towards the lorry and then turned away.

Footsteps clattered on the pavement and he heard the door of the truck being opened. Reilly realised that the driver had arrived and the truck was about to be driven off. Above his head he saw the spare wheel fixed to its bracket at an angle to the chassis. There was just enough time for him to squeeze himself length ways across it with his feet on the chassis and hang on The truck moved off and stopped at the soldiers, who had a cursory search of the cab and body before it moved on. They were checked at three more roadblocks before the driver finally stopped in a quite cul de sac and parked the vehicle. After locking the truck his footsteps faded into the distance.

CHAPTER 4

George Reilly was soaked to the skin and numb with cold. His fingers gripping the metal bar seemed not to belong to him at all. He doubted if he would have been able to hang on much longer. The pain in his body from being bounced against the steel was something else. Gently he eased himself from under the truck and stood up. For a moment he felt dizzy. Shaking his head he tried to massage his hands and legs. Gradually some form of life came back into his tired body. It was raining again. That soft Irish rain that soaked into his already wet clothes. He was cold, oh so cold. Willing himself to move he walked towards the corner of the street. It seemed to be the main street of a town. To his right was a tall building with a clock tower which told him it was just after nine p.m. He looked to the left. There seemed to be more lighted windows in that direction. He started to walk towards them. The odd person he passed had no thought for the sodden figure that glanced at the shop fronts in an effort to find the name of the town. Then suddenly there it was. In black lettering it said Bray Sub Post Office. At the same time he heard a bus approaching, on the destination board the word Dublin stood out. He had covered some twelve miles since his escape from the city.

He passed a cafe. The smell of the food made him realise how hungry he was. His mouth watered at the thought of eating. There were only two people at the tables. Hell, there was no point, he did not have any money. As a prisoner you were not allowed to carry money when in court. He started to move on down the street. Suddenly he was aware of a man walking behind him. Without turning he listened to the footsteps. Stopping at the brightly-lit window of a radio shop he stood looking in. The footsteps stopped. Glancing sideways Reilly saw the man gazing at the unlit window of a building society. He was of medium height with dark raincoat, scarf and cap pulled down to one side of his face. George moved on. The footsteps followed. At the next corner a man stepped out of a doorway, blocking his path.

"Have you got a light Mack?"

He asked.

Without taking his hands out of his pockets George replied curtly,

"I don't have a light or a match or a cigarette, I'm cold hungry and wet through and not a penny to my name, so just leave me alone."

A voice came from behind him,

"You're lucky then because we have the lot, George Reilly, it is George Reilly, am I right?"

George could only nod accent to the man in the raincoat. They bundled him into a car, which had drawn up at the kerb and explained that they had been on alert since the escape had been announced. When they saw him first he was looking at the post office. The Garda description had been very accurate. It was good that there were no Patrol cars around or he would certainly have been picked up. They drove for about half an hour, before turning into the grounds of a detached house where the driver entered a large garage. The doors were shut and the other two ushered George into the house. He slumped down on a chair shivering.

"Wait here."

The older man ordered. The other man went to a sideboard and came back with a bottle and glass. He filled the whiskey to the brim and handed it to Reilly.

"Here, get that down, it will warm you up."

At that moment the other man returned with a bundle of clothes and towels.

"O K. upstairs and have a hot bath, get out of those wet clothes, before you catch pneumonia, afterwards you can have something to eat, we'll say good bye now and wish you the best of luck"

George shook hand with both men who brushed off his thanks.

He went up the stairs. The bathroom was directly in front of him, the steam rising from the clear greenish water. After he had soaked himself for a quarter of an hour he shaved and dressed. The clothes fitted perfectly. Going downstairs he could hear the sound of a tel-

34

evision or radio coming from one of the rooms. He gave a knock and entered.

In the centre was a table laid for a meal. The television in the corner was showing a late news summary with details of his escape.

"All airports and seaports were being watched and an early recapture was expected."

George looked at his own face staring at him from the screen.

"You're not as bad looking as that picture."

The voice was female with a Northern Irish lilt to it. A girl had come in wheeling a food trolley. She took a plate and expertly filled it with meat and vegetables. Placing it on the table she asked,

"Would you like beer or wine?"

Reilly asked her for a lager. She left the room and returned with two cans, which she placed in front of him. Then sitting down opposite she lit a cigarette and watched him eat. She did not speak.

He judged her to be about twenty-three or four. She had very black hair, which hung, about her shoulders. Her face was long and narrow, not pretty but pleasant thought George as he drank his lager. He finished his meal and sat back.

"That was very nice, thank you very much, I'm afraid I don't know your name"

Without answering him the girl collected the dishes and placed them on the trolley. She disappeared into what must have been the kitchen. He heard her moving around. Ten minutes later she returned, looking at him as she spoke.

"My name is Francis, that's all you need to know for the moment, our orders are to get you out of the country. Tomorrow we will have a visit from an important member of the inner council. In the meantime you can have anything you want, within reason that is."

She looked at him with a faint smile,

"The one thing I want now is a good sleep,"

He replied, yawning. They went upstairs and the girl showed him his room.

"If you want anything I'll be in there."

She said pointing to a door across the way. He was asleep almost as soon as his head hit the pillow.

Someone was shaking him by the shoulder.

"George, George, it's nine o clock we've to be ready by ten,"

It was the girl. He lay there for a few moments trying to adjust to his new surroundings then showered and shaved and went downstairs where the girl had breakfast ready.

At ten-o clock sharp a blue Datsun saloon drove up and a man carrying a briefcase got out to be greeted with a hug by the girl. George rose and went forward. The girl introduced him.

"George this is the man from the inner council, you can call him John, he will explain all"

The man shook hands and sat and looked at him for a moment, then began,

"First let me congratulate you on your escape, secondly we are getting you out of the country this evening. You will travel by Dormobile from Dun Laoghaire on tonight's eight fifteen sailing. Francis here will go with you and you will be travelling as man and wife. In England you will meet up with one of our men who will pass you on. Your final destination is Moscow. There you will meet a certain Colonel Gudenuv. We are making plans for a final phase to make this country into, a thirty-two county republic. Of course we require some help from the Ruskies. From time to time they will be sending arms and ammunition. We want you to oversee that part of the operation and I can think of no one better suited. Eventually when everything is ready you will return with the final arms shipment.

He reached into his briefcase and took out an envelope.

"All your tickets, papers, passports and money are in there so are your instructions for contacting our man in England, you and your wife are going home after a touring holiday. The tickets are dated three weeks ago, learn the dates and the times and change your hairstyle a little. It's dead simple getting you out, you probably won't even be asked any questions. Learn your new identities, remember from now on you are Mr. and Mrs. Holmstairs from London. The Dormobile will be here at six o clock, any questions?"

He was fastening the briefcase as he spoke. Reilly gathered up the papers and examined them carefully. He stuffed them into the envelope.

"Just one thing, how do I make contact?"

John gave him a smile.

"Leave that to us we will keep in touch and send you orders as required, good luck and safe journey."

He shook hands and walked from the room. George watched as the girl went with him to the car. She gave him a hug and a kiss before he drove away.

At seven thirty that evening they joined a slow moving line of cars at the Ferry port. Their tickets were checked in by a bored staff member who tore them off without as much as a glance at their faces. The open doors of the ship swallowed them up and they were aboard. One of the two men, who were leaning casually on the pier railing, wrote down yet another registration number on to his list. While the ship was on its way to Holyhead the Irish registration numbers would be checked through the computer. British police would check the English ones before the ship reached the other side.

They drove off the ferry at about twelve thirty. The customs man waving them through and stopped the next car. Turning right at the entrance to the docks they found a large car park where they tried to sleep until eight a.m. They had breakfast and a clean up in a roadside cafe. Afterwards they set out to make their rendezvous with their contact. It had been arranged that he would meet them in a lay-by on the A47 on the Eastern side of Norwich. Here a white Transit van waited. The Volkswagen pulled in behind it. A young man in overalls and cap came towards them.

"Hello, I'm Mick, we haven't much time so follow me carefully. First we must get rid of the Dormobile. When you see me turn right follow, it'll be a bit rough so for God's sake don't get lost."

After about fifteen miles they turned on to a narrow track leading into what George could see was marsh country. By now it was dark with heavy rain showers. The Transit stopped and Mick waved them on by. They stopped with the headlights showing a vast expanse of water in front of them. Reilly stepped out of the Volkswagen into a foot of water. The girl stepped out the other door and George heard her squeal at the coldness. Mick joined them with a large stone in one hand and a small branch in the other. First, he put the V.W. in second gear. Then he wedged the accelerator with the stone. Cutting a slot in the branch, he reached in through the driver's window engaging the ignition key in the slot. A quick turn, the engine fired and the Dormobile shot forward out over the bank, a few bubbles arose as it sank beneath the water.

"What a terrible waste,"

Mick grinned at them,

"Come on we still have some miles to go."

They skirted a small village and drove for about ten miles before turning on to a narrow country road with high hedges on either side. A rutted overgrown track brought them to some derelict buildings. Here he drove the van into the shelter of what was left of a Nissan hut and got out.

"This used to be an old airfield during the last war,"

Volunteered Mick.

He was taking some small bicycle lamps from the van. The rain had stopped now and he led them down to the old runway. At the edge he placed two lamps and switched them on. They gave off a green light shining into the black sky. At approximately two hundred-yard distances he placed four more. Sometime later the sound of an approaching aircraft could be heard. Out of the night sky a small Cessna landed. George Reilly climbed aboard and two minutes later it took off out over the North Sea. They landed in Holland. After a few days stay in the house of a Dutch- Irish couple he became an American student travelling around Europe. He reached Berlin without incident and crossed into East Germany through that most famous of crossings, Checkpoint Charley. From there he was flown to Moscow and Colonel Gudenuv. Now at last he was going back to Ireland.

He lay there gazing at the ceiling. This was to be the big one. A complete take-over of the country The realisation of the Irish dream. A thirty-two county Ireland In three days? Gudenuv's plan sounded good, there was no doubt, but three days? There was bound to be a foul up somewhere. What if Britain and America intervened? Then the cat would really be among the pigeons.

He hoped he would not have to kill anyone, the sweat broke out on his forehead. Down the years he had never killed or hurt anyone during his bank raid days. Even at the last one he never made any attempt to fire his revolver. He had been horrified to discover some months after his escape that the bodies of the couple who had owned the Dormobile had been found in a lake in the middle of the country. He put out the light and went to sleep.

Five stories overhead the man with the damaged hand had been sleeping. He awoke to the gentle buzz from his wristwatch. In almost total darkness he picked up the transistor radio. Removing the back he connected a wire to the antenna. The other end he passed through a tiny hole in the window frame where it connected with the metal rainwater pipe, which joined up with the guttering around the roof, thus making one giant antenna. Taking what looked like a calculator from his pocket he connected it to the radio. Then he began to tap out a message in code. High above in the night sky visible only, as a pinpoint of light from earth the American spy satellite held to its orbit. It picked up the coded message and relayed it to its monitoring station in the frozen wastes of Alaska. Half an hour later in the Pentagon in Washington the decoded message was passed to Maurice J. Curley head of Special Operations Branch of the C.I.A. It read as follows.

Mos. Three Irish leave tomorrow for home, something big.

Curley studied it carefully for some moments. He picked up a blue telephone on his desk.

"Henry, arrange a staff meeting for ten o clock tomorrow morning and get me a line to the President."

He lit a cigarette and looked again at the paper in his hand.

CHAPTER 5

Joe Kearns arrived at the newspaper office at about seven thirty p.m. By eight thirty he had completed his report on the parade and riot. The Editor read it through and looked at him.

"This is a bit strong Joe, was it really organised? How can you tell, if we print this we could find ourselves in trouble."

Joe sat on the edge of the desk.

"Look, I was there, I saw what happened and I can tell you it was an organised riot. Rent a mob or whatever you like, what's in that report is the truth, what you want to print is your business but there is more to this thing than meets the eye, now I'm off to get something to eat.

He left the man reading through the report again. Walking down the street he entered a small restaurant where he usually dined when he was in the newspaper office or working in the area. Jack McConnell, the owner, gave him a wave and came over.

"Joe, its good to see you we've missed you for the past few weeks,"

They sat down at a corner table and May, Jack's wife, took Joe's order and welcomed him back. The two men talked about things in general and Joe's last assignment. May arrived back with the meal and placed it in front of him. Jack McConnell started to move and then said.

"That was a rough session in O'Connell Street today Joe."

"It was rough all right Jack, I know, I was there, I can tell you there was something very strange about it as well"

Jack looked around before speaking quietly.

"Joe, there were a couple of Northern blokes in here last night. I happened to overhear a bit of their conversation one of them was saying something like,

"We'll have to make this thing tomorrow into a bloody good row."

"That's all I could heard Joe, do you think they could have had something to do with today's trouble?"

Joe stopped eating and looked at his friend, a feeling of excitement starting to rise in him.

"What did these fellows look like Jack?"

Jack thought for a second or two.

"One was about five foot six or seven, medium build, a short beard and reddish hair, the other was taller, I'd say six foot or over, with a moustache, and a scar on his left cheek. He had jet black hair and was wearing one of those creamy coloured raincoats, except it wasn't creamy it was filthy dirty."

A picture flashed into Joe's mind of a man in a raincoat hurling a brick at the Garda Inspector. That man also had a moustache. He felt the adrenaline starting to flow. It had to be the same man. Then the whole thing had been planned in advance, but for what reason? Just to cause trouble in the city centre on a Saturday afternoon. No that would not make any sense. Jack's voice broke in on his thoughts.

"Joe, your food is getting cold, it's my fault let me get you something else.

He took the plate and went towards the kitchen. Kearns mind was racing. What was going on? Why a riot on a Saturday afternoon. It did not make any sense. Jack came back with some hot food which Joe finished off and left the restaurant to go back to the newspaper office and the Editor.

As he approached his car two figures converged on him from either side. The taller of the two spoke.

"Good evening Mr.Kearns, I'm Detective Sergeant Holmes, Special Branch, and this Detective Garda Willis."

Both men showed him their I.D. cards.

"Can you come with us? I must emphasise that you are not under arrest, you are free to refuse, however I am to tell you that this is a matter of great urgency and that your co-operation would be greatly appreciated."

All three stood in silence for some moments. Joe felt that this was a very strange request, yet something about it intrigued him, who knows there could be a story here. He looked at the men and asked,

"Can you tell me where I'm going? Who I'm going to see?"

The detective sergeant shook his head,

"I'm afraid not sir, but I can tell you that it is of National importance."

Joe considered for just a moment more then nodded accent.

The younger man said.

"Will you come this way sir, it will be better if you leave your car here, we will drop you back."

He led the way to a black car almost invisible in the shadows a short distance away. The younger man got behind the wheel and Joe and the sergeant sat in the rear. Joe noticed that the windows were so darkened that he could not see out. He tried to look forward but there was a screen between them and the driver made of the same material. The sergeant chatted pleasantly about mundane things during the twenty-minute journey. When they alighted, Joe found they were in a walled courtyard. He did not get time to see anything else as he was ushered through a door into a passageway guarded by two men with Uzi sub machine guns and up a flight of stairs. At the top was a richly carpeted area with rooms to each side. One on the right had two oaken doors and the sergeant knocked on one of these and entered. A moment later he emerged and holding it open said,

"Will you go in please Mr. Kearns."

Inside Joe found himself facing three men sitting behind a desk. One was in the uniform of a Garda Commissioner. The other was an Army Commandant. There was no mistaken the third man, it was Victor Fitzgibbon, the Taoiseach and leader of the Irish Government, who rose and came forward shaking Joe's hand.

"Mr. Kearns, good of you to come, please take a seat"

Joe sat in the chair, which had been placed opposite the three men. The Garda Commissioner looked at some papers in front of him and addressed Joe.

"Mr. Kearns, first, let me welcome you here tonight. I know this is a strange way for us all to meet. Believe me we think this meeting is absolutely necessary, first I want to ask you some questions, you were at this meeting in O'Connell Street to day, we would like you to tell us exactly what your impressions were of what happened there."

Joe Kearns started into an account of the happenings in front of the Post Office. He refrained at this stage from saying anything about the possibility of the whole thing been rigged. At times one of the men would interrupt to ask a specific question. All three were making notes. When he had finished they held a muttered conversation among themselves. Then turning to Joe the Taoiseach asked.

"Mr. Kearns, was there anything else you noticed there, anything out of the ordinary, anything at all?

Joe then gave them his opinion that the whole incident had been stage-managed. The three men looked at each other and nods were exchanged. For a moment there was silence in the room. The Taoiseach looked directly at Joe, his eyes boring into him.

"Mr. Kearns, I must ask you now not to speak a word of this meeting to anyone outside this room. It is imperative that anything spoken of here this evening be regarded as top secret. From scraps of information we are aware that some sort of coup is being planned for later this year. At the moment it's only rumour, a word or two here and there. We are aware of your ability as an investigative journalist. I am now going to ask you to take on a job that will tax your abilities to the utmost and put your life at great risk. You will be dealing with people who are completely ruthless. They will kill without mercy any one who gets in their way. I am asking you now if you are prepared to try to find out what is happening. You are unconnected with the Gardai so people might talk more freely with you. Any information however small will be of help. As I have told you it is of the gravest National importance that we learn of what's going on as soon as possible, of course you are free to refuse, if so that will be the end of the matter."

He never took his eyes off Joe, whose brain was spinning over his words. This man, the leader of the Irish Government was asking him to do a job that could end up with one very dead Joe Kearns. On the other hand it could be very interesting. What a story he could get out of it. It would be the sensation of the newspaper world.

"How long do I have to think about it Sir?"

"I must have your answer now."

"Right, I'll do it,"

The Taoiseach sat back, a look of satisfaction on his face and nodded to the Commissioner who now spoke.

"You will appreciate Mr. Kearns that you will be entirely on your own in this, we will not be able to interfere if you get into trouble. You will have to be very careful. If you have anything for us you can ring this number and the message will be recorded. Do not mention your name, your call sign will be 'Magpie'. Memorise that number, don't write it down. If you want a meeting, leave a time and date. This line is fully protected from interference. All your calls will be scrambled, the only one that will be able to read them is me. Are you clear on all that?"

Joe nodded. The Taoiseach stood up. He held out his hand to him.

"Goodbye Mr. Kearns and thank you for doing this, I wish you the best of luck, we can but pray that you will be successful, the fate of this Nation may well depend on it, The sergeant will show you back to your car."

He pressed a bell on the desk.

Travelling back with the genial Holmes, Joe felt as if in a dream. He felt sure that these people knew everything about him. They must have had him in mind for some time. This whole thing could not have been set up as quickly as all that. They dropped him opposite the newspaper office and he walked to his car and drove back to his flat.

Next morning found him in a large square near the city centre. The Sunday morning bird market was crowded. It had been frosty earlier but now, at twelve, midday, the weak winter sun was shining on the colourful scene. Joe Kearns wandered around until he found the man he was looking for. He was standing at the corner of a stall, his head bent, as he tried to light a cigarette with one hand, the other was missing from the elbow.

He was about forty years of age and looked sixty. Some years previously he had been brought into a hospital with a badly mangled arm, the result of a motor cycle accident some said. The arm had to amputated at the elbow. Joe had known him for some time. They had met in Dublin some years ago shortly after he had lost his arm. Joe had tried to help him and since then he had been the source of information on many an occasion. Needless to say Joe always parted with some cash. At that moment the man looked up and his leathery face broke into a grin.

"The bould Joe, what the hell brings you here on a Sunday morning?"

Frank O'Brien blew a cloud of tobacco smoke out of his lungs. Joe grinned back at him.

"Hello Frank, I'm looking for you of course, don't you know you'll kill yourself if you keep smoking those coffin nails."

"Sure I'm half dead already, what does it matter, but that's not what you want me for, your looking for info."

He stared Joe squarely in the eye before breaking into a fit of coughing. Joe brought him to the car and they both sat in. The coughing subsided and Joe explained that he was doing an article about the Republican struggle to free the six counties from British rule. He was looking for people to interview. Maybe Frank could suggest some names. What could only be described as a mask seemed to slip over the man's face. He gazed out through the car windscreen.

"Tell me Joe are you on the level? Is it the political boys you want to talk to? I can tell you a name. He's supposed to be the headman for the organisation, at the moment he's in the Government as an Independent T.D. and likes to keep everyone thinking that's all he is, but I can tell you he is very high in the movement, his name is Michael McCall. I could probably arrange a meeting with one of the active members as well, but you'll have to get to McCall yourself"

He looked at Joe with a grin,

"Of course this will cost you a few quid."

Kearns smiled to himself, money, it opens all doors.

"Okay. Frank, see if you can arrange a meeting, I promise you you'll be paid."

O'Brien looked at him sheepishly.

"I don't suppose you could give me a tenner now, I'm broke, I'll fix the meeting, by the way your man is fond of the Jameson, don't ask him too many questions, or you could find yourself in a lot of trouble."

Joe passed over a tenpound note and O'Brien let himself out of the car.

"Thanks Joe, I'll give you a ring at the paper when things are ready".

He walked away into the crowd his body shaking from the coughing.

Monday morning found Joe Kearns in the newspaper office reading up on the T.D. Michael McCall. He had a political history of local council work before being elected to the Government and although his politics were left wing he was apparently not connected to the Subversive movement. He was known as a tireless worker on behalf of his constituents. Married with four children he lived in an old red brick house in Rathmines. A photograph showed him as a tall man, round faced and wearing horn-rimmed glasses. His face gave him a studious expression, rather like a college professor, thought Joe. As he read on, the picture formed of a dedicated socialist who was viewed with grudging respect by friends and enemies alike. He was also a man who liked his share of publicity. This was evident from the numerous statements which he gave to the newspapers, most of which were accompanied by a photograph. When not attending the Government sittings he could be found in his office in Wisbeck Street not too far from Government buildings.

At three thirty that afternoon Joe Kearns rang the bell of the door marked Michael McCall. There was a buzz and a girl's voice told him to come in. He entered a room with a desk and some chairs lined along the wall. The girl looked up from some papers.

"I'll be with you in a second-------!

Her voice trailed off,

Joe smiled at her. It was the girl from the riot, Jean McKay.

"It's true you know, you never know who you are going to meet when you're working."

He told her.

"How are you Jean and young Joanna?"

The girl started to blush.

"We're fine really Mr. Kearns, thank you, but what are you doing here?"

Joe looked at her, she's really lovely he thought.

"I came to see if Mr. McCall would give me an interview for an article I'm doing on the Northern situation and by the way, you promised to call me Joe, remember."

"You're out of luck to day, he's gone to Dundalk for a meeting, he will not be back until tomorrow, I'm his secretary, if you like I'll ask him and give you a ring".

She was making notes on a pad. Joe found himself staring at her. On Saturday he had found himself attracted to her and now a couple of days later here she is again. He felt a sudden urge to prolong the conversation.

"Can you tell me anything about him at all?"

He asked her,

"And please call me Joe."

The girl gave him a disapproving look.

"There's really nothing I can tell you that you don't know already, I've been working for him for the past year, I can only say that he is very nice to work for."

Joe felt she did not want to say anything more about the man. He arranged to phone her the following morning at about ten to find out if he could have the interview.

Later sitting in the Volkswagen he though about the girl again. She was a real good looker. He had to admit that this second meeting did have quite an effect on him. No, better forget it, what about young Joanna, she must be married, there was probably a husband around somewhere. Too bad Joe old son, you could have fallen for her she's so nice and very much her own woman too. He was surprised at his own thoughts. For the first time since the accident he was actually considering the possibility of dating a girl. Suddenly it just felt good to be alive. He spent the rest of the day looking around, gathering a bit of information here and there. When he got back to the office there was a message from One Arm. He had arranged a meeting for eight P.M. in the Black Cat public house on the coast road near Blackrock. He was to carry a copy of his newspaper for recognition purposes.

Joe walked into the Black Cat at five minutes to eight. A blast of hot air hit him as he entered. The place was almost empty. There were four customers sitting on high stools at the bar. One young fellow of about twenty was engaged in animated conversation with the barman. Two others talked quietly while sipping their pints. The fourth was reading a newspaper from behind a glass of whiskey. Joe bought a Coke and sat down at a table under the cynical eye of the barman. He placed the paper on the table and waited.

Half an hour later he was beginning to think that he was wasting his time when the door was thrust open and a man came in. He was wearing jeans and a leather jacket and was unshaven. His eyes searched the room and focused on the newspaper in front of Joe. He came straight over.

"Are you Kearns?"

He almost spat the question out.

Joe nodded and the man sat down opposite, he leaned forward, his voice low.

"I hear you're looking for a story and there might be a few bob in it, is that right?"

"Yes I'm doing an article on the situation in the North and its effect down here, by the way would you like a drink?"

"A large Jameson would go down nicely."

Joe went to the bar and returned with the drink. The man took a gulp of the liquid.

"How much is in this for me? Times are hard."

His bloodshot eyes stared into Joe's.

"That depends on what you've got to tell me, if it's good you'll be well paid."

Joe was beginning to wonder if the meeting was a mistake. The man took another drink and emptied the glass.

"I can tell you plenty Mister, I know whose doing the bank robberies, where the arms come in, who the head men are and a lot more."

He rolled the empty glass around from hand to hand. Joe signalled to the barman who brought a refill. There was silence until he had gone. The man emptied a third of the glass at a swallow. He started on a rambling tirade of historical rhetoric about the North of Ireland. Another glass later and Joe decided to call it a day. This man was telling him nothing. He signalled for more whiskey and prepared to leave.

"I don't think you've anything to tell me that I don't know already, I've got to go but here's another whiskey for you."

He started to rise. The man reached out and caught his sleeve.

"Sit down"

He hissed through clenched teeth.

"I'll tell you, by God I'll tell you, you don't know the half of it."

Surprised by his venom Joe sat down. Raising the glass the man swallowed it in one gulp. He leaned across the table until his face almost touched Joe's nose.

"There's going to be a take over by the boys sometime at the end of March. We're going to make this place a socialist republic, now what do you think of that? We'll be taking the six counties too, so at long last Ireland will be totally free and everyone has been told to stand to. Even oul fellows like me."

He stared at Joe triumph in his eyes. Kearns had heard this rumour several times over the past years but this was the only time he had heard a date suggested.

"Are you sure about this?"

He looked at the drunken man across the table.

"Sure I'm sure. Hard to believe isn't it. They've been saying it for years, now it's really going to happen, Kathleen Mo Voureen, a nation once again, and it's only going to take three days, three bloody days and we'll be a thirty two county republic, how much is that worth to you Kearns, what?"

His eyes were misty, his voice a drunken slur. The voice trailed off and he twisted the empty glass in his hands. Joe signalled and the barman brought another glass of the amber liquid. Two men came into the bar and looked casually around. One was quite short with blond close cut hair and a pleasant smile. The other was taller with a thin face and a high sloping forehead. Joe guessed them about thirty-one or two. The blond one came over and slapped the drunken man on the shoulder.

"Jem me ould son, how are you? How are things? We haven't seen you for a while"

He looked at Joe.

"Who's your friend Jem?"

His eyes were cold steel. Jem was looking at him owlishly.

"Friend, old friends, I'm drunk Sean, will you take me home?"

He looked from Joe to the blond man. Joe offered to bring him home. Sean laughed.

"Not at all we'll look after him, we're well used to him, we often bring him home, we'll just have one ourselves and then be off."

Joe said good night and left the three sitting around the table. Driving back towards the city he pondered on the information he had gleaned from the man called Jem. The Taoiseach had said that something was about to happen, if what Jem had told him was true, it was a bombshell. Yet how was it possible? The Subversives did not have that much support to be able to take over the country in three days. Unless of course they had outside help and that could only be from the Russians. He would have to see Jem again, perhaps he could get a little more out of him. He parked the car and went to bed remembering as he did so that he was supposed to have left the V.W. with Paddy McKenna that same morning. Well, the repairs to the wing would just have to wait. Putting on a Brahm's symphony he fell asleep before the tape finished.

CHAPTER 6

In Washington that January morning, the weather was snowy, with an icy wind blowing off the Potomac River. Harry Grant drove into the Pentagon at nine forty five. He had got home to his apartment at five a.m. after a party. There was a message on his ansaphone to call Dad, who was one Colonel Maurice J Curley of Central Intelligence. Grant, had been discovered by Curley, when he was serving in the State Police as a young trooper. He had previously been a Green Beret in the American Special Forces. After rigorous CIA training he had passed out head of his bunch. His various undercover jobs in Europe and Asia made him one of the most experienced man under thirty in the service. At twenty seven he had seen more action than most of the older men had in their lifetime. Presently he worked in the Pentagon keeping tracks on agents throughout the world. Curley would not have left that message unless something important had come up. Well, he had been getting a bit bored lately. There had been no serious work for him for the last six months. Maybe this was a new job. The old feeling of excitement came back to him. Where would he be going this time? It just had to be something big for Curley to summon him like this. He stepped into the elevator and went up to Curley's Office on the sixth floor. The wooden faced Marine on duty at the door, never moved a muscle as he went in.

Inside Curley was talking with four more high-ranking intelligence men. He turned at Harry's entrance.

"Morning Harry, take a seat, hard night? You look a bit green".

He grinned, motioning to the table around which the others were seated.

Maurice J Curley was tingling with suppressed excitement. He had spoken to the President, briefing him on the message received from Moscow. He felt sure that this was the start of a move to set up a Soviet base in Ireland. It would be up to him and his team to try and stop it in its tracks. It was essential to obtain more information, hence this meeting. He would dispatch these men to Europe. Grant he would send to Ireland. He started to explain the position to the group at the table. They listened carefully to his instructions. No notes were taken, memory alone would serve them. Their tasks appointed the men started off to make preparations for their departure leaving Grant and Curley making their way back to the Colonels office.

"Shut the door Harry."

Curley sat in the high-backed leather chair and picked up the phone.

"Henry, bring us some coffee, ever been to Ireland Harry?"

Grant shook his head. Curley went on.

"A beautiful country Harry, scenery you just will not believe, you'll step back twenty years when you get off the plane. The Irish people. Well, they're something else, friendly, gracious and for the most part very easy going. Yet if you start to talk politics you could have a war on your hands in no time at all."

He paused as Henry arrived with the coffee.

"My grandparents came here from Mayo along with hundreds of others, maybe I'll get a chance to go and have a look at the old place someday."

He was pouring out two cups of coffee as he spoke.

"Harry I want you to go to Ireland, try and get a lead on the situation that's developing. You can be a student of history doing research into the whole Irish question. If you need any help there's an electronics factory outside Kildare town. We operate a radar station there as part of the works. There is also a direct radio link to here by satellite. Of course the Irish authorities know none of this. As far as they are concerned it's just an ordinary electronics factory producing parts for computers. Our Embassy in Dublin will help you all they can, there's a couple of good men there too."

He took a drink of his coffee and looked across at Grant. Harry put his cup down. His head was throbbing and he felt definitely queasy.

"Okay. Sir, I've never been there, from what I gather it's supposed to

52

be to be a quaint place, never thought much about it until now. I suppose I had better read up on it before I go, it will be a bit of a holiday after the excitement of the last six months."

He grinned across at Curley who glowered back.

"I'll remind you that this is not an ordinary job, we have heard rumours that the Russians are going to try and turn Ireland into another Cuba. We can't let them succeed. If this is not stopped it could very well lead to world war three. Think of the catastrophe that would be."

Curley dropped his eyes to some papers on his desk. Grant whistled softly.

"It's that bad Sir?"

Curley nodded and pushed a large envelope across the desk.

"Your ticket is in there, its for the Air Lingus flight from Boston tomorrow evening, you'll be in Dublin at about eight a.m. their time on Thursday morning. The fountain pen is a knockout spray, the cigarette lighter is a camera and by pressing the filler cap it gives you one shot of a bullet the size of a match head. This is an explosive bullet and can kill. It must be used at close quarters, maximum range one yard. Try for a head shot if you can, you do know that firearms are taboo in Ireland. They get very upset about people carrying guns, even the police are unarmed, that is except the Special Branch men, one more thing, Good Luck."

The two men shook hands and Grant picked up the envelope. Putting it inside his jacket he stood up and winced as his head reeled. Curley looked at him with a frown.

"Harry I think you should go and read up on Ireland and the situation there. The subversives there are a tough lot, people who get in their way tend to disappear or are found shot in the head, don't underestimate them, if they think you are spying on them they will have no mercy, I don't want you ending up dead. It's not too bad in Dublin as they try not to antagonise the authorities to much or they might introduce internment, the same as in the nineteen forties, now take yourself off and get something for that head of yours."

He waved him out. Harry made his way down to the pharmacy where he was given a sedative which cleared the headache inside the time it took to get from there to the library. Here he engrossed himself in learning as much as possible about the country he was about to visit. By evening he felt he had absorbed enough knowledge of the place to be able to move around Dublin and talk to the local population without making a complete fool of himself. An hour spent with an ex member of the staff of the Embassy in Dublin gave him more up to date information on the scene there. He had returned some weeks ago and was sorry to come home to Washington. The Irish people were so friendly. There was no great trouble with the subversives in Dublin, apart from the odd bank robbery. Bombings and shootings were mostly confined to the six Northern counties, which were under the control of the British Government. Mind you there were certain areas in Dublin where you did not go at night. He was sure that Harry would like the people, and the girls, well, they were something else, he himself reckoned they were the most beautiful in the world. The pace of life was slow compared with America, a bit like Italy he supposed if it could not be done today, well, there was always tomorrow. Harry left the building at five-o clock and made his way to his apartment. Here he packed his bags and added a few documents and books, headed Harvard University, and a small lightweight typewriter. These would lend authenticity to his story that he was a student doing research on the troubles.

He boarded the Aer Lingus Boeing that evening at Boston's Logan International. The two hostesses in their immaculate green uniforms welcomed him aboard and directed him to a window seat where a husband and wife of about forty joined him. The woman started to chat to him as the plane taxied out for take off. They were from County Wicklow. He should try and visit there; the scenery was only wonderful. Was he staying long in Ireland? The man wanted to know. Most Americans only came for a week or so, sure you could not see anything of a country in that short time. The woman insisted on giving him her address, saying that he would be most welcome if he chose to visit them. The hostess came round with the headsets for a film so he excused himself and took a pair to watch Earthquake. Later he fell asleep. When he awoke they were touching down at Shannon for a half-hour stop. They landed at Dublin Airport about half an hour later.

In the Customs hall a red bearded officer examined his passport. Sitting at the desk with him was a well-built man with a long face, which gave him a rather sad appearance. He looked as if he was about to fall asleep but Grant noticed that he was viewing each passport as the Customs man held it at just the right angle for him to see. Redbeard looked up at Harry.

"How long will you be staying in Ireland, Mr.Grant?"

Harry explained that he was here as a student to do some articles on the troubles in the North and their effects on the Republic, he would be moving about, getting the opinions of the people. The officer stamped his passport and handed it back.

"Enjoy your stay Mr. Grant."

Harry got the feeling that he had not believed one word of what he had told him. As he walked away he saw the older man reach for a telephone. Grant he thought, you're really slipping, there's no way they could suspect anything or know anything about you and here you are starting to imagine things already. He walked out into the cold of an Irish January morning. On the bus into the city he viewed the people and buildings as they passed. He arrived at the Embassy at about ten, where he was given breakfast. The First Secretary who was the CIA man in Dublin brought him up to date on events. He advised Grant to stay in a small guesthouse in nearby Baggot Street. At the embassy they too had heard rumours of an impending coup but nothing concrete. Of course that demonstration last week was been talked about. One paper had even gone so far as to suggest that it might have been an organised riot, but no definite evidence had emerged to prove this was so. Grant mentioned the man at the Airport that morning and the Secretary looked startled.

"From your description that was Inspector John Maguire, Head of the Special Branch here, I wonder why he was there?"

The First Secretary went on.

"He's a tough one, very efficient, he was there for a purpose, make no mistake about that, I'd sure like to know what, keep out of his way or he'll have you back on a plane out before you can say Davy Crockett. Now go and book into that guesthouse, a lot of our fellows use it. The woman that runs it is a widow, her husband was shot in one of the subversives bank raids, you might get a lead or two from her, bye the way there's a bar along the quays in the city. It's called the White Horse, some of the Subversives drink there. I might be a good place to start."

Grant walked the short distance from the Embassy to Baggot Street. He had no trouble finding the place. There was a large sign, which said St.Ultans Guest House fixed to the front railings. What had once been the front garden was now a tarmacadam car park. He stepped into the hallway and rang the bell on the desk.

"Good morning, can I do something for you?"

The voice was soft with a musical lilt to it. Grant turned. The woman was about his own age with jet-black hair and grey eyes. Her face was pleasant and she wore no make up except for a little lipstick. She was tall for a woman and well proportioned. Grant thought she was very beautiful except for the sadness in her eyes. They hadn't told him at the Embassy that she was as young as this. He introduced himself and told her he was doing some research into the situation in Northern Ireland and its effect on the South. She looked sharply at him when he told her this. All the time she was writing his particulars into a ledger.

He was allocated room eighteen on the top floor. There was a sitting room on the ground floor. Breakfast was from eight till nine. Evening meal from six to seven. She brought him up and showed him to his room. He unpacked and placed his clothes in the wardrobe. Lying on the bed he read the paper he had been given on the plane.

CHAPTER 7

In Moscow the three Irishmen presented themselves in Gudenuv's office. The Colonel greeted them warmly in his perfect English. He gave them a rundown on the whole operation. It would, he told them, result in a thirty-two county Ireland. Theirs was a most important part of the operation. They were to take the largest shipment of arms and explosives ever sent to any country home to Ireland. This evening they would leave Moscow for Split, in Yugoslavia. There they would board the freighter. This would have on board about five hundred tons of arms, ammunitions and explosives. They would sail at midnight and head for the Italian mainland. Tomorrow they would begin the long haul under an Italian flag down the coast, around the toe of Italy, into the Mediterranean, then through the Straights of Gibraltar into the Bay of Biscay, up the coast to France and then across to Ireland. He pushed a sealed envelope across to George Reilly.

"Those are your final instructions and landing place. You will not open them until instructed by radio contact when you are within seven miles of the Irish coast. At this point you send out the call sign 'Sweep' at ten-minute intervals until contact is made with your people. If you run into trouble destroy them, the ship is wired for demolition, in that event you will have about ten minutes to get clear. You George are in full command, I wish you the best of luck."

He was careful not to mention the fact that payment for this would be Russian missile bases in the new state. Opening a bottle of vodka he filled four glasses. They all drank to the success of the mission. Then he shook hands with each of them in turn.

"Now, you will leave here immediately for your flight to Split, it will depend on weather conditions when the pilot can take off but I'm sure there will be very little delay. When you get to the ship you can familiarise yourselves with it and your crew, now go and have a good meal, then my driver will take you to the airfield."

George Reilly thanked him and picked up the envelope the others echoed the sentiments. The Colonel saluted all three as they left. They were in jubilant mood as they entered the canteen and ordered their meal. The conversation buzzed about the forthcoming trip and its implications. The young man with the damaged hand was eating at a table some distance away. He reached up and adjusted his hearing aid touching a tiny projection on the plastic. The sound amplified, he could now hear the conversation from the other table quite clearly. Tonight he would send a message to the CIA He would have to be extra careful. The satellite would be in range for only a short time after midnight. Tomorrow he was to leave for Bolivia. He had an uneasy feeling he was been watched. The secret police were always wandering around the complex checking on the students. He had admired the Irishmen, they had no regard for authority and always tried to make the police look foolish when stopped and questioned. Soon he rose and left to join his comrades for a final lesson.

Gudenuv's driver picked them up an hour later and drove them to the military airfield some twelve miles away. It was a hair-raising experience as he skidded and swayed the car through the snow. They were greeted by a cheerful air force Colonel who was to fly them. The snowplough was busy sweeping the runway. Half an hour later the Tubeluv rose into a leaden sky and a short time later they broke through into sunshine. Two hours later they landed at Split. There they were taken by two KGB men and driven to the port area where the car stopped before a pair of huge steel gates. One of the men rang a bell and the gates swung open. They drove along the quays for a time before stopping beside a rusting ship which looked about fifty years old. The KGB men ushered them out and pointed towards the vessel. Bewilderment written on their faces the three stood looking at the hulk. Fergus Doyle spat on the ground.

"Jesus Christ if that damn thing is going to get us to Ireland, my name is Dicky, what happens if we run into rough weather, I'll bet the bloody thing would break in two."

The three picked up their bags and went slowly up the gangplank. The secret police drove away towards the gates. Stepping on to the deck the trio were confronted by a line of Ursus tractors which were taking up most of the space.

"Welcome aboard George,"

The voice came from behind them. Turning quickly George recognised the man called John whom he had last seen before he escaped from Ireland. He came forward and shook hands with the three men.

"Come, I'll introduce you to the crew"

He led them into a small lounge. Seated around the walls were four men and to George's great surprise, the girl Francis. One of the men was wearing a sort of uniform complete with a cap with an indecipherable badge on it. John pointed at him first.

"This is our Captain Gregor Makirious, the fellow on his left is Abdul Kemil, He's Turkish and the first mate, the fellow with the red hair is Sean McConville, from Kerry, and that fellow grinning at you over is there Shamus Tynan from Donegal,"

"I want you to meet George Reilly, he's in command of this operation, those two with him are John O'Shea and Fergus Doyle."

George noticed the he made no mention of the girl. John took Reilly's arm and steered him from the room. The others were passing drinks around. The two men made their way to the wheelhouse and John shut the door. He looked at Reilly for a moment before speaking.

"George, I need not tell you how important it is to get this ship home. I know it looks like a wreck but believe me its perfectly seaworthy. It has been completely overhauled and strengthened by the yard here. They did not paint it so as not to attract too much attention. It's supposed to be Italian. The deck cargo is for delivery in Portugal. After its unloaded, the Captain and mate are paid off and you and the rest sail it to Ireland. You have your final instructions in the envelope. You will not open it until you get radio clearance, all right? Now come with me and I'll show you the cargo."

They went down into the forward hold. Reilly whistled softly. Every inch of available space was taken up with packing cases. From floor to ceiling John showed him crates of rifles and machine guns, hand held missiles, hand grenades. Heavy calibre machine guns were in crates of five. Other boxes contained ammunition. The other holds were similarly loaded. All the boxes were labelled as farm machinery, tools and spare parts and addressed to a firm in Dublin. The two men climbed back to the deck where John collected his briefcase and said,

"Well George, I'm off now, I'll see you in Dublin, one thing more, keep a eye on Francis for me, you look a bit puzzled, didn't you know? She's my daughter."

He walked down the gangplank and disappeared through the gates. Reilly went back to the cabin and spoke to the man in the uniform.

"Captain Makirious, what time are we sailing? And I'd like to know about our course and times, for instance when do you expect to reach Gibraltar?"

Makirious rose and came forward. In fairly good English he told George,

"Come vee go to the cabin,"

Here he unrolled some charts.

"Vee are sail at midnight, by dawn vee off the Italian coast, I dunno ven vee reach Gibraltar, maybe three veek, vee can't go vast, the boat, she very heavy."

He looked at George grinning, with his little piglike eyes. Reilly looked at the course set out on the chart. If we get to Gibraltar in a month he thought, we'll be doing well. I don't think I trust this fellow very much, there's something about him I don't like. Aloud he said.

"Good, you do your best, I'll sort out shifts for my men, they'll take any orders you give them."

He made his way back to the others. The mate had gone down to the engine room. George gave them details of the journey and suggested they familiarise themselves with the ship McConville and Tynan told him they had experience of fishing trawlers and would be able to sail the ship on from Portugal. George and the other two would look after everything else. The girl would act as cook and general factotum. Reilly took John O'Shea outside and walked around the ship. From up in the bows the two men could see the Captain in the wheelhouse. George turned to O'Shea.

"John I'm not too happy about our friend up there, I wouldn't trust him as far as I could throw him. I know we'll be getting rid of him with the tractors in Portugal but keep your eye on him, any sign of anything suspicious, let me know."

O'Shea looked at him with a grin.

"What the hell could he do George, there's six of us and two of them, Does he know what we're carrying?"

"I don't think so the cargo manifest says its farm machinery, tools and spare parts. He could suspect something else, he's been bloody well paid to get this boat as far as Portugal, after that he's supposed to leave with the mate, no questions asked, maybe its nothing but I have this feeling about him."

He shrugged his shoulders and they started back. Halfway along they met the girl, huddled into a heavy parka several sizes too large for her. Reilly smiled at her.

"You'll get lost in there Francis, how are you?"

He held out his hand and she shook it, answering rather sharply he thought,

"I'm fine George, you look well, I suppose my father has asked you to look after me, well, I can do that myself, I'm over twenty one and here to do a job, so just treat me as one of the boys."

O'Shea made a grimace at Reilly from behind her as he went aft. George turned and leaned on the rail looking down at the quay, the girl stood with him. He was aware of her perfume.

"I suppose you realise Francis what a dangerous journey this could prove to be. We could run into all sorts of trouble. Your father was only trying to make sure I would look out for you if there's any trouble."

She looked at him without any signs of wilting.

"I suppose your right but I can look after myself, in fact I've done the whole training course, so you see I will not be any trouble, in fact I might even be of some help."

She turned abruptly and walked towards the stern. Reilly watched her go. If that lassie is as tough as she sounds he thought, someone is in for a hell of a surprise. She was quite a looker too. He found himself wondering if she had a lover.

At one minute past midnight the Christopher Columbus, for that was the faded name painted on her stern, slipped her moorings and moved away from the quay. Her bow swung round and she headed down towards the open sea. Soon the twinkling lights of the port faded into the distance. George Reilly watched as the speed slowly picked up to nine knots before retiring to his small cabin.

In Moscow the Bolivian student had rigged up his transmitter. He had just finished tapping out the first few words of his message, ship leaves Split, when the door was forced open and three burly KGB men burst into the room. One snatched the wire from the transistor and smashed it on the floor. The others grabbed the student, one of them swung a heavy cosh, which connected with his forehead. He collapsed on the floor. The other man felt for a pulse and found none. They dragged the body over to the window and opened it, pushing the corpse out to fall on to the concrete below. Tomorrow it would be described as a tragic accident. The only thing that bothered the KGB men was that they had failed to take the Bolivian alive.

In Washington, Curley was dining with friends when he got the message from headquarters. He pondered over it for the rest of the evening. It had been given to him as, 'ship leave split', which did not make much sense. The message had been interrupted suddenly so their man had probably been caught in the act, it was almost certain there would be no more messages from that source.

CHAPTER 8

Joe Kearns arrived at the newspaper office a little late. There was a message from the editor to see him immediately. He looked up as Kearns entered and motioned him to a chair.

"Morning Joe, what are you working on now?"

He was looking at some papers on his desk as he spoke. A bit taken aback Kearn's mind raced.

"I thought you knew chief, I've started to follow up on that riot on Saturday, I think it would make an interesting story."

The editor shuffled his papers and looked at him.

"It has been decided to drop that one and concentrate on the stolen car racket."

This was a reference to a racket in stolen cars whereby cars stolen in Dublin found their way out of the country for resale.

"But chief, this is something big, this bloody riot was organised, I know, I have found out a lot more since. There's a sort of jigsaw here which needs putting together, I think we should keep on to this one."

The editor looked at him over his glasses.

"Not on this paper you won't, drop it Joe, I'm telling you to forget it, do the other story, if you don't like it, you know what to do."

He bent over the desk and started to write notes on the pages in front of him. Joe felt the blood pounding in his head. He had never in his career heard anything like this. The man was actually telling him to pack in the story or go. He made another attempt to argue his case.

"But chief I'm definitely on to something here."

The editor cut in.

"You heard me, I said forget it, go and do the other one."

He returned to the papers on his desk, at that precise moment Joe Kearns, lost his cool.

"Fair enough, if that's the case I would rather go, you can send on what ever money is due to me. I'll do the thing myself, There'll be no bloody way I'll sell it to this blasted paper."

Without looking up the editor enjoined,

"Have a nice day."

Kearns nearly took the door of its hinges as he hurtled out. The editor picked up the telephone and dialled a number. He waited for a connection, then spoke into the mouthpiece. He was smiling as he replaced the instrument on its cradle. In the Taioseach's office, Victor Fitzgibbon toyed with his pen making little doodling marks on the paper. His eyes bore a faraway look. He was thinking about a young man whom he might be sending to his death.

After storming out of the paper's office Kearns backed his Volkswagen out of the line and drove off. He needed time to think. Down by the river he parked near the water's edge. Time was when ships were lined up here loading and unloading. Now they called to the new container port at the mouth of the river. Here and there an abandoned and rusty crane pointed its jib towards the sky as if in some form of supplication. After a while he calmed down sufficiently to make some decisions First there was the interview with McCall the T.D. He had probably missed the message from the girl. Looking at his watch he saw that it was now eleven thirty, maybe he would try now. He parked the car on Merrion Square and walked the short distance to the man's office and rang the bell. Jean was typing when he entered. Her face lit up with a smile.

"Good morning Joe, Mr.McCall has just come in, I've asked him about your interview but he hasn't given me an answer yet, that's why I didn't ring you."

This was all in one breath. Joe was looking at her and she reddened under his gaze. As for him all he wanted to do was talk to her, about anything.

"Maybe he would see me now Jean."

She pressed a speaker on her desk.

"Mr. McCall, Mr. Kearns is here, will you be able to see him now?"

She was looking at Joe as she spoke.

"You can go in now Mr. Kearns."

Jean pointed to a door to her left, which opened and Michael McCall came out.

"Mr. Kearns, nice to meet you."

He proffered a hand and ushered Joe into the office.

"Take a seat Mr. Kearns, I don't believe we've met before, now what can I do for you?"

Joe sat down in front of him and took out his notebook.

"Thank you for seeing me at such short notice Mr. McCall. I'm doing a feature on the situation between the South here and the situation in the Northern six counties. I would like you to give me your impressions of what's happening both in Dublin and the North, also do you think that a thirty-two county republic is possible in the near future?"

He was watching the man closely as he spoke. For just an instant the eyes startled in the round face, then he looked towards the ceiling.

"I think that the situation in the North is getting worse. I've just come back from a meeting in Dundalk. Some of our people from Belfast were there. They were telling me of the harassment the nationalist people are getting from the British army and RUC.

Joe Kearns looked at the man in front of him and phrased his next question carefully.

"Mr. McCall, this riot in O'Connell Street last Saturday, I wonder what you thought of it?"

McCall joined his fingertips before replying,

"I wasn't there myself but according to reports it was very rough, I'm tabling a question about it in the Dail later today as to why it was allowed to get out of hand, this kind of thing can't be allowed to go on in our capitol city."

His voice had taken on an indignant tone. Joe delivered his next question with a casual smile,

"Do you think Mr. McCall, that the riot could have been organised?"

The T.D.'s faced changed perceptively. A startled look flashed across his features. His right hand went up to his forehead and brushed back a lock of hair. There was a moment's silence before he spoke.

"How do you mean, organised, Mr. Kearns? Are you of the opinion that it was caused deliberately, what makes you think that?"

Kearns had to admire the way the man parried the question.

"I was there, Mr. McCall, I saw a few things that made me question what happened. The impression I got was that it was stage managed, For what end I don't know, give me your thoughts on it."

McCall looked at him over his desk. His eyes were cold.

"I can't say anything about it as I was not there, If what you say is true, there must have been some reason for it, I do know this, It can be very dangerous dealing with these people. I would watch my step if I were you, now I must go, I'm due in the Dail for the afternoon session, perhaps we will meet again, goodbye Mr. Kearns."

He started to put papers into his briefcase, signalling that the interview was at an end. Joe felt like a schoolboy being dismissed by the headmaster as he left the office. In the outer room Jean McKay was putting on her coat. She turned as Joe came out.

"Hello again, you got your interview then, you've not been in there long, was it satisfactory?"

He looked at the clock on the wall, it was twelve-o clock and he gave her a grin,

"Not bad, it was interesting anyway, are you finished for the day now Jean?"

"Yes,"

She went into McCall's office and returned some moments later. In that time Joe Kearns had made a decision.

"Jean would you like to have lunch with me? There's a place I know. That is unless you have something else to do."

She looked at him for a moment smiling.

"Thank you Joe I'd love to and I haven't anything else to do, at least not until four o clock."

Joe drove to his favourite restaurant. Jack McConnell greeted him with a surprised look. He found a table for them in a secluded corner. As the meal progressed they talked about various things. Joe told her about his work and how he had left the newspaper that morning. He would now be a freelance reporter, selling his stories to the highest bidder. She would not be able to contact him at the paper so he gave her his home number. From her he learned she was twenty-five. Her father had died about three years ago. The secretarial job with McCall earned her enough to live on. She was a member of her local musical society and was learning French two nights a week. Not very politically minded she found the bombing and killings in the North terrible. Travel was something she enjoyed, mostly spending her holidays in France on rail and cycling trips.

This girl intrigued Joe. He wanted to ask her about Joanna. So far she had not mentioned the child. He wondered where she fitted into the picture. Throwing caution to the winds he said.

"By the way how is young Joanna? Has she recovered from Saturday yet?"

Jean looked at him, her eyes dancing with laughter.

"O' she's fine, she was talking about you last night, I told her I might be seeing you today."

She took a sip of her wine and played with the glass.

"Joe I'd like to thank you for the lunch, I've really enjoyed myself, I don't know when I've been out to lunch with a man, it must be about three years, it was really nice, thank you."

Her voice had become somewhat husky and her head was lowered. He reached across the table and took her hand. It was warm to the touch. She made no effort to pull it away.

"Jean I've enjoyed it too, I haven't felt so good for a long time, we'll have to do this again soon."

Jean looked up at him without speaking, he was surprised to see a tear in her eye. She dabbed at it with a small handkerchief.

"It's almost four Joe, I'll have to go I have to collect Joanna."

She got up to leave.

"Wait a minute Jean, why don't we go in my car, I'm not doing anything, besides young Joanna wants to see me. Come on, I won't take no for an answer."

He went over to McConnell to pay for the meal.

"Thanks Joe, that's a nice girl you have there, the best of luck."

Joe took his change with a nod. They drove to the school where Jean collected an excited Joanna. In the car she kept up a ceaseless chatter from the rear seat. At the house in Sandymount Jean's mother greeted him warmly after some surprise and invited him in. This time he accepted immediately.

They were sitting in the front room, looking out on the white breakers of Sandymount strand. Joanna was showing Joe her books and games. The lively five-year-old intrigued him. Mr's McKay looked at Joe across the room.

"She's my son's daughter Joe, she lives with us Her parents were killed in an air crash in America two years ago. So Jean and I look after her, Jean is wrapped up in her and for that matter so am I. The world can be a very cruel place Joe, we've had our share of trouble in this house. First my husband died suddenly from a heart attack. Then the air crash, shortly after that Jean was about to be married and he broke it off, this was a week before the wedding, yes it can be a very cruel world."

Listening, Joe felt a surge of excitement, Jean wasn't married. He would definitely be asking her out again. Mrs. McKay returned from the window where she had been drawing the curtains and sat down by the coal fire. For all her troubles, thought Joe, she's a very pleasant person. He found himself sympathising with her. Soon he was telling her his own story. Joanna was busy with a colouring book on the floor. Jean came in and switched on the television as she passed.

"You two are having a fine old chat, I hope your not talking about me."

She smiled at her mother and Joe, who stood up.

"I'll say good bye for the present, I'll see you again soon Jean."

She broke in on him.

"You can't go just yet Joe I've just made some tea, why don't you stay a little longer."

At that moment Joe caught a news item on the television screen.

"The body of an elderly man was taken from the sea today near Blackrock. The victim has been identified as a local man James Somers who lived in Sandycove."

Kearns felt a shiver, the man in the pub, his name was Jem or James, could it be possible? Something told him he was right.

"Joe, Joe, are you all right? You look as if you have seen a ghost, what is it?"

Jean's anxious voice broke in on his thoughts. Mrs. McKay was looking at him, a frown on her face. He shook his head.

"Sorry, I was lost there for a few minutes, it's just that I think I knew that man. I'm not sure, but I think I was talking to him last night. I'm sorry but I'll have to go, there's a few things I have to do, Goodbye Mrs.McKay, bye Joanna."

Jean walked to the door with him. She watched as he put on his heavy anorak.

"Joe, your not in any trouble are you? I know it's none of my business but if I can help."

Her voice trailed off, Joe looked at her and took her hands in his.

"No, I'm not in any trouble, at least not yet, I'll give you a ring before the weekend."

He gave the surprised girl a kiss on the cheek and stepped out into the rain. In the car his thoughts were on the body taken from the sea. There was a detective in the Merrion station whom Joe knew well enough to approach. On previous occasions they had swapped information about various criminals and their methods along with the seeming inability of the law to stop them. In one particular case Joe was able to provide information which led to an arrest. Parking the car in the station yard he entered the day room and went up to the counter. The young

Garda on duty was writing at his desk. He rose and came forward. In the background the radio crackled its messages of traffic accidents and other incidents.

"Yes sir, what can I do for you?"

"I'm looking for John McQuillen, do you know if he's in? My name is Joe Kearns."

The man at the radio spoke without turning his head.

"John's upstairs in the detective office."

Picking up a phone the young Garda spoke into it, with sidelong glances at Joe.

"Go straight up sir, first door on the left."

Finding the door marked Detective Office Joe knocked and entered. John McQuillen rose from his chair and came to meet him with out-stretched hand.

"Come in Joe, how are things, it must be six months, what have you been up to? Here, sit down."

He indicated a chair. They exchanged pleasantries and short talk for a few minutes before McQuillen paused and said.

"Come on Joe spit it out, there's something bothering you, what is it?"

"It's about that body you fellows fished out of the sea to day, John, I'd like to know what he looked like."

A cautious look came over McQuillen's face.

"That's an easy one Joe we've already identified him, he was a local man from Sandycove, he was about thirteen stone, was wearing a leather jacket and jeans, The boys reckon he was stoned out of his mind and fell in, why? What's your interest?"

He spoke casually as if it was an everyday occurrence. At the same time he was watching Joe closely. The description certainly tallied with the man Joe had met in The Black Cat. One more question remained.

"John, tell me, was he connected with the Subversive movement?"

McQuillen gazed at him eye to eye for fully half a minute. He knew

Joe was not one to ask such a question unless he knew something, he answered in one word.

"Yes."

McQuillen listened as Joe unfolded his story of last night's meeting, carefully avoiding any reference to whom he was working for, McQuillen interrupted here and there to ask a question. When Joe got to the part about the two men who were to leave Jem home, he asked for descriptions. When he told him he sat the table toying with his pen.

"Joe, this is beginning to look like a murder, our two friends are well known to us, It looks as if Jem was killed because he could not keep his mouth shut, unfortunately it will be impossible to prove anything. One thing you should realise, you are likely to now be a target also if they know who you are. This crowd is ruthless. If they think your interfering in their affairs they won't hesitate to kill you, so start looking over your shoulder, they won't shoot you or anything like that, they'll make it look like an accident, all I'm trying to tell you is, for Christ's sake be careful"

He doodled a bit more with the pen. Joe said nothing. McQuillen went on.

"Those two in the bar, the blonde one is Sean Mahon, he's a psycho. The other is Martin Farrel, he's an explosives expert. We know he's done several jobs in the North that has resulted in deaths. I didn't know that they were back in Dublin, I wonder where they're staying? If you happen to find out anything I would appreciate if you would let me know."

Joe thanked him, promised he would keep in touch and left McQuillen still playing with the pen. As he left the young Garda wished him good night.

Kearns stopped the Beetle in front of his flat. He was just getting out when he heard a low whistle. It came from a clump of bushes in the garden to his left. Joe fiddled with his key and sat back into the car. A voice softly called his name. It was One Arm, who slipped into the passenger seat.

"Jesus Christ Joe, what the hell have you been up to? That bloke I sent you to see is dead, The word is he talked too much about something that's going to happen at the end of March or beginning of April. I'm

71

not sure which, They know it was you he was talking to and the order is out to get you. You had better look out and don't try to contact me anymore, I don't want to end up dead. You should try and disappear for a bit, I'm even taking a chance coming here to night, but I thought I had better warn you. I'm going now, so long, remember what I told you"

He stepped out of the car and into the bushes. Kearns sat there. Things were certainly starting to happen, this was his second warning inside a few hours. Locking the car he went into the house.

"Joe? Is that you?"

Mrs. Black came from the kitchen she was wiping her hands in a cloth.

"Joe there were a couple of men looking for you earlier, I told them I didn't know when you would be back."

Joe gave her a grin.

"Thanks Molly, What did they look like? Was one small and blonde, the other taller with a moustache."

"Yes, yes, that's them, you know them then?"

"Yes I know them Molly, If they come back say I've gone away for a few days on a job, tell them you don't know where."

She looked after him as he went upstairs. He threw a few things into a bag before making a phone call to the number he had been given. There was a click and he could hear a faint hum as the message was recorded. When he came down Molly was waiting.

"Joe, come and have a cup of tea, I've just made it."

They went into the kitchen. As she poured, she never took her eyes off his face.

"Joe there's something wrong, isn't there, you're in some kind of trouble, is there anything I can do?"

He looked at her anxious face and gave her a smile.

"Molly I'm all right, you just tell anyone that looks for me you don't know where I am, I'll be in touch from time to time, I'm on a special job at the moment, that's all, I have to go now, all the best."

Picking up the bag he went out to the car. There was very little traffic as he drove south over the Canal Bridge and towards Rathgar. His destination was a cottage near Ballingeary, which belonged to a friend of his who spent most of his life at sea. He had asked Joe to keep an eye on the place and use it occasionally if he wished. Now he would stay there until he formulated a plan of action. Then he noticed the lights in his mirror. At first he thought it was just a following car. He slowed to the regulation thirty miles per hour. The lights remained behind. A few streets on he stopped at a late night shop and bought some cooked ham, bread, butter and a couple of cartons of milk. As he pulled away the lights followed, there was now no doubt in his mind, he had grown a tail. Across Churchtown they went and Joe decided he would head for the mountain fastness of Glencree and try to shake them off. They reached Enniskery and Joe swung the car right, up the steep Kilgarron hill. The other car made no attempt to gain on him. As they climbed the houses got scarcer and scarcer. Kearns realised he had made a mistake, he should have stuck closer to civilisation, well it was too late now. The road was narrower now as they climbed the wild and desolate Glencree valley towards the top. Now the other car started to close up. The bonnet was almost touching the rear bumper of the Volkswagen when Joe shoved the accelerator pedal to the floor and the car surged forward. Swinging the car round the bends like a madman he watched for the lights in the mirror. Now the other car closed on him without any effort, It nudged the rear of the V.W. and it took Kearns all his skill to avoid hitting the low stone wall which prevented him from going over and down into the valley below. Then they were round the last bend and the stone walls were gone. Nothing but bog land on either side. Sparse clumps of pine trees dotted the countryside in the light of the moon. They were racing downhill now, Joe's hands were sweating as he fought to keep the VW ahead. He knew that at the bottom the road swung sharply to the right. Straight-ahead was a parking spot where tourists and others could admire the view. A rough stone border about two feet high protected sightseers from a thirty-foot drop into a small bog lake. The speedometer was reading seventy-five now as the bottom of the hill came up to meet them. The other car was only about six feet behind him. Joe left his breaking until the last minute before slamming them on and locking the car into a four-wheel skid into the bend. The other driver was taken completely by surprise and swerved to miss the V.W as it braked and veered to the right. He shot by across the small parking area. Joe had a brief glimpse of brake lights shining before the car hit the granite stone border. Its momentum carried it onwards and it tumbled into the dark waters of the lake. It had vanished from view when Joe ran back from where he had stopped the Volkswagen. Apart from the skid marks and a few missing stones there were only some small ripples on the almost still waters. A shiver ran through him, these boys certainly played rough. The driver of that car had been trying to kill him. Now he was dead, buried in a boghole in the Wicklow Mountains. He drove on until he reached the village of Laragh before stopping at a phone box and dialling his contact number. He left a report of the night's events before resuming his journey, cutting across country until he reached the cottage at Ballingeary.

This was situated at the end of a narrow lane and invisible from the main road being tucked away behind a small hill among a clump of pine trees. It backed right on to the beach, which was about one hundred yards away. There was a large garage with room for the V.W. beside the Cortina GL belonging to his friend. In the house he made himself a meal of ham sandwiches and tea before climbing into bed at about three a.m. He was asleep almost at once.

CHAPTER 9

Harry Grant took a bus into the centre of Dublin. He walked along beside the river until he saw the public house called The White Leprechaun. All over the world in pubs and bars he had collected information. You could always rely on someone dropping a word here or there when the conversation flowed. It was as good a place to start as any. He pushed open the door and went in. Inside a long mahogany counter ran the length of the room. This was divided into partitioned sections. At this time of day it was sparsely occupied. In the first section a tall thin man with a morose expression sat reading a paper, a half glass of black liquid stood in front of him. Harry moved up to the bar and asked for a beer. The barman asked him if he would like a Guinness, this being the national drink. The morose man interrupted to say.

"Try it Yank, it's very good, over here on holiday are you? Go on give it a try."

The barman placed the glass of the dark liquid in front of him. Harry gave it a tentative sip.

"Well, it sure is unusual, and no I'm not here on holiday, I'm doing a story about the troubles here and in the North, my name is Harry Grant, I'm a student."

The man put down his drink and looked at Harry.

"Now isn't that the job, you fellas come over here and try to sort out a problem that's being going on for the last three hundred years. You know they'll never solve that problem, what's more we can't afford them down here anyway, so it'll go on and on."

He took another drink from his glass, looking more morose than ever.

"My name is Mick, I'm glad to meet you Yank, you know you're going to have your work cut out."

Grant grinned at him and sipped the Guinness, he wasn't mad about the taste.

"Where would I find someone to talk to about it Mick, Is there anyone who could give me a line on what's happening?"

"Well I suppose you could talk to some of the crowd that meets here sometimes, there supposed to be mixed up with the Crowd in the North, isn't that so Paddy."

He appealed to the barman who had been listening to the conversation. Paddy wiped the bar top with a cloth before replying.

"Yes I suppose they would be about your best bet, as a matter of fact there's a couple of them come in here for a drink and a chat most nights, they will probably be here to night, if you come back about eight."

He walked up the bar to serve another customer. Mick turned to Grant.

"Yer men will be here tonight, they're always here on a Thursday night, that's when you'll catch them Yank."

Grant finished his drink.

"Thanks Mick, I might see you later."

Outside he started to walk in the direction of O Connell Bridge. The neon signs flashed garish coloured lights advertising Japanese motor cars and televisions. The crowds hurrying home from work were huddled into raincoats and anoraks to shield them from the wind and rain. One red sign stood out from the rest. It read, The Irish Sentinal, Ireland's first newspaper. Making his way to the building he was just in time to meet a girl in a raincoat and head-scarf coming out.

"Excuse me Miss, are there any of your reporters in the building, I'm an American doing an article on Northern Ireland, I'd like to talk to someone."

The girl looked at him with something akin to pity.

"I'm sorry, there's no one there now, They've all gone home, why don't you come back to morrow morning."

Just then footsteps sounded behind her and a portly figure resplendent in dark overcoat and Russian type fur hat came into view. The girl turned to him.

"Mr. Martin, this man is an American reporter, he wants to talk to someone about the North, you might be able to help him, I've got to go."

She vanished through the doorway leaving the two men face to face. Martin spoke first.

"From the States are you? Where?"

Grant told him Boston and that he was a Harvard student over here for three months to study the situation North and South. He was looking for help in finding out what was happening. Martin though for a moment.

"There's one man who could help you, He worked for this paper up to a couple of days ago, had a row with the editor over a demonstration that broke into a riot here last Saturday. He had some crazy idea that the whole thing was rigged, wanted to print it, mind you. There wasn't a shred of evidence. After the row he just walked out, I can give you his address, you might get something from him, he's a very good reporter and in my own opinion, if Joe Kearns said that demo was rigged he must have a very good reason."

As he spoke he was writing into a page of his notebook, tearing it out he handed it to Grant.

"There you are, 14 Norris Street, its off Heytesbury road, he has a flat there."

Grant took the paper and read it aloud.

"Say sir thanks very much, I'll look him up."

Martin broke in.

"Look for a yellow Volkswagen Beetle, find the car and you've found the house. Good night Mr. ER?"

"Grant Mr. Martin, Harry Grant, and thanks a million. Good night to you too sir."

He watched as Martin hailed a taxi, which drove off into the traffic. This was good. First day and he already had a lead or two. He found

McDonalds and ordered a burger, French fries and coffee. As he ate he thought only for the different accents he might have been back in the States.

The White Leprechaun was crowded when he went back. Mick was nowhere to be seen but the barman, Paddy nodded to him as he entered. He stepped from behind the bar and indicated a door. They passed through into a hallway, up a flight of stairs to the first landing. Paddy knocked twice on a door and entered. He introduced Harry as the American student. Three pairs of eyes viewed him. One of the men stood up and held out his hand.

"Hello, I'm Eamon Morris, that's Peter Donnelly, our friend in the corner is Joe McCann, Paddy tells us you would like to talk to us about the North."

Grant shook hands with them and took a seat. He gave them his cover story about being a student from Harvard University. Morris pressed a bell on the panelling, as he said.

"We're always glad to talk to someone interested in the cause, particularly someone from America, you ask the questions and we'll try to answer them. You know we can't tell you much about the military side of things, we're only interested in the political end, what will you have to drink?"

This was in response to the arrival of Paddy. Grant asked for a lager, the others were ordering Brandy's. He suggested to Morris that he tell him anything he thought relevant, as Grant himself had very little knowledge of the subject. He was then given a description of the aims of the organisation towards the making of a thirty-two county free Ireland. Asked by Grant if he thought this was possible in he near future, he seemed taken aback. Morris looked at the other two before replying.

"You know Harry it might just be possible, yes, it just might."

He looked at Grant across the table.

"Now tell us a bit more about yourself, you're a Harvard student, I've heard of that place, its one of the great American Colleges. I've never been to America my self, maybe some day."

He took a drink of his Brandy. One of the others, Grant thought it was McCann, broke in.

"Is there much sympathy for our cause in America, Harry?"

Grant thought he was trying to change the subject.

"Not very much I'm afraid, it gets very little publicity over there unless there's some carnage, then there will be some television reports, maybe a few comments from some politicians chasing Irish American votes, then it all dies down again."

The other man, Donnelly, had not spoken at all. Grant felt he was there to observe only. Without a doubt he was from the military wing. They were always suspicious of strangers asking questions about what they were pleased to call The Armed Struggle. Furthermore Grant had been struck by the coldness of his eyes. They were killer's eyes. He had seen them before in various parts of the world. Ice cold, with a psychotic stare, they radiated evil. The others gently probed him with questions, where was he staying, how long did he think he would be in Ireland, would he be going to Belfast if so they would arrange for him to meet some of their friends to show him around. Up there he would learn all about British injustice. Grant had been making notes throughout the meeting. McCann now asked to see them and corrected some points here and there. He rose from the table.

"Well now Harry, its been nice talking to you, if there's anything else you'd like to talk to us about, drop in here and Paddy will arrange a meeting for you, good night to you now."

He stood up and guided him to the door. Harry made his way downstairs. In the hallway he found a door leading into the street. The rain was sweeping up the river now, driven by a cold North Easterly wind. He hunched his shoulders and walked towards the bus stop. On the other side of the road in one of a line of parked cars, Inspector John Maguire watched the man who had just emerged from the White Leprechaun and nodded to his companion.

"Well now, there he goes, this is getting very interesting, we'll leave him alone for a few more days, then maybe I'll have a chat with him, slow and easy Hugh, slow and easy. Come on, let's go home, your wife will think you're lost."

The younger man grinned and started the car.

Next morning Harry Grant came down to an early breakfast. There was no one in the dining room. Peggy Noone came in and gave him a smile.

"Good morning Mr. Grant, did you sleep well? Is everything all right?"

Grant nodded thinking, she really is very good looking, and aloud he said.

"Everything's fine ma'am, thank you and please call me Harry."

When he had finished breakfast he asked her if she knew where he could hire a bicycle, as he wanted to journey around the city. She thought for a moment.

"There's a bicycle out in the garage, it belonged to my late husband, you can borrow it, the tyres might need to be pumped, otherwise it's alright."

Taking a bunch of keys she led him through the house and into the garage. Against the wall stood a man's bicycle. It was covered in a coat of dust, which she proceeded to clean off with a cloth. As he pumped the tyres she stood with a wistful expression on her face.

"My husband was a policeman Mr.Grant, Harry. He was killed during a bank robbery three years ago. It was a bunch of Subversives who did it, he didn't even have a gun, they shot him down like a dog."

There was bitterness in her voice. Grant looked at her.

"I'm sorry about your husband, this is the kind of thing I'll be writing about, I'd like to hear the whole story sometime, thanks for the bicycle, I'll take good care of it."

His first stop was at the nearest newsagents where he bought a couple of Irish papers. Finding a park he sat in a shelter and read them through. At about midday he started to try to locate the man called Joe Kearns. He eventually found the quite cul-de sac known as Norris Street and cycled slowly down towards the end. There was no sign of a yellow Volkswagen. In fact the only car on the street was parked facing him as he looked for number fourteen. It turned out to be the one with the car outside. Leaning the bike against the wall he approached the front door. It was partly open. He could hear a man's voice asking,

"Where is he? Come on you old bitch where's Kearns?"

This was accompanied by the sound of a slap. A woman's voice whimpered,

"I don't know, I tell you, I don't know. He doesn't tell me where he goes, he just said he was on a job, that was yesterday, don't hit me again, please don't hit me."

She was crying hysterically.

Grant came slowly into the hall. There was a glass door into the kitchen. Inside he could see a woman of about sixty. She was sitting in a chair. Two men stood in front of her, one short, with blond hair had his hand raised to strike her, the other was taller with a moustache. He was grinning at the woman. Grant could hear him saying,

"Come on Grandma, tell us, it will be easier on you, otherwise we might break up everything in the house including you."

Grant moved back and pressed the doorbell. There was silence. He pressed it again and stood to one side around the corner. Moustache came to the door and opened it wide. Grant stepped forward and grabbed his jacket pulling him forward. He drove his knee into the man's groin. A right fist went into his solar plexus and Moustache was writhing on the ground. At that moment Blondie ran out of the door. Seeing Grant he made for an inside pocket. Now Grant's special training in unarmed combat came to the fore. With a leap over the gasping figure on the ground he grabbed Blondie's arm twisting it up behind his back. There was an audible crack and a scream of pain. A small handgun dropped on the concrete path. A left-handed punch to the jaw followed and the man sank to the ground. Picking up the gun Grant ran into the house. The old woman, blood trickling from her nose and with a swollen right eye was half lying against a table. She shrunk back as Grant entered.

"I'm not going to hurt you where's your telephone?"

She made a gesture to the corner of the worktop. The phone had been ripped out. The woman muttered through battered lips.

"Upstairs, Joe's rooms, phone."

Grant was up the stairs two at a time, The first door he opened had a phone on a small table. On the wall was a list of numbers. He dialled 999 for police and reported the situation asking for a doctor and Ambulance. Outside he heard a car start up and race up the street. The two had made good their escape. Back in the kitchen Grant tried to make the woman as comfortable as possible. A short time later a siren announced the arrival of a Garda squad car and an Ambulance. The two young Gardai were first in. They looked from Grant to the woman at the table. A doctor came in with the ambulance men. Grant took one of the policemen outside and told them what had happened. When he produced the gun the young Garda's face changed perceptively. He was writing in his notebook as they spoke. By now the ambulance men had got Mrs. Black into the vehicle and departed. The doctor was talking to the other Garda who came out to them.

"The Doctor says she will be all right, I'll check back with headquarters."

The man with Grant closed his notebook after giving his companion an almost imperceptive nod. He turned to Grant again and spoke.

"It's a good thing you happened to come along Mr. Grant, or that poor woman might have been dead, It's getting worse and worse here, bye the way what were you doing here any way?"

Harry explained how he had been looking for Joe Kearns who lived there and that he was here doing a story about the troubles in the north.

The policeman put away his book and almost as an after thought turned again to Harry.

"I wonder Mr. Grant would you mind coming back to the station with us, you could make a statement now and it would save you having to come in again, maybe you could look at some photographs, our friends may be on file, It might save a lot of trouble later."

Harry smiled to himself. This was Irish blarney at its best. Yet he knew he could not refuse. He mentioned about the bicycle. It was wheeled in and left in the care of a neighbour who was going to look after the house.

The two Gardai chatted to him on the short drive to the station. They entered the courtyard of a large modern building. A lift whisked them up to the fifth floor. In a small office Grant sat while one of the men typed up his statement on a word processor. He asked Harry for his home address. Grant handed him his passport. When the statement was finished the Garda read it over to him and he signed it. He then left the office with the statement and Harry's passport. The other man came in with a large photograph album and said.

"Have a look through that Mr.Grant, see if you can spot either of those men."

He left Harry turning the pages. It wasn't long before he had found Blondie and Moustache. When the men returned he pointed out the pictures to them. One said.

"Will you come this way Mr. Grant, there's someone wishes to speak to you."

They went up a flight of stairs and into a larger office where Grant sat down near the window. He could hear the murmur of traffic from the street below. On the ledge a pigeon looked in and stared at him curiously. The door behind him opened and someone entered. He came into sight and sat down behind the desk. A pair of sleepy blue eyes gazed at him for a moment from out of a craggy face.

"Well now, Mr. Grant is it?"

He reached into a drawer and took out a paper bag. Standing up he walked over and opened the window. He shook some seed on the sill and the pigeon walked up to him and started to eat. He sat down again and remarked.

"That's Clarence, he comes around fairly regular for a bit of grub. Now, what have we here?"

He glanced at the paper in his hand, his voice was quite, with a Dublin drawl to it. He went on.

"This is a very interesting situation you got yourself into today Mr.Grant, if you hadn't been there that old lady might well be dead, would you go over the details with me again, I believe you have already picked out our two friends."

Grant had recognised the man as soon as he had sat down. It was the Special Branch Detective Inspector he had seen at the Airport, John Maguire. He went through the statement again, the Inspector asking the odd question here and there. A Garda entering with the photographs of the men and their folders interrupted them. Maguire pushed the photos across and looked directly at Grant.

"You're absolutely sure Mr.Grant that these are the same men."

Grant nodded yes. The Inspector rose and stood looking out of the window Grant waited in silence as the minutes ticked by. Presently the Special Branch man sat down. Reaching into his briefcase he took out a file. He looked at it for a few moments then pushed it across to Harry.

"Will you please have a look at that Mr.Grant."

As Grant started to read the first page he could not believe his eyes. It was a detailed account of his every move from the time of his arrival to his fight at Joe Kearn's flat. He looked up at Maguire who nodded. In that soft voice, with just the trace of a smile he handed Grant another file.

"Read that Mr.Grant, if you will and tell me if I'm right or wrong."

Harry Grant reached for the papers and started to read. His eyes could barely believe the words. It was a complete description of him and his work. Included were some of the incidents in which he had been involved in various parts of the world. He looked across the desk at the face opposite. Admiration showing on his own. Putting the file down he said.

"Okay. Sir, you've got me dead to rights, I suppose I'll be on the next plane home?"

The Inspector was stuffing tobacco into an old briar pipe.

"That might not be necessary at this time Mr.Grant. First let me introduce myself, I'm Detective Inspector John Maguire, head of Special Branch here, It's the same as your CIA. Now I have a good idea what you are here for, if you are willing to work with us you can stay, that is for the time being. Trouble is you've stirred up a hornet's nest now with that bit of a scrap. Those two fellows you tangled with are highly dangerous. If you meet them again, look out, they'll try to kill you for sure, although from what I know you can take care of yourself, but no firearms, you're not carrying any I hope."

Grant shook his head. Maguire struck a match and sucked at the flame, blowing out a cloud of blue smoke. He went on.

"We want to find out what's going on as quickly as possible. If you have any more information we would like to share it. We know that the man you went to see, Joe Kearns, had an attempt on his life last night, it failed. At the moment we don't know where he is, those fellows were trying to find him, I don't need to tell you what for. If you think you can help I would appreciate it."

He looked at Grant expectantly. Harry's mind was a whirl. This man had him in a vice. He either co-operated or he would wind up back in the States on the next flight out of Dublin.

There was only one answer and he could not give it. It would depend on one Maurice J Curley. Looking across at the pipe smoking Inspector he could only grin.

"Sir I'm willing to do all I can, but you must appreciate that I must talk to Washington first. They will probably give me the green light, but maybe you could talk to them first."

He could imagine Curley's face when he found out that Grant's cover was blown. What had he said, step back twenty years when you stepped of the plane, boy, was he in for a surprise? He looked at his watch, Curley should be in his office now. Maguire nodded his approval.

"You can use our phone here Mr. Grant, or maybe you'd like to go down to Kildare?"

Maguire's face was a picture of innocence. So he knows about that too, Grant mused. Somehow Curley had vastly underestimated these Irish. It was funny and his ancestors coming from here too. He reached for the phone and dialled the number in Washington.

Curley's voice was as clear as if he were in the room. Grant took a deep breath and spoke.

'Colonel, this is Grant, I'm in a police station in Dublin, there was a bit of a scrap today and I'm here making a statement. They know everything about me, I've been asked to help them with this business so I decided I had better call you before saying yes."

Curley gave a little chuckle.

"Who's there with you Harry is it Maguire?"

Grant managed to answer yes.

"Put him on Harry."

Grant handed the phone to Maguire and the Inspector started to speak.

"Maurice, how are things, nice to talk to you again. Don't you know better than to send a boy on a man's errand, are you going to tell me what this is all about?"

There was silence as Maguire listened to Curley describe Grant's job of work and how he came to be in Ireland. He was jotting down notes as the conversation went on. Grant sat back and waited. Maguire exchanged a few more pleasantries with Curley before handing Grant the phone. Curley was very precise.

"Harry, do whatever the man tells you, He's a wily old bird but as straight as they come, good luck."

The phone went dead and Grant handed it back to Maguire.

"There now Harry, wasn't that very civilised, Sure we've been telephone friends for years the Colonel and me. Now the lads will drop you back to St.Ultans, if you need any help ring this number. Memorise it and destroy this."

He passed a piece of paper and pressed a bell on the desk. Two well-built men in plain clothes came in.

"Drop Mr. Grant back to Baggot street lads then come straight back here, good evening Mr. Grant."

They dropped Harry in a side street and he walked back to the house. Inside the front door the bicycle was lying against the wall. He had forgotten all about that.

"O, Harry, you're back, a young man dropped the bike in, said you'd be along later, come on in and I'll make you some dinner."

Peggy Noone's quite voice came from behind him. He followed her into the dining room.

CHAPTER 10

It was late morning when Joe Kearns awoke from a troubled sleep. For a moment he did not move. Then a flash of last night's chase came back to him. He shuddered, thinking of the man in the car going into the bog. Well, it had been his own fault, after all he had been doing his best to kill him. He got up and dressed. Looking in the mirror he decided to let his beard grow. It would be a helpful disguise in days to come. Going outside he opened the garage doors. He found the keys of the Cortina and checked it for fuel and water. The tax disc and Insurance were current. It took a little time to start but it soon settled down to a healthy purr. Satisfied he went into the house, switched on the radio and spent the next couple of hours tidying up. Later he drove to Ballingeary and stocked up with groceries. He would lie low here for a few days before restarting his investigation. Certainly he had become a target so perhaps Jem had been right, there was something going to happen at the end of March. Well, he would keep on trying.

That evening he watched the nine o clock news on television. There was a report of a break in and attack on an elderly woman in Dublin. The screen showed the front of a house with a uniformed Garda standing outside. It was number fourteen Norris Street. The woman was believed not to be seriously hurt. There were no more details.

Joe felt the anger rise in him. Those bastards had been there looking for him he was sure. But to beat up his landlady, Jesus, he hoped she was all right. Picking up the phone he rang his old paper and got on to Ken McGuiness.

"Joe, where the hell are you? You've heard about your landlady, yes she'll be all right. They're keeping her in hospital for a few days. It appears two blokes came looking for you. When she told them she didn't know where you were they started to knock her around. This American fellow arrived on the scene and ploughed in. Did quite a good job too according to accounts. It was he who phoned the police. That's all we know at the moment. The Gardai don't want any publicity, they are asking us not to give the story much space. What's happening Joe? Is this something to do with that riot?"

Joe did not answer directly.

"I'm glad Molly's all right Ken and I certainly don't know anything more than you do. What was the American doing there anyhow?"

"He was looking for you Joe. The old man was talking to him a couple of nights ago here and gave him your address, apparently he's doing some kind of story about the troubles here. The boss told him you might be able to help."

"I see, thanks Ken I'll be in touch."

Before the man could ask any more questions Joe had replaced the receiver. He pondered the facts. The Subversives were very definitely after him. He could expect no mercy if they caught up with him. Molly had certainly been lucky. If that American had not come along she could well have been killed. A sudden thought struck him, Jean he wondered if she was all right. Dialling her number he found himself excited at the prospect of speaking with her.

"Jean, its Joe, how are you? Good? I'm away for a few days, I just rang to see if you were all right."

She sounded glad to hear from him and assured him that she was fine. There was no mention of anyone looking for him. He told her he would ring again in a couple of days.

Three days later his appearance had changed. The stubble beard gave him a completely different face. On the trip into Ballingeary he had bought a bottle of black hair dye. The assistant had smiled when he told her it was for his wife who had noticed some grey hair. This he washed into his hair and changed from dark blond to black. Looking in the mirror he was satisfied. He had changed completely, no one would recognise him unless after very close scrutiny.

Next morning he drove the Cortina to Dun Laoghaire where he booked into a small hotel. Leaving the car, he took a train into Dublin. In the market in Francis Street he bought a ragged second hand anorak and a pair of faded jeans. A pair of rubber boots completed his purchases. In another part of the building he found a public toilet where he changed into the clothes he had just bought. With his beard and scruffy clothes he looked like a building worker. He stuck his own clothes in a plastic bag and set out to find One Arm. After searching for over an hour he spotted the man on a piece of waste ground tinkering with something under the raised bonnet of an old Ford van. Joe shuffled towards him one hand stuck in the anorak pocket.

"How are you Frank? Are you still playing around with that old thing?"

Frank O'Brien straightened up so quickly that his head hit the raised bonnet. He looked at Joe his face white with fear.

"Jesus Joe, you frightened the living daylights out of me, what the hell are you doing in Dublin, don't you know every bloody Subversive is looking for you, you're a marked man if they catch up with you, you're dead."

He slammed the bonnet down.

"Get in, we'll go somewhere where we can talk."

With a crunch of gears he drove out into the traffic. Joe was intrigued by the man's dexterity in driving with only his left hand. They followed the river and up into the Phoenix Park. One Arm drove across the grass into a clump of trees. No words had passed between them on the short journey. Joe turned to the man in the driving seat.

"Frank those bastards beat up my landlady trying to find out where I was. I don't like that Frank."

O'Brien lit a cigarette with the dashboard lighter,

Joe could see that his hand was shaking.

"Joe if they find out I was talking to you they'll kill me too. All I know is that there's to be a take-over here at the end of March. There's no definite date yet. I was talking to someone the other night and he told me that the final dates and time would only be issued about twenty four hours before. Another thing is they are expecting a big shipment of arms and explosives, again no dates or times. You know I couldn't ask too many questions."

He took a drag of the cigarette,

"Those two fellas that roughed up your landlady. That Yank did a good job on them, one has a broken arm and the other three broken ribs."

He gave a bit of a chuckle,

"The joke is, a couple of nights previous he was talking to some of the boys in the White Leprechaun. They told him to come back anytime, now they're wondering what the hell he was doing at your house and who he really is."

Kearns saw the irony of the situation and grinned to himself.

"Frank is there anything else you can tell me, anything at all, I promise I'll keep away from you unless its anything urgent."

O'Brien sat, smoke curling up from the butt of his cigarette. With a quick movement he flung it out through the open window and started up the motor.

"Joe, you know your man McCall the T.D., well he's supposed to be the new Taoiseach after the take-over."

He let in the clutch and the van jerked forward. As they drove back into the city Joe digested the information. McCall was obviously the key man in the whole affair. Then there was Jean. If McCall found out that they were friends she could be in extreme danger. His thoughts were interrupted by One Arm stopping in a dark side street. Frank O'Brien reached down under his seat and came up holding a bundle wrapped in a rag. He opened it up and held something out to Kearns.

"Did you ever handle one of these Joe? For your own protection I think you should take this and learn how to use it, you never know when it will come in handy."

Joe looked at the small black sinister looking revolver in the dim light from the dashboard. He had often seen the like in gangster movies on television. Never having handled one and certainly never having fired one he shied away, besides if he were found with one by the Gardai there would be hell to pay. He looked into O'Brien's face.

"Frank there's no way I need one of those things, it could get me into all sorts of trouble, thanks very much all the same."

O'Brien shoved the gun at him angrily.

"Take the bloody thing Joe its for your own good. You don't know what your up against, its not that hard to use, particularly if someone is coming at you with one in his hand don't hesitate, just point it and pull the trigger. Go on take it. It might save your life. Don't ask me where it came from, if I didn't feel you needed it I wouldn't be given it to you, Now fuck off out of here."

He started up the engine as Kearns stepped out on the roadway and started to walk back towards the railway station. The gun in his pocket weighed a ton. He felt that everyone was looking at him. Seeing a uniformed figure approaching a flash of panic went through him until he realised the man was a postman. He had to get a grip on himself. O'Brien would not have given him the gun if he had not been sure that he was in mortal danger. Reaching the station he changed back into his own clothes. He wrapped the gun in the anorak and stuffed the lot in the carrier bag. On the platform he gave the appearance of a man who had been doing a bit of shopping.

Later in his hotel bedroom he examined the gun. It was fully loaded. He could see the shells in their chambers. It fitted comfortably into his hand, his finger on the trigger. He looked at himself in the mirror, the gun pointing out at him. This had gone far enough. He would have to talk to someone about the situation. Dialling his contact number he left a message asking for a meeting and where to contact him. At eleven thirty he rang Jean McKay's number. She answered almost at once.

"Jean, its Joe here how are you?"

"Joe, where are you? I was beginning to think you were never going to ring again, it's so nice to hear from you, is everything all right?"

"Everything's fine Jean, I can't tell you where I am, except to say not too far away. Now I want you to listen to me carefully. If anyone asks you about me you don't know anything, is that clear? You haven't seen me, you don't know me, you just met me once at McCall's office, Is that clear?"

"Yes Joe but why? Are you in trouble, you know if you need any help you have only to ask."

Her voice sounded concerned. He wished now he had said nothing. How could he tell her that her own safety was at stake if they linked her to him.

"Jean just do as I say, I'll contact you again in a few days. Good night, I'll be thinking of you."

He rang off before she could reply.

Next morning he sat around the hotel awaiting his request for a meeting. By midday he had heard nothing. It was getting on for three p.m. when a call to his room from the desk told him there was a taxi there for him. He stuck the revolver in his jacket pocket and went downstairs. Outside the taxi was waiting with the engine running. Kearns sat inside and it moved off. They drove into the city in silence. Somewhere near Government buildings the driver turned down a narrow lane and faced a pair of garage doors. A soft honk on the horn and they drove through, the gates closing after them. They were in a large underground garage. The driver got out and opened Joe's door.

"Will you come this way sir, please."

Joe followed him to a lift, which left them outside an office. Sitting inside was the Commissioner whom Joe had last met with the Taoiseach. He stood up and came forward and shook Joe's hand.

"Joe you wanted to talk to me, what can I do for you?"

Joe went through a summary of all that had happened since their first meeting. When he got to the part about the car chase the Commissioner interrupted.

"Yes that was a lucky escape for you Joe. We fished the car out of the bog. That fellow was well known to us, he had killed at least three people that we know of and probably one Garda, Don't have any qualms about him, he killed himself you were just the catalyst."

Joe went on to tell him of the meeting with One Arm and about the expected take-over. He then produced the gun. The Commissioner took the weapon and examined it with a practised eye.

"I think the man is probably right Joe, you should keep this, have you ever fired a gun?"

Joe shook his head.

"I've never even held one until I was given that, I don't think I would be much use with it."

"I'm afraid Joe if you are going to stick with this investigation you had better learn to use it and fast. Come with me."

The Commissioner led him out of the room to the lift where they descended to a lower level. Here they entered a room, which was set out as a firing range. Picking up some earmuffs he gave Joe the gun and pointed to the target. Kearns pointed the weapon and fired. It bucked in his hand missing the target entirely. The Commissioner took the weapon and fired three shots rapidly at the target figure. All three went into the chest area.

"Remember Joe, point the gun down to allow for the kick, try to aim for the body, the object is to stop him so aim for the biggest area. Now Freddie here will give you some lessons, when you feel you've improved come back to me."

He indicated a man who had emerged from the shadows. Freddie gave him a lecture on the weapon and some of its faults and showed him how to load and fire it. After an hour he could hit the chest area two times out of three, which Freddie said was very good for a beginner. He reloaded the gun for Joe and gave him a box of ammunition before returning him to the Commissioner. Here he was told that his landlady was home from hospital. Her sister was staying with her and the Special Branch was keeping a discreet eye on the house. Joe then asked about the American, did they know anything about him. The man behind the desk toyed with a pen for a few moments.

"I suppose you might as well know now as later, he's a C.I.A. man trying to do the same job as you. It might be a good idea if you two got together. He's staying out in Baggot Street, Here's his address."

He passed a piece of paper over with the American's name and where he was staying.

"What do you intend to do now Joe? We're still very short on information."

"I don't exactly know Commissioner, the first thing I'm going to do is visit Molly, I feel I'm responsible for what happened, then I think I'll find our American friend and see what we can come up with after that. Thanks for the lessons, at least I feel I'm not completely useless if it comes to a fight."

The Commissioner told him that he would get a message to the American telling him that Joe would phone him tonight about midnight. The taxi left him in a street some distance from fourteen Norris Street. He walked the rest of the way and rang the bell for the benefit of anyone watching. The woman who answered it was obviously Molly's sister, she looked so much like her. She had the same hair and eyes.

"Hello I'm Joe, Joe Kearns, I've come to see Molly."

He gave her a smile and she opened the door wider.

"Come in Mr. Kearns, she's in the kitchen."

Joe followed her in. Molly was seated at the table. The bruises on her face were still shades of yellow and black. She looked up as Joe came in.

"Joe? Are you all right?, I nearly didn't recognise you with that beard."

"Molly, I'm glad you're all right, I just dropped in to say hello and make sure you were okay. You won't be seeing me for a bit, Don't ask any questions, I can't answer them, now I don't want to be seen around here so I'm off. Those people will not be back as long as I'm not here, I'll be all right, I'm just doing another job, now goodbye for the present."

He squeezed her hand and got up to leave, she clung on to him.

"You're a good man Joe, for God's sake be careful and look after yourself."

He got back to his hotel about nine and looked at television to wile away the time until he could ring the American.

CHAPTER 11

On the Columbus, Reilly made his way to the bridge. He could feel the ship shuddering and heaving as it drove through the waves. John O'Shea was looking out towards a faint black line on the horizon parallel with the ship.

'Morning George, sleep well? That's Italy over there, we're making about eight knots, heading south, There's a hell of a swell running."

He gestured out through the front windows as the bows dipped into another wave and rose again like a large whale sporting itself. Reilly steadied himself against the roll of the ship.

"Morning John, where are the others?"

"Sean and Seaumus are turning in now, the Mate has already gone, They kept the old tub going during the night, it's our turn now."

Reilly nodded and picked up a pair of binoculars. He could pick out the buildings on shore with the Italian flag flying from the odd flagpole. The Captain was at the wheel, he grinned at George as he approached.

"Vee cannot go any faster, the sea, she too rough to day, maybe quieten down to morrow."

He stuck a small cigar in his mouth and lit it with a lighter taken from his pocket. George nodded to him and made for the galley to find some breakfast. Francis was the only one there when he entered, she flashed him a smile.

"Good morning Mr. Reilly, what would you like? Bacon and egg, or cereal?"

George who was feeling the motion of the ship settled for toast, marmalade and tea. He got the feeling that the girl was laughing at him. When he started to ask her questions about her life he found her strained and evasive.

As the days passed she seemed to become friendlier. They walked around the deck together and spent time sitting in the small lounge when the wind and rain made it a trial to go outside. They had all settled down into some form of routine. There was not a lot to do to keep the ship moving. The monotony of daily chores led to a sort of lassitude. On the fifth day out the weather started to improve, becoming a little warmer with odd bursts of sunshine. The speed went up to ten knots. They were now just below Pescara still hugging the coastline just outside the limit. The old ship had covered some six hundred miles since it left Split. For the most part the journey was going well. The Captain seemed to have taken no notice of O'Shea's constant presence in the wheelhouse or if he did choose to ignore it. They were all beginning to feel the strain of living together at such close quarters. Reilly reminded himself that once they got rid of the Captain and Mate in Portugal the rest would be facing the toughest part of the trip.

At the speed they were making it would be another three weeks before they reached Gibraltar. That is if everything went well. Then to Oporto to unload the tractors and the Captain and his Mate. After that it would depend on the weather when they could set out for the Irish coast.

"A penny for them George."

Francis had come up behind him unnoticed and stood at the rail.

"I don't know if there even worth a penny, girl, I'm thinking about what's ahead of us, and how slow this trip is going to be."

Taking a packet of Russian cigarettes from his pocket he offered her one. As he held the match to her their eyes met and held until she looked away. There was an awkward silence. George looked over the side.

"Look Francis, I've got to ask you this, I've grown quite fond of you these last few days, if there's anyone else just say so and that will be that."

He flung the cigarette into the waves. She caught his hand in hers and gave it a squeeze.

"There's no one else George and I'm beginning to like you a little bit too."

With a wink she started towards the cabins leaving Reilly with mixed feelings staring after her. At that moment O'Shea arrived, grinning from ear to ear.

"Having woman trouble George?"

Seeing the look on Reilly's face he immediately switched to serious again.

"The Captain's complaining about the radar, say's it's not working properly, thinks we should call in somewhere for repairs."

Reilly looked at him sharply.

"No way, we can't do that, it'll have to wait until we get to Portugal, I'll go and talk to him myself."

He started towards the bridge. There, Makirious was sitting at a desk. Fergus Doyle was at the wheel.

"Captain, O'Shea tells me there's something wrong with the radar, that it's not working properly."

Makirious looked at him with a grin,

"Come I show you, sometime it vork okay. Then it go all funny and see nothing, this very dangerous, vee have to get fixed, maybe vee go in Brindisi, eh?"

He grinned into Reilly's face. Who answered grimly.

"No, radar or no radar this boat keeps going until we reach Porto, is that clear?"

With a flash of tobacco stained teeth the Captain shrugged his shoulders and turned his attention to some charts. Reilly went out and up towards the bow where O'Shea was lying on a hatchway in the weak sun. He sat on the edge watching a seagull, which was flying parallel with the ship.

"John get Tynan to have a look at the radar, he ran a trawler at home he should know something about it, tell him to do it when Makirious is off duty and let me know the result."

He stood and watched the distant coast slip by. O'Shea said nothing a faint movement of the hand was the entire acknowledgement he gave. Reilly went back to the stern and started to check the supplies and fresh water tanks. It would relieve the monotony and pass a few hours before the night.

George Reilly awoke suddenly from a deep sleep. He had been dreaming. The ship was on fire and he was trapped below decks with its deadly cargo. The flames were reaching out to him and he was screaming in panic. He could feel the terrific heat. His hands were bloody from trying to open the steel door. Running his hand over his face he found he was covered in sweat. He lay there for some time. The dream had been so real. Swinging out of the bunk he stood looking out the porthole. He knew now with certainty that this whole venture was about to go disastrously wrong.

It was almost a week since Seamus Tynan had carried out checks on the radar equipment. He had told George he could find nothing wrong. Three times at night he had done checks and the results were the same. George wondered again what the Captain was playing at. The monotony was getting to them all now. There was that hint of tension everywhere. It was the little things. The odd sharp word here and there. There were ridiculous arguments over trivial incidents. The ship was now off Bari and doing a steady ten knots. If they kept up this pace they could top up their fuel tanks when they reached Oporto. He was sure the Captain was up to something. On one occasion he had come on him and the mate huddled together over the charts talking animatedly. They had stopped on his entry into the wheelhouse. Well O'Shea was watching Makirious like a hawk. So far he had not put a foot wrong. Maybe he was wrong, but then again maybe not.

After a shower and a shave he felt better. Out on the deck Francis was reading a book, sitting in a deck chair and wearing a bikini, which left a lot of space for a tan. George climbed up to the bridge. O'Shea was sitting with his feet propped on the rail his sunglasses reflecting the rays. One of the others, Tynan, was at the wheel. There was no sign of the Greek Captain. Reilly nodded to O'Shea.

"Where's our friend?"

"He went off about an hour ago, said he wasn't feeling well, George I'm getting fed up to the teeth with this bloody ship, it's driving me crazy, the sooner we get off the better."

He stood up and with his back to the rail facing Reilly.

"I know how you feel and believe me I feel the same way, but we have a job to do and we'll just have to stick it out. I still have this feeling about our Greek friend, so keep on the alert, In another couple of days we'll be round the Cape San Maria, from there on its a straight run across to Sicily, at least the weather is getting warmer and sunnier, that should be some consolation."

The two men walked around the ship and finished at the stern watching the white wake stretching into the distance. A single engined aeroplane passed overhead and travelled in the direction from which they had come. It turned and came in the direction of the ship waggling its wings and turned towards land. Reilly had just got back to his cabin when O'Shea burst in.

"George it looks like we've got trouble there's an Italian naval boat coming up fast towards us, I think they're going to stop us."

Reilly made for the deck. Everyone was standing at the rail watching the approaching ship. It was an Italian navy destroyer, long and rakish and sending up a high bow wave. It circled the ship and pulled alongside. Makirious had reappeared on the bridge and was shutting down the engines. An Officer and some men came aboard. Captain Makirious went to meet him and to George's amazement greeted him in fluent Italian. They went up to the Bridge together where Reilly saw them sometime later toasting each other. The Captain produced some bottles, which he gave to the young officer who returned to the destroyer. The patrol boat turned and headed back to shore. Reilly went up to the Captain.

"What was all that about?"

Makarious grinned into his face.

"A small trouble, vee have the oil leak De aeroplane she see it, vee go and look."

It had to be fuel oil. They made their way down to the tanks. There were drain cocks fitted to the fuel system in order to drain out the tanks of water and sludge, which accumulated over periods of time. When Reilly and the Captain checked them they found one valve about two turns open. This was allowing a trickle of the precious fuel oil to leak away, The Greek turned it down tight and turned to George.

"They never close it fully in port I theenk."

Reilly's face was indifferent,

"I just wonder how much fuel we've lost, I'll check on it and see how much we have left."

He looked at the gauge on the tank. It was reading nearly a third full. The other tank read half. A quick calculation showed they had lost nearly five hundred gallons of fuel. So it must have been leaking for some time. It could have been an accident, maybe it had not been fully closed before they left, or was it another trick of the Captain's to get them into port. In the bridge room he spent the next hour calculating how far they could get with the remaining oil. If they dropped the speed down to eight knots they should just have about enough to get to Oporto. That was provided the sea remained as calm as it had been for the last few days. If they had to run against a heavy sea it would eat up fuel. He wondered about going into one of the Italian ports and stocking up. The trouble was that you were then inviting Customs examination. Perhaps someone would decide to question what five Irishmen and a woman, with a Greek Captain and a Turkish mate were doing on a ship in the middle of the Adriatic. In Oporto it would be different, the tractors were to be unloaded there. The Captain would see to all that, George and the rest would keep out of everybody's way until they sailed again. The Captain and Mate would be paid off and dropped in a small boat near the coast.

Reilly decided to carry on and recheck the situation when they reached Sicily.

CHAPTER 12

Joe Kearns dialled the American's number at exactly twelve, o clock.

"Mr.Grant? This is Joe Kearns. I believe we have something in common, perhaps we could meet, say tomorrow morning, I could pick you up at about ten."

"That would be fine Joe, I'll be in the lobby, what colour car?"

Joe told him and put down the phone. When he drove into the Guesthouse entrance next morning the man was standing on the steps. He was in the car almost before it stopped. He turned to Joe and stuck out a hand.

"Hi Joe I'm Harry Grant, glad to know you, got a call from the Specials to expect you to contact me,"

Joe drove out towards Dun Laoghaire where he parked facing the water, protected by an iron railing from the edge of the pier. On the way he had told Grant what had happened to him since he had started to cover the demonstration. How he had contacted Jem. How the police had found Jem's body next day. He described the meeting with his detective friend and the warning from him. When he mentioned the attempt on his own life and the death of his assailant Grant looked at him in appreciation. He did not mention about the Taoiseach or the Commissioner. In return Grant told him of his orders and arrival and his meeting with the men in the pub. Joe thanked him for saving his landlady. Grant turned to Joe.

"I reckon that the key to this, lies with that bloke McCall, we'll have to try and get into his office, there's a chance we might find something there."

He suddenly sat up and was looking in the side mirror. Joe looked in his centre one. A large truck had come over the hill leading down to where they were parked. The driver seemed to be having some kind of trouble, as he was out on the roadway leaning into the cab. There was a sudden roar of engine and the truck started down the hill towards them. Grant shouted.

"Get out."

Joe had the door open in a flash, hurling himself out of the car. He caught a glimpse of Grant going out the far side before with a terrific bang the truck hit the Cortina and pushed it through the railings into the water and toppled over. Joe stood up and looked for Grant. There was no sign of him. Thinking the truck had hit him, he rushed to the edge where the truck and car had gone into the water. There was no sign of Grant. He looked around. A figure was running alongside the wall of the boatyard from where the truck had come from. As he watched, it disappeared from sight. By now a small crowd had gathered and were peering at the wreckage, which could be just seen under the water. Kearns quietly left and made his way after Grant. In a corner of the boatyard he found him sitting astride a young fellow of about twenty, who was dressed in a blue boiler suit. As Joe approached Grant drew back his fist. He heard the crack as it connected with the young man's jaw and he went limp. Grant stood up as Joe reached him.

"Glad to see you got out Joe, this is the bastard who tried to kill us, he waited around to see if the job was a success. I came up behind him and dragged him in here."

He rubbed his knuckles.

"We'll have to get him out of here and see if he'll talk, I'd say he won't wake up for about half an hour."

Joe thought quickly. There was no time to ring his contact. That left John McQuillen. In the meantime Grant had found a piece of dirty tarpaulin and covered the body with it. Joe made his way to a phone box and called McQuillen's office. The Garda that answered said he did not know when he would be back. Joe suggested he try the radio and when he demurred told him unless he wanted to be stationed somewhere in the wilds of the West of Ireland he should get the message to McQuillen immediately to come to the boatyard in a hurry. Joe waited at the bridge for about fifteen minutes before a car pulled up and McQuillen jumped out.

"Joe, what the hell's up I got a panic message to get here as quick as possible? What's that crowd doing down there?"

He was looking towards the harbour. Kearns caught his arm.

"John, come in here a minute."

He took him into the boatyard where Grant was sitting on the bundle in the tarpaulin. He pulled back the cover to reveal the young man. McQuillen looked at Joe.

"John this fellow tried to kill the two of us a short time ago. We were sitting in a car down there and he sent this truck at us. It was the mercy of God we got out in time. Harry here is American C.I.A., your people know about him."

Grant stood up and said to the stunned McQuillen.

"I'm afraid Joe's right sir, if you care to contact Detective Inspector Maguire of Special Branch he'll fill you in, can we take this fellow somewhere I'd like to ask him a few questions."

McQuillen looked from one to the other. He walked some distance away and took a radio from his pocket. Turning his back he began a conversation, looking an odd time at the two men. By now a squad car had arrived at the pier and two Gardai were talking to the crowd. McQuillen put the radio away.

"Wait here, there'll be a van along in a few minutes, I'll go and sort them out down there."

He walked towards the crowd. A short time later a black Transit van drove into the boatyard. Two men in working clothes got out, casually picked up the bundle in the tarpaulin and threw it into the back of the van. McQuillen spoke with them and they drove off in the direction of the city. Grant and Joe got into McQuillen's car and followed.

Later behind a one way glass they watched as the young man regained consciousness. A doctor was in attendance and after checking him out declared him to be in no danger. McQuillen then started to question him, the man, sullen faced, maintained a stony silence. After about half an hour McQuillen came out. Looking at Joe and Harry he told them.

"Look lads, we're going to get nothing out of this bloke and we've basically got nothing on him, so I'm going to have to let him go. Now I suggest that you two go on home. Don't worry about the accident, you will not be mentioned in any report. It appears that the car was unoccupied at the time it was hit."

Grant looked from McQuillen to Joe who was staring at the detective in disbelief.

"But John he tried to kill us, Harry saw him putting the truck in motion, you can't just let him go like that"

"I'm afraid so,"

Said McQuillen, as he guided them towards the door. Outside Grant stood for a moment a grin forming on his face. He grabbed Joe's arm.

"Come on, let's find ourselves a taxi."

They moved up to some traffic lights and waited. Soon they spotted a taxi coming from the direction of the city. Grant signalled for it to stop. Grant told the driver

"Joe and myself are a couple of press men, we would like you to drive us where ever we want to go, you'll be well paid, so maybe you will sign off now, here's my press card."

Grant showed him his card. Joe did likewise. The driver looked from one to the other and shrugged his shoulders. He took the radio and told the controller he was finishing for the evening. Grant then told him to park in a side street where they had a good view of the front of the Garda station. It was a good half-hour later when the young man emerged and stood for a moment looking at the traffic. He then walked to a phone booth and made a call. When he emerged he stood on the edge of the kerb looking up and down. A short time later a black Mercedes stopped and the young man hopped in. It rejoined the traffic and drove towards the city. Grant tapped the taxi driver on the shoulder who moved off in pursuit.

"Keep well back but don't lose him,"

Grant advised the driver, who nodded. They followed the black car to where it turned to follow the canal. Here it stopped at the next bridge to pick up two men, one with his arm in a sling. Grant recognised them as the two who had attacked Joe's landlady. The car then turned and they followed it on to the Blessington road out into open countryside. It finally turned in between the stone pillars of a wooded driveway leading to a large house set well back from the road. The taxi drove by and stopped in a small lay-by about one hundred yards further on. Here it was hidden from view by some large banks of gravel used by council workers for road repairs. Harry gave the driver another twenty pound note. Then he took a fiftypound note from his wallet and tore it in half. One part he handed to the driver.

"Wait here for us, you'll get the other half when we get back. We'll try not to be longer than an hour."

The driver nodded, he looked decidedly unhappy at the prospect of sitting for an hour in the cold frosty night. Joe and Harry climbed over the wall and dropped into the grounds of the house. It was bright moonlight and the frost was making crackling noises under their feet. They reached the gravelled avenue, leading up to the front door and started in the direction of the house where there were lights in the bottom windows. Just as they neared the building they heard the sound of a car approaching, They quickly ducked behind a rhododendron bush almost opposite the door. As the car swept into view a series of security lights came on making the place as bright as day. When it stopped a tall figure got out and went into the house. It was Michael McCall, the T.D. Almost immediately the lights went out. Joe and Harry crouched behind their bush. Harry let out a low whistle.

"If that car hadn't arrived Joe, we would have set off those lights. We've got to get over to the windows."

They could see figures silhouetted against the curtains of a room to the left of the main door. Just then another car arrived and the lights came on again. This time they noted where the car was when they lit up. Harry reckoned that there was probably a blind spot for about three feet out from the wall all along the front of the house. If so, they could possibly get to the wall without activating the lights. There was one chance. At the end of the house a gravel path led around the corner to the rear. Lining this was a growth of young conifers about ten feet tall. If they could circle round behind them and come in from that corner they might just avoid the beam from the sensor. They crept around the bushes until they were behind the trees. It was about two feet from the wall of the house. If the beam reached that far when they stepped forward the lights would come on. Grant moved his right foot slowly forward, twelve inches, pause, no lights. He followed with his left, nothing. Now he was against the wall of the house. He beckoned Joe who gingerly followed. On hands and knees they crept forward until they were under the window. They could hear the murmur of voices. Grant raised himself up and peered through a gap in the curtain. He could see figures seated around a table. At the head sat McCall. On his left sat one of the men Grant had met in the White Leprechaun. Beside him sat another man whom Harry did not recognise. The young man whom they had followed was standing facing McCall. He seemed to be arguing. McCall said something to the others and heads nodded in agreement. The man with the sling and his companion moved forward. At that moment Joe became aware of a sound behind them. Two men brandishing heavy automatics were standing there. One of them motioned for them to rise. Slowly Kearns and Grant came to their feet, their hands in the air. One of the men spoke, he had a clipped Dublin accent.

"Into the house."

He prodded them with his automatic. The other covered them from the side. Inside they halted in the hall. One of the men went into the room where McCall and the others were. The other stood them facing the wall while he searched them for weapons. Joe decided he had done the right thing in leaving One Arm's gun in the Cortina. Moments later they were ushered into the other room. McCall looked at them.

"Well now, it's our American friend Mr.Grant and despite the disguise our other friend is Mr. Kearns, the interfering reporter. I'm afraid that you have caused us enough trouble, I did try to warn you Mr. Kearns, now I regret we must take the necessary steps to protect our operation. Take them upstairs and tie them up well, I'll have another chat with them later".

The guards expertly trussed them up. Then kicked their legs from under them. Leaving them lying on the floor. One of them looked at them as he went out, grinning at them he said.

"You fellas better say your prayers, you won't be walking out of here, we hate spies."

He slammed the door and the key was turned in the lock. Grant rolled across the floor and propped him-self into a sitting position against the wall. Kearns followed his example. They were sitting one facing the other. Grant was in one corner while Joe was in another. Here he lay in the corner, which was formed by the fireplace and the main wall. Grant looked around the room, which was bare of any furniture.

"Joe we sure are in a mess this time, its my fault, I should have realised that they would have guards, I only hope we can get out of this one."

He shifted his position slightly. Joe was about to say something when he caught the faint murmur of voices. The sound seemed to be coming from the fireplace. Grant watched in some surprise as Joe twisted himself around and stuck his head in the grate. Now he could hear every word that was been spoken in the room below. Someone was saying,

"We've no option only to execute them, they know too much, if they escape they could ruin the whole plan, I say shoot them now."

Then came McCall's voice.

"No if we kill them now it could provoke a hue and cry, but what's puzzling me is how Kearns met up with the American, there could be more here than we know about. Let's see if we can get some more information from them before we do anything."

There was a murmur of assent. Another voice broke in.

"Let's get on with the meeting, we've agreed on the dates for the coup then, it is definitely the week end of the end of March, beginning of April. When will the arms ship arrive?"

McCall's voice floated up.

"That is the correct date, the ship will arrive about a week before hand, this will give us time to distribute the stuff. No one is to know about the seizure of the Government except us here in this room. To all intents and purposes we are going to arrest them and charge them with crimes against the State. However we can save ourselves a lot of trouble here and also give a warning to the public. When we use the gas at the castle it will be lethal. We can then announce that all of them were found guilty and executed after a quick trial during the weekend. Remember that no one outside this room is to know about this, is that clear?"

There was a chorus of accent. Another voice then asked where the ship would unload. McCall replied that this was still a secret for the moment but that the ship was already on the way. Joe Kearns listened aghast. They were planning wholesale murder here. At least they now knew when and where. He and Grant would have to make every effort to escape and warn the Taoaseach. He shook his head out of the fireplace and rolled across to where Grant lay against the wall. When he told him of what he had overheard, Grant was stunned.

"Joe we've got to try and get out of here, the Russians must have a hand in this, there's no way these people could even attempt this on their own. I can't move those bloody ropes, these blokes knew what they were doing, at least we know that they're not going to kill us for the moment."

Sitting in his taxi the driver looked at his watch. It was now two hours since the men had left. He stamped his frozen feet, agonising for another few minutes. After all, they had said one hour. It was now two. He looked at the torn fiftypound note. Just my luck he mused, a, well, he had already got forty pounds and it was getting colder. He shivered slightly and blew on his hands. Then with a quick movement he started the engine and drove back towards the city.

CHAPTER 13

George Reilly could not sleep. He could feel the throb of the engines as the freighter ploughed through the Adriatic. Every beat seemed to echo inside his head. It was stuffy in the small cabin. He swung his legs out and stood for a moment in the darkness. He pulled on shirt and trousers and went out on the deck. Leaning on the rail he watched the lights on shore slip past. The girl's voice broke in on his reverie.

"What's the matter George? Could you not sleep either?"

She moved over to the rail beside him. Looking at her Reilly wondered how long she had been standing behind him.

"Francis, yes, I suppose you're right, it got terribly stuffy down there, I just came up for some air."

He was looking at her face, side on, as she gazed towards the shore. The moonlight shone on her black hair lighting it up with silvery flashes. Reilly had been thinking a lot about her recently. He had become even more curious about her in the last few days. She for her part had shown no sign that she found him in any way attractive. Now she gazed into the night at the far off lights.

"George, have you ever been in love? Do you have a girl friend?"

Reilly laughed quietly.

"No Francis to both questions, I suppose I never did have the time or the inclination to indulge, especially in my line of work, or maybe I just never met the right girl, but what about you?"

She turned to look at him.

"No George, there is no one, I never felt the need for any one, that is until now."

It took him a short time to realise what she was saying. He reached out and took her in his arms and kissed her, a long lingering kiss. She responded twining her arms around his neck. Their kisses got more passionate. Francis took his hand and led him down to her cabin.

The first streaks of dawn were starting to light up the horizon as Reilly made his way back. He had left Francis sleeping. They had stepped over the threshold and become lovers in the last couple of hours. He turned a corner of the passageway and collided with someone. Something hit him hard on the forehead and he went down in a heap on the floor.

When he came round some two hours later O'Shea was sponging ice water on his head. Raising his hand he felt the large bump. He could not focus his eyes properly and kept blinking at O'Shea, who grinned at him.

"We thought you were a goner there for a bit George, any idea what happened, Fergus heard something and found you lying in the passage, he thought he saw a figure disappear around the corner but he's not sure, where were you going anyway?

Francis came in and looked at him anxiously. O'Shea grinned at her and told George.

"Your nurse here has been giving us orders for the past two hours, she was very worried about you, in fact if you hadn't wakened up she was going to put into port for a doctor."

Reilly's head felt as if it had been hit with a sledgehammer. Flashes of lightning were shooting in one side and out the other. Francis was mixing something in a glass. She held it to his lips and told him to drink. He did so and lay back closing his eyes. Some ten minutes later he began to feel a little better and he was able to think a little clearer. For the moment he pretended that he could remember nothing about what had happened. Telling the others he must have walked into a door he told them he wanted to sleep.

He must have dozed off because as he found out later he had been asleep for three hours when he awoke to a cool hand on his brow. Reaching up he caught it. She gave a start of surprise.

"I'm sorry George, I didn't think you were awake, I only wanted to see if you were okay."

She gave him a smile. Sitting up he put his hand to his head. Feeling the bump, he winced.

"Someone really clouted me Francis, it was either the Captain or that bloody mate of his. The question is, what were they doing, I'll go down later and have a look in the holds, for now I'm going to play the idiot, I don't recall anything, is that clear?"

"Would it not be better George if I went and had a look, If I find anything I'll come back to you."

Before he had time to reply she had gone. With a muttered curse he put his legs to the floor and stood up. His head swam. Splashing himself with cold water over his head and face made him feel better. Going out on deck he climbed up to the bridge. Makirious was at a table working on some charts. Fergus Doyle was at the wheel. George went over and stood looking down at the charts.

"Where are we now Captain?"

Makirious glanced up at him and pointed to the map.

"Vee be off the coast of Sicily in a few hours, then vee head for Gibraltar, is good no?"

He flashed tobacco stained teeth at Reilly who leaned over the table swaying slightly. He put his hand to his forehead and leaned over the chart table. Straightening up again he put his hand on the Captain's shoulder and deliberately slurring his voice said.

"Very good Captain, very good, keep us on course I'm going to lie down now, I don't feel so good."

He saw Fergus Doyle looking at him curiously. Giving another stagger he lurched out on deck. He lay across the rail for a few minutes, then like a drunken man staggered towards his cabin. Out of the corner of his eye he saw Makirious looking down at him from the window. Francis was waiting for him inside. She gave him a quick kiss and a hug.

"George there was no sign of anything having been disturbed down there, I looked everywhere, but I found this in the passageway where you were lying."

She handed him a small coin about the size of a penny, it had Turkish writing on it. Reilly turned it over in his hand. It might have been there for some time, on the other hand the Mate was Turkish. He smiled grimly. There had to be something going on with the Captain and the Mate. That coin had probably been dropped during the struggle. Then there was that intersecting line on the chart on the Captain's desk. It had bisected the ship's line of travel. At the time he had not given it much thought. Now he was sure it was a rendezvous. It was at a point where the ship would be at its nearest point to the coast of Sicily. The Captain must have sold them out to the Mafia. Francis was tugging at his sleeve.

"George what's going on, what is it? Tell me."

"I'm not sure Francis, I think we're going to have a problem, go and find O'Shea and bring him here, do it casually, just tell him I want to see him."

She made to say something but he waved her out. A few moments later John O'Shea came in. Reilly nodded to him. Francis made to enter but he told her to go and keep an eye on the Captain. When he told O'Shea what he thought was about to happen. O'Shea whistled soundlessly.

"When do you think they will make their move George, is it tonight?"

Reilly nodded.

"As far as I can estimate it has to be tonight, we'll be off the nearest point to Sicily, Capo Passero, at about three thirty hours. What better place and time for an attack I'd say the plan is to take over the ship and kill us all. Now the question is what are we going to do about it. Who's on shift tonight?"

O'Shea grinned at him.

"I'm on the wheel from midnight with the Mate, I'll take a couple of automatics with me and tell Fergus and the others to be ready, if they hear anything to come running, by the way does Francis know anything about this?

Reilly shook his head.

"I don't want her to know anything about it, it could turn out very rough and I don't want her getting hurt, say nothing to her about it, just make sure the lads have weapons, do it quietly, Makirious mustn't suspect anything."

After O'Shea had gone Reilly pulled his bag from under his bunk. From it he took a heavy Russian automatic. He pulled the magazine

112

and checked it was fully loaded. Placing it underneath his pillow, he shoved spare magazines into his pockets. The door opened and Francis came in. looking at George she put her hand on his arm.

"Are you going to tell me what's going on George, what is it? I want to know."

He gave her a kiss on the cheek.

"There's nothing going on Francis, not a thing, I was just telling O'Shea to watch the Captain and that Mate of his, I just don't trust them, that's all".

He took her in his arms and they kissed, she clung to him and whispered in his ear.

"I'll leave the door unlocked in case you might like to kiss me goodnight."

He looked at her in mock horror.

"Isn't it the shameless hussy you are Francis, lock your door, I'll knock three times when I get there, now run along and I'll see you later."

He gave her a playful pat on the rump and steered her out into the passageway hoping he had sounded convincing. She would be safer locked in her cabin if anything did start. He went down to the engine room. Sean McConville was sitting in a chair reading in front of the mass of gauges. George had a few words with him about the situation. He would come off watch at midnight and Shamus Tynan would take his place. Reilly climbed back to the deck and walked down the line of tractors. They would provide some cover he thought. He noticed there were two rope ladders coiled one at each end of the line of tractors. This would be where they would come aboard he reckoned. Going back to his cabin he armed himself with an electric torch and made his way down to the holds. Looking at the rows of packing cases he walked along each of the aisles checking each box. He had almost finished when he saw the broken sliver of wood. The lid on this case had been removed and replaced. Except for the broken splinter of wood sticking out from the lid he would not have noticed anything. He got his fingers under the lid and pulled. It rose with a slight groan. Someone had examined the contents, which were hand grenades. Reilly stuck four in his jacket and pushed the lid back home.

O'Shea was in his cabin, getting ready to go on the twelve-o clock shift. He told Reilly that each of the others had been briefed and were ready. George told him about the opened crate and patted the bulges in his pockets. O'Shea showed him his two automatics under his jacket. They heard footsteps and Fergus Doyle came in with a trio of Kalashnikovs and ammunition and left them with Reilly in the cabin. George lay down on the bunk and thought about the coming fight. He was feeling very tired.

Something made him open his eyes. He lay there listening. By the dim light of the cabin he looked at his watch. It was a couple of minutes past two. He had been asleep for over two hours, damn. Slipping off the bunk he moved to the door. Someone was standing at the other side. He could hear him breathing before he moved off quietly along the passageway. Reaching for the handle, George tried to open the door. It would not budge.

"Jesus Christ it's started, that was bloody stupid of me falling asleep, Makirious is locking us in, damn damn damn."

He swore fluently, he had to get out and quickly. He grabbed the automatic from under the pillow and stuck the butt behind the door handle. Catching the barrel he levered upwards. Nothing happened. Looking around the cabin he saw in its case on the wall a steel fire axe. Grabbing it he inserted it behind the lock and heaved. There was a tearing sound and the door handle came away with a piece of the door. George got the head of the axe behind the lock and gave it a twist forcing the lock out of the door. Stepping out into the passageway he made for Doyle's cabin it too was locked. With a couple of twists of the axe he soon had it opened. Doyle stepped out and collected the Kalashnikovs one of which he threw to Reilly. As they passed McConville's cabin the door was ajar. Reilly looked in. In the dim light he could see the figure in the bunk. In the blanket was a hole with burn marks around it. He checked for a pulse. Mc Conville was dead. They made their way down to the engine room. Shamus Tynan was sitting watching the gauges. George reached out and tapped him on the shoulder. He toppled over on to the floor his sightless eyes staring up at them, the handle of a knife stuck out from his chest. Grim faced, Reilly motioned Doyle up the ladder leading to the deck. They had just time to duck around the corner when the Turkish Mate stepped onto the ladder and went down to the engine room. Reilly and Doyle crept out among the lines of tractors and crouched behind one of them. It was bright moonlight and they could see everything as clear as day. One of the rope ladders had been dropped over the side. So the Captain was expecting company. Looking towards the bridge they could see him talking to O'Shea who was at the wheel. Then he produced a revolver from his pocket and pointed it at O'Shea. At first they thought he was going to shoot him but he motioned him to raise his hands. The Captain then searched him, dropping the two guns on the floor and kicking them away into a corner.

Now the engines slowed down and then stopped. The ship started to lose headway. Makirious was speaking into a hand held radio keeping O'Shea covered as he did so. The Mate came back and climbed up to the bridge. He picked up one of O'Shea's guns and forced him down the ladder and towards the stern of the ship. Among the tractors Reilly and Doyle could only watch as the two passed out of sight. A few moments later a shot rang out and there was a cry and a splash.

They heard the sound of an engine and Reilly raised his head cautiously over the side. A small fishing boat was approaching from the starboard side. There appeared to be eight or ten men on the deck. The Captain leaned out and greeted them in Italian as the boat pulled along side. Fergus Doyle whispered in Reilly's ear.

"What will we do George, wait until they come aboard? I'll go to the other side,"

Reilly nodded and checked his Kalashnikov. He looked up and saw a figure moving back from the stern towards the steps leading to the bridge. It must be the Mate yet Reilly thought there was something familiar about it. Doyle had disappeared to the other end of the line of tractors. He could hear the Italians climbing the rope ladder now. His hands were sweating and his heart was thumping in his chest. He aimed the rifle at the top of the ladder and waited, better let them get on board first then shoot, his mouth was dry. He was going to kill someone. He wondered vaguely could he really do it. If he did not they would surely kill him. He gripped the rifle tighter. After all McConville and Tynan were already dead and O'Shea, that bloody Mate had probably killed O'Shea, a wave of hatred went through him and suddenly he was icy cool. He waited, listening to the ladder and its load hitting off the iron side as the Italians climbed up from the fishing boat.

A pair of hands reached over the rail and a man heaved his body, over to stand on the deck. Two more men climbed aboard. A fourth joined them almost immediately. The Captain had come out on the bridge and was watching the boarding. As Reilly looked a figure climbed up the steel ladder towards the bridge. Stepping on to the deck, it moved towards Makirious. George thought it was the Mate, yet it looked smaller. He saw the Captain back away, the figure raised its arm and fired twice and Makirious tumbled over the rail and into the sea. A burst of fire from Doyle tore into the group of men on the deck. Two of them went down and a third fell across the front wheel of a tractor. Reilly felt the gun buck in his hand and shots poured towards the men still standing, two of whom were firing revolvers at Doyle. He raised a hand to George. A head appeared over the rail and Reilly fired at it. It vanished in a bloody mess. One of the men to his left fired at them and George heard O'Shea cry out and slide to the deck. A tractor tyre exploded beside him and the force flung him against the steel rail. He fired at another man and saw him go down. The figure on the bridge was shouting at him now. It was Francis.

"There's more coming up the ladder George get them, get them."

He ran to the side and looked over. Two more men were coming up the ladder. They were about halfway up. Pulling out his automatic he fired at them. One fell into the sea the other hung on to the ladder, Blood spurting from a wound in his neck. His eyes pleaded with Reilly as he muttered over and over.

"Cristo, Cristo."

There was a movement beside him and the girl was there. Almost casually, it seemed to George, she shot the man between the eyes, his body falling back into the fishing boat below where two more men stood looking upwards. Reaching into her jacket pocket the girl took out two grenades. Pulling the pins she dropped them onto the boats deck where they exploded with a roar. The cabin and the two men vanished in a sheet of flame. Doyle joined them at the side. There was now a deadly silence broken only by the crackling flames below. A moan behind them reminded them of O'Shea. He was lying on the deck half under a tractor blood seeping out of a hole in his left shoulder. Reilly and Doyle lifted him out and propped him against the steel side. The girl knelt beside him and took his hand away from the wound. She turned to Doyle.

"See if you can find a first aid box or something to bandage him with. George, check that boat, see what's happening, we've got to get rid of these bodies too".

Reilly looked over the side at the remains of the fishing boat. It was down by the head and slowly filling with water. Little tongues of flame flickered from the remains of the cabin. Two bodies were lying face downwards in the debris. He walked across the deck to where the other bodies lay. They were all aged between twenty or twenty-five, all were very dead, the decks, slippy with their blood. He shuddered at the carnage. In the moonlight the whole scene looked unreal. The girl was bandaging O'Shea's shoulder from a first aid box, which Doyle had found. She looked up as Reilly came over.

"That boat is sinking Francis, the others are all dead, how's is his arm?"

She finished tying the bandage.

"He's lost a lot of blood, he could do with a doctor, I wonder did anyone hear the noise on shore?"

They were about five miles off the coast where lights twinkled. The remains of the fishing boat were on the seaward side of the freighter. Reilly thought for a moment.

"We'll have to get moving, the best thing to do is head for Libya, we certainly can't go into Sicily, let's try and move out of here fast. Fergus, see if that boat has sunk yet if not put a couple of grenades into it. Then get back here. I'll get the engines started. See if you can get something to cover those bodies, we'll weigh them later and drop them overboard as we go."

Doyle disappeared over the side. George and the girl managed to get O'Shea into a cabin where they put him on a bunk. Then Reilly went down to the engine room. He pressed a green button on the panel and was rewarded by the slow thump of the engines starting. Back on the bridge, Doyle told him the boat had sunk. He worked out a course south towards the Libyan coast. The he moved the telegraph to full ahead and the ship started to move forward. He lashed the wheel on course and went down to help Doyle get rid of the bodies. It took them over an hour to do this. Then they washed down the bloody decks with a powerful hose. Francis was nursing the restless O'Shea who was now running a temperature.

Ten miles away the British Submarine Gadfly cruised on the surface recharging her batteries. The lookout was attracted by the flames in the distance and reported to his Captain, Peter Pritchard. He ordered full speed ahead to investigate. The Gadfly arrived shortly after the freighter had started away south. Around the submarine the debris from the fishing boat floated by. Some of the crew fished two bodies from the water. One wore a kind of uniform. On searching his pockets they identified him as one Gregor Makirious, Captain, resident of Athens. There was a neat hole in his forehead just above the right eye. The back of his head was missing. The other body had no identification he had been shot through the heart. To Pritchard's eyes he looked Italian. They weighted the bodies and after a short prayer slid them into the sea. A report was sent to the Admiralty of the incident with a description of the vessels involved. A short time later Pritchard received the following message.

'Imperative ascertains name and possible destination of ship and number of persons aboard. Please obtain photographs. Observe utmost secrecy. Pritchard gave an order and the Gadfly moved south in the direction taken by the freighter.

CHAPTER 14

Peggy Noone stood uncertainly outside Harry Grant's bedroom door. She had not seen him since he had left the previous morning. She was sure he had not come in the previous night. Knocking on the door she called his name. There was no reply. Taking a bunch of keys from her belt she opened the door, the bed had not been slept in. She re-locked it and went downstairs. A few moments later she was on the phone to John Maguire head of The Irish Special Branch.

When John McQuillen entered the station after having been out on a robbery detail there was a message to ring Special Branch Headquarters. Maguire then asked him about Grant and McQuillen felt a cold chill go down his spine. He explained about Grant and Kearns setting out to follow the man who had tried to kill them. At the end of the line, Maguire gazed out over the city. He told McQuillan that it was imperative that the men were found. An all points bulletin was issued to all Garda stations in the Dublin area stating that the men were wanted for questioning. For three days the enquiries continued without as much of a trace. Everywhere they were met with blank stares and a shaking of heads. Then on the fourth day a young motor cycle Garda was driving his machine when the engine suddenly died and he slowed to a halt beside a taxi rank. A couple of drivers came over and stood around as he tried in vain to restart engine. He radioed for a pick up and sat back to wait. Pulling out the picture of Grant and Kearns the Garda asked the drivers if anyone had seen or picked up either one of the men. The drivers looked and shook their heads. Then one of them told him.

"One of our lads picked up a couple of fellows a few nights ago, they got him to drive them somewhere and asked him to wait, but they never came back. They gave him the half of a fifty pound note, told him he would get the other half when they returned but they never came so he went home, he still has the note, maybe it has something to do with the fellows your looking for."

The Garda made some notes including the driver's name and address.

The pickup truck arrived and took him and the bike back to the station. His report passed along the line eventually reaching Maguire's desk some hours later.

John McQuillen went to investigate it. He parked some distance from the neat semi detached house. The taxi was parked in the driveway. A girl of about ten was hopping a ball off the front wall and catching it in some endless game. He rang the bell and waited. Inside a dog barked and a woman's figure was outlined against the glass. The door was opened cautiously.

"Yes?"

"Could I speak to Mr. Sam Duff please?

The door opened wider, she called back,

"Sam, There's someone here to see you,"

To McQuillen,

"Won't you come in,"

He was led into a sitting room and offered a seat. A stout man of about forty-five came in and looked at him curiously. McQuillen stood up and held out his card.

"Mr.Duff, I'm Detective Garda McQuillen, I'd like to ask you a few questions about a couple of men we're looking for."

He took out the photographs of Grant and Kearns and showed them to Duff. The man nodded and handed them back without a word and left the room coming back almost immediately. In his hand was the torn half of a fiftypound note. He handed it to McQuillen with a trace of a smile.

"Those two fellows hailed me in Merrion on Monday night, got me to follow this car out to a house on the Blessington road. They went off after giving me that note, told me I would get the rest when they returned, said they would not be more than an hour. I waited two and decided they weren't coming and went home. Besides I was frozen with the cold, that's it.

McQuillen was making notes, he looked up at the man.

"Can you describe exactly where you left them, better still could you come with me now and show me?"

120

Duff nodded and stood up.

"I'll just tell the wife I'm going out for a bit, I can't stay too long, I have to go to work about six."

They drove out to the place on the Blessington road where he had dropped the men. He showed McQuillen where he had parked and they had climbed over the wall. Before they got back to Duff's house, McQuillen impressed on him the need for absolute secrecy about the affair. Back at headquarters a check was carried out on the ownership of the house. This turned out to be an Irish American millionaire who was believed to be somewhere in the Pacific at the present time. He only used the house about twice a year, mostly in the summer months. It was looked after by a married couple, who were employed as caretakers. They lived in a newly built cottage a short distance from the main gate. The man usually drove a Range Rover while the woman owned a Red Nissan Micra car. They were well known and liked in the area. Maguire stuffed tobacco into his pipe and lit up. McQuillan, a non-smoker, gazed in awe at the cloud of blue smoke and wished he could open a window. Maguire sucked at his pipe and blew more smoke towards the ceiling. Taking the pipe from his mouth he stood up.

"John, there's no point in charging in there to night, we don't know what to expect. Put a discreet watch on the place. Meet me here in the morning, we'll go out and have a good look at the place then, go on home and get a good night's sleep. I'll see you here at nine."

They parted company outside and McQuillen made his way home. His wife, May, met him at the door. He could hear the two boys playing in the front room. Dropping into his favourite chair, he picked up the evening paper.

Grant and Kearns had been left alone for almost two hours after their capture. Suddenly the door opened and McCall came into the room. He looked at the two captives on the floor.

"Well gentlemen I must apologise for your discomfort but you have placed us in a rather difficult position. I know that Mr. Kearns is a reporter but I'm curious about you Mr. Grant, for instance how do you and Mr. Kearns come to be together?"

He looked from one to the other like a schoolteacher questioning children. Grant decided to play along his role of research student.

"Why that's sure an easy one, I came here to research the troubles, at Joe's newspaper they gave me his address, I went there to meet him and those two monkeys were laying into his landlady. I stopped that, afterwards he found out I was looking for him. We met and someone tried to kill us, I caught him and the police let him go. We followed him to here, the rest you know."

McCall seemed to accept the explanation.

"I see, well I must tell you that unfortunately you have stumbled on something which we cannot let you interfere with. Normally we would dispose of you immediately as spies but as you Mr Grant are an American and Mr. Kearns is a newspaper reporter, we will spare you for the time being. You may be of some use to us later. However we must move you out of here, have a pleasant journey until I see you again."

He called the two men who had first found them. They untied them and then cuffed their hands behind them bringing them downstairs. Here McCall gave them final instructions.

"Take them to Nevin's place, make sure they don't escape. Then come back here and clean everything up we don't want anyone to know we've been here, then report to me at the office, is that clear?"

The two nodded accent. Grant and Kearns were then taken out to an old Transit van and put into the back. Here they were fastened to the ribs of the body with two short chains while the men tidied up the house. A short time later they returned and the van drove out of the gates and turned left. Joe Kearns reckoned that they were heading out the Blessington road towards West Wicklow and away from the city. Some two hours later the van slowed as it drove for a time over a rough track, which then smoothed out. It finally stopped and the rear doors opened. They were ushered out. Looking around Joe saw they were at the front door of a large old country house. One of the men pressed a bell and the door opened to reveal a large rough looking man carrying a Uzi who stood aside as they entered. One of the men handed him the keys of the handcuffs. In spite of the situation Joe almost laughed when he noticed the man was dressed in full butler's regalia.

"There you are Ned, you know what to do, fix these two up for the night we have to get back to town. Bye the way you had better inform them of the situation here, just in case they get any ideas about walking away. We might see you again in a couple of days."

He grinned at them as he and his companion went out closing the door behind them. Ned pointed his gun at them and moved them into a room off the hall. He watched a television monitor which showed the van's progress until it stopped at what looked like a double security fence. The gap in the centre was occupied by a pack of snarling Rothweilers. Ned pressed a button and two sections of fence swung across separating the dogs from a gate section, which then opened and the van moved through. The fence swung back and the dogs were in command again. They watched on another camera until the van left through the main gates. Looking at the two men Ned gave them a bitter smile. He opened their handcuffs and spoke.

"Gentlemen as you have seen its next to impossible to escape from here, the dogs patrol that area which runs around the house. There are also armed guards stationed in the grounds. There is a bedroom prepared for you, the Boss sends his apology for not being here to meet you but he will see you in the morning, please do not try to do anything foolish."

The men stood rubbing their wrists. Neither could think of anything to say. Ned showed them up stairs and into a large bedroom with two large double beds. On a table stood a tray with some cans of beer and coke and packets of prepacked sandwiches.

"I'm sorry that's all for now but we had rather short notice, but sure you will be all right tomorrow, good night now."

He left them standing at the table. Grant picked up a can of beer and opened it. He took a sandwich from its pack and sat down.

"Well Joe we might as well make the best of it and see what happens next."

They slept until about eight next morning. The room contained a bathroom where they showered and Grant shaved. It was about ten a.m. when the men came down stairs. Ned met them in the hall.

"Will you come this way gentlemen please."

He led them into what was the dining room. Here at a long table sat a man and a woman having breakfast. The man was about forty-five or fifty. He wore an immaculate navy pin striped suit and white shirt. His face was pleasant with a jolly smile and his dark hair was carefully combed in a slight wave over a broad forehead. It was the woman however who caught their eyes. She was much younger. Grant thought about thirty, with thick long black hair. An oval face with high cheekbones and hazel eyes made her a picture of beauty. She looked curiously at the men as they entered. The man rose and wiped his mouth with a napkin.

"Gentlemen, good morning, I trust you slept well, darling, this is Mr. Kearns and Mr. Grant, they'll be staying with us for a few days, sit down please gentlemen and have some breakfast."

He waved them to the table. Kearns and Grant took their places, nodding to the woman. This was unreal. Both were surprised at the treatment they were now receiving. Kearns could not remember where he had seen the man before although his face seemed very familiar. He soon found out. The man gave a short laugh and spoke.

"I'm sorry I haven't introduced myself, my name is Conor Nevin, in the last Government I was Minister for Defence, this is my wife Valerie, I call her Val, It's Joe and Harry, isn't it?"

He looked from one to the other. Grant rose to the occasion.

"I'm Harry, glad to meet you sir, madam."

The woman gave him a smile.

"What do you do Harry? What part of America do you come from?"

Grant gave her his cover story. Nevin listened to the conversation, a half smile on his lips. Turning to Joe he asked.

"I believe Joe that you think that demonstration a few weeks ago was stage managed, is that so?"

Joe gave him his impression of the event. Nevin shook his head.

"I'm afraid I can't agree, what purpose would it serve, I must leave now but Val and Ned will look after you. By the way you can go anywhere you wish around the house and gardens but don't try to cross the guarded section, we must preserve security here."

He rose from the table, gave his wife a peck on the cheek and left the room. A few moments later they heard the sound of a Helicopter engine as the machine took off from somewhere at the rear of the house. The woman looked at them and by way of explanation said.

"He's off to Dublin to the Dail, he won't be back till late tonight."

She excused herself and left the room. The two men ate the rest of their meal in silence. Afterwards Grant suggested a walk outside. They found that the house lay on the floor of a narrow valley. On two sides the walls of rock and shale reached upwards for about two hundred feet. At the back of the house, about a mile away, a river tumbled down in a cascade of white to the valley floor. Grant surveyed the scene with practised eye. In a quiet voice he spoke to Joe.

"Nothing very difficult about climbing up those hills out of here, the biggest problem is the dogs. Don't look now but there's a fellow with a gun pointing in this direction in that clump of trees to our right, see if you can spot him.

Kearns bent and picked up a handful of stones, which he proceeded to throw half heartedly at the fence posts. For a while he could see nothing, then a movement in the topmost branches of one of the small trees told him where the man was positioned. They followed the fence around to the front of the house. The dogs, which were keeping pace with them on their side of the fence were growling and showing their teeth. Joe was looking at the macadam drive. He turned to Grant.

"There must be another way in to this place. We were bumped all over the place last night, that drive is dead smooth."

He was looking around as he spoke. They walked on, Grant with his head down, Kearns talking nonsense to the slavering Rothweilers. Then they came on it, another smaller gate in the fence. The rough track leading out of a small forest of Ash trees. In the distance over the trees they could see the tops of buildings. Joe turned to Grant.

"That must be old farm buildings or stables. They probably keep the transport there. If we could get as far as there we might be able to get a car or Jeep and run it through the fence."

Harry kept on walking his head still on his chest. He caught Joe's arm and pointed towards the river. Then, as if describing something he said.

"We're on candid camera there are four cameras on the roof of the house, I'd say they are infra red at night, so it's going to be tough getting out. Come on we'll go back to the house and see if we can learn anything further there."

A resplendent Ned met them at the door. He bade them good morning and asked if there was anything they wanted to which Joe replied with no little sarcasm, a way out. Ned glared at him and moved off. Inside he wandered into the library and started to examine the books. Harry Grant moved off on a tour of the house.

It was three days later. It had been an uneventful time. Nevin had been missing most of the time. His wife was seldom around. Yet they knew she was somewhere in the house. It seemed as if she had been told to keep clear of the two men. Grant was looking out from the corner window of a sitting room at the waterfall in the distance when he heard a sound behind him. It was Val Nevin.

"It's very beautiful, isn't it.'

Harry turned and looked at her, She gazed into the distance. Without looking at him she continued.

"Mr.Grant, Harry, what are you doing here? I want to know. There have been people here before from time to time but this is different. I was awake when you arrived the other night. I saw those men bring you and your friend in. You were in handcuffs. Please tell me what it's all about."

Outside Ned appeared coming towards the house. Grant stepped quickly behind the curtain and moved backwards into the room. The woman made pretence of adjusting the lace curtain and moved back to join him. She told him quickly.

"Come to my room later its the white door on the top landing, watch Ned, he'll be going out for about two hours, we can talk then."

Grant hurried to the billiard room and was lining up a shot when Ned came in. He looked at Grant and went out. In the library he found Joe Kearns asleep an open book on his knees.

At about three o clock Grant saw Ned drive out towards the guard fence in a Range Rover. He watched as the automatic gates opened, first closing the dogs into the two sections. The car moved through and the gates swung back. He waited a bit before going upstairs. Val Nevin was waiting on the landing and guided him into her bedroom where they sat on two antique chairs.

"Thank you for coming Harry, as you can see I'm almost as much a prisoner here myself. My husband doesn't allow me any sort of freedom, I can only go out if accompanied by him and that's usually to some official functions. I would like to know what's going to happen, what are you and your friend here for? I know there's something going on, please tell me."

Grant looked at her, her face was anxious. She is a beautiful woman he thought, Nevin must be at least twenty years her senior. There did not appear to be any children. He decided to tell her what he knew. Her face grew pale as she listened. She twisted her hands together in a sort of desperation.

"This is terrible Harry, I didn't realise that anything so awful could happen here, they've got to be stopped. You must get out of here and warn the authorities. If this takes place as you say there could be hundreds of people killed. I know Conor is power happy, but I can't believe he would do anything like this. You know he married me because he wanted a wife to show off. It was unbecoming of a Government minister not to be married. My father was facing bankruptcy when he offered to marry me and pay off the debts, there wasn't much I could do only go along with it. Shocked Harry? It happens quite a bit in dear old Ireland, even in this day and age. I suppose he's been a good husband to me, at least he doesn't hit me or beat me up, That's something to be thankful for. As you can see we sleep in separate rooms. This is the way it was from the start, sometimes I think he's a homosexual although I've no evidence of it. Enough of this, how are you going to get out of here? Promise you will take me with you, I don't think I could stand it here any longer, not after what you've just told me, I'll help you all I can."

She was crying now wiping away the tears with a small handkerchief. Grant moved over to her and took her hands in his.

"I promise you that we won't leave you here, when we go, you go with us."

She stood up and turned a tear stained face towards him.

"O thank you Harry, thank you, I know I just couldn't stay here."

127

Her voice trailed off, Grant was looking down into her dark eyes, his head moved lower and their lips met. He kissed her and she responded passionately. Their lovemaking was slow ecstasy Afterwards they lay holding each other. Grant felt that she had been awoken like a flower in sunshine after a shower of rain. He felt a wonderful feeling for this woman, something he had never felt before. It would complicate things but there was no way he would leave her behind when Joe and he made their escape. She kissed him again and said.

"We had better get back before Ned comes back Harry."

He left her and went downstairs where Kearns was still sleeping. Harry shook him awake. As Grant explained about Val, Joe listened in a kind of daze. At least now they had an ally of sorts. They heard the sound of the Range Rover returning.

CHAPTER 15

Detective Inspector John Maguire and several cars with armed Special Branch men arrived early at the house where the two men had been held. During the night some Gardai had moved into position and kept watch. They reported there was no sign of life around the place. Maguire, McQuillen and four more officers armed with a variety of weapons moved cautiously along the avenue to the front door. In the grey morning drizzle the house looked completely deserted. All the lower windows were shuttered. A solitary black cat sat on the steps and fled as it saw the men. Moving up to the front door Maguire rang the bell. They could hear it ringing loudly. Two detectives who had gone to the caretaker's house came up and told Maguire.

"There doesn't seem to be anyone at home down there either, will we break in?"

Maguire shook his head and reached into his pocket. Taking out a bunch of keys he started to try them in the front door lock. The third one clicked the levers over and the door opened. Maguire gave a slight grin and gently pushed the door wide open.

"Well now, there's something for you, would you go off and leave a place like this with no burglar alarm on. I think our friends are gone, some of you search every nook and cranny, even the dustbin, if there is one."

They walked into the room where Grant and Kearns had seen the meeting being held and stood. McQuillen moved around the room his eyes searching for any sign of the two men. Everything seemed to be in order. Maguire was lighting up his pipe. He gave a few puffs and blew out a cloud of smoke. McQuillen pulled the large fire screen back and looked in the grate. There was a mass of charred paper in it. Taking a poker he rummaged in it and found a piece of unburned newspaper. It had a date on the corner of three days previous. Maguire studied it for a moment.

"Now John what have we got here? Why would anyone be burning bits of paper. It looks as if someone must have tidied up. I think they were here all right and pulled out, they must be holding Kearns and Grant somewhere else, but where? I only hope there still alive, I wouldn't give much for their chances, it's almost a week now, the odds are we could be looking for their bodies, you know what that shower are like, I'm also worried about the caretakers, where are they? Here take these keys and try the house, see if you can find anything."

McQuillen took the keys and made his way down to the caretaker's house. He opened the front door and went inside. Nothing seemed to be out of place. Upstairs he went into the bedrooms. The beds were neatly made up and clothes hung in the wardrobe. Back downstairs he looked in the kitchen. A woman's handbag lay on the table. It contained some money, a driving licence and the usual bits and pieces. Beside the bag was a bunch of keys. McQuillen tried them in the locks and found they fitted the front and back doors. He opened the back door and walked the short distance to the garage and tried the door. A faint whimpering came from inside. He tried another key and it opened. Lying on the floor was a black and white sheepdog. It was very weak and had not been fed for some time. The smell of the place made his stomach turn. He went back to the kitchen and filled a bowl with water. The dog lapped it greedily and seemed to revive somewhat quickly. He found some dog food and fed it before continuing his search. One thing was sure he felt, these people would not have gone off and left their dog to starve, nor would the woman have left without her handbag. He called Maguire on the hand radio and told him what he had found.

"The forensic boys will be here shortly John, come back up here, we think we have found the room where they held Grant and Kearns."

As McQuillen started towards the house he heard a whimper behind him. The dog was staggering slowly after him. He ordered it back but it turned off to the left along a narrow pathway through clumps of high rhododendron bushes, McQuillen watched as the animal staggered on giving little whimpering cries. Something told him to follow and he walked in the same direction. Around a bend he found a Range Rover and a red Micra. The dog was sniffing around them and seemed to be excited. It moved off again nose to the ground McQuillen following. Soon they came to what looked like an old stable. The dog scraped and whimpered at the heavy door. McQuillen tried the keys. None would fit. He brought up the Uzi and fired a burst, blowing off the lock. Kicking the door open he moved inside, the dog beating him to it by a head. In a corner, two bodies lay face downwards. Black hoods covered the heads from which a trail of congealed blood told its own story. The dog licked the man's cold hand and whimpered gently. Sick at heart McQuillen went outside and called Maguire.

George Reilly lay in his bunk and went over the last twenty-four hours. It had been an incredible session. A vision of Francis shooting the Italian in the head flashed into his mind. How cool she had been. She had also killed Makirious and the Mate who was going to kill O'Shea. Only for her the rest of them could all have been killed. She certainly was a tough one. She seemed to have grown in stature since and was buoyed up with confidence. As for him self he remembered firing the rifle and seeing men fall. He must have killed one or two of the boarders. He gave a shudder, yet he felt a strange exultation. They had prevented the seizure of the boat and cargo. It was tough about O'Shea's arm. They would get help for him in Libya. When they got there he would try to contact Dublin for further orders. There was a tap on the door and Doyle came in.

"George, she want's you up on top"

Reilly found her in the wheelhouse. She greeted him with a smile.

"George we should be off the Libyan coast sometime tomorrow morning, when we get there I'll contact my father and get further instructions, do you think we could manage to get this old tub home?"

Reilly rubbed a hand over his face.

"It might be possible Francis, after all we haven't done too bad up to this, we really could do with O'Shea, how is he by the way?"

"He lost a lot of blood and he's a bit weak but I think if he gets a transfusion and some medical help he will be okay. I think I'll go and have a sleep now, will you carry on?"

He nodded and watched as she went down the steps towards her cabin. She certainly was on a high, and was issuing orders as if it was she and not him that was in charge. There was no trouble keeping the ship on course. It was practically a straight line to the coast. There, the

Libyan navy would pick them up. Doyle relieved him at midnight and he slept until dawn.

When he came out on deck again the sun was shining and a hazy mist covered the horizon. After a bit this lifted and a black line was visible on the horizon. Looking through the binoculars he could see buildings and palm trees down to the water's edge. Doyle's voice broke in.

"Don't look now but we've got company."

Reilly turned and watched as two fast frigates flying the Libyan flag swept towards them, one circling around behind them. The other drew in line, there was a flash and a bang and a shell landed in the water a hundred yards in front of them. Doyle threw the telegraph to stop and pressed the emergency stop button. He grinned at George.

"They don't look too friendly to me, I hope they can speak English."

The ship had practically stopped now and the frigate was coming alongside. Reilly was lowering the rope ladder. The first man up was an officer, revolver in hand. He pointed the gun at Reilly and waved him back. Ten sailors followed and took up positions around the deck. Francis appeared and spoke to the officer in French, explaining who they were and what they were doing. The man listened impassively, looking at their passports and then back to Francis. In quite atrocious French he ordered them over the side. Francis tried to tell him about O'Shea. He shouted something and two sailors went towards the cabin area. Once on board the frigate the ship sped in the direction of land. They drew alongside a jetty where a van with military marking waited. They were taken to a military barracks. Inside the building they were searched and then marched downstairs and Doyle and Reilly found themselves in a filthy cell. The door clanged shut and a key turned in the lock. Both men sat down on the floor with their backs to the wall.

In the Gadfly Captain Pritchard had drawn close to the freighter when it stopped. Photographs had been taken through the periscope camera, which showed the name on the stern and the transfer of the crew. Then the sonar operator reported.

"Vessel approaching, bearing thirty degrees starboard."

Pritchard swung the periscope. The second frigate was bearing down on them. It must have made radar contact. He gave the order

"Down Periscope, dive, prepare for depth charge attack."

At one hundred feet he levelled off and ordered slow forward. The sound of the frigate's engines could be heard now. There was an explosion and the lights dimmed and the submarine rocked. Pritchard had an idea he raised the submarine to within thirty feet of the surface. There were more explosions behind them. He gave the order for half speed astern. The sound of motors again passing overhead. Pritchard ordered full astern. There were more explosions. This time, from in front of them. He raised the periscope, the frigate was about two miles away and starting to circle. It evidently was not equipped with lock on radar. As he watched two more depth charges exploded behind it. It would have been an easy target for his radar guided torpedoes but that would probably cause an international incident. Setting a course Northward he dropped the Gadfly to one hundred feet and set course for Gibralter.

Next morning the photographs were on the desk of Admiral George Pervis, Chief of Naval Intelligence in Whitehall. Here they were subjected to a minute scrutiny. He was particularly interested in the photograph of the three crewmen climbing down onto the frigate's deck. One of them had presented a full facial view as he turned to look for the deck of the Libyan ship. Pressing a bell on his desk summoned a Naval rating, who saluted and stood to attention. The Admiral handed him the photographs.

"Take these to the lab, See if they can get a few pictures blown up of his face in particular and close ups of the rest of them, we might be able to find out who he is. Find out if we have a report on that Greek Captain yet and the ship, ask Captain Clark, he was dealing with it."

The rating made his way to the lab and threw the photos on the desk. The figure in the white coat picked them up and looking at them said sourly.

"What am I supposed to do with these?

The rating grinned in his face.

"HE wants you to blow them up so as HE might be able to identify the people and HE want's them Yesterday, Got it? I'll be back in an hour."

Whitecoat stood up and walked into the back muttering insults. The rating grinned and went and found Captain Clark watching a telex, which was coming off the machine and told him of the Admirals request. Taking the tape and file Clark went to the office. Here he read out the report on Makirious, which had just come in from Interpol. From all accounts it appeared that he had been a most unsavoury character. He would carry anything for money. His main forte was smuggling cigarettes and other goods and people all around the Mediterranean. Interpol had a file on him as long as your arm. It was also believed that he was involved in the white slave trade. It was rumoured that he could come and go as he pleased into Yugoslavia and Albania. The Admiral raised his eyebrows and looked at Clark.

"Mr. Makirious was quite a character, I wonder what he was up to this time? As our literary friends would say, the plot thickens."

Clark looked out of the window and into the distance over the London rooftops.

"You know sir I would give anything to know what that ship is carrying and where it's going."

The Admiral was leaning back in his chair, his eyes closed. He remained that way for some time. There was a knock at the door and the rating came in with an envelope. The Admiral opened it and slid the contents on to the desk and he and Clark looked at the photos. They showed a well built man of about thirty. His face was three quarters on to the camera as he hung on a ladder hanging down the ship's side. The other man was in profile and his face could not be seen clearly. He was much smaller in stature. On one picture of the deck area, in the background, Clarke could see another figure half hidden by a Libyan sailor. Picking up a magnifying glass he took a closer look. It almost dropped from his hand as he realised he was looking at a girl. He handed the glass and picture to Pervis who studied it for some minutes and then handed it back.

"Circulate that photo of the man on the ladder, perhaps some one will recognise him. Try the Anti Terrorist boys in the Yard, they might know him, When you find out anything let me know immediately. Send a message to Gadfly to take station off the port where the ship had been taken. If it leaves, it is imperative that he follows it until we find out what and where it's bound for."

Clark took the pictures and left.

It was after lunch when a portly gentleman in hard hat and carrying a briefcase arrived to see Admiral Pervis. To the Security Officer on duty at the door he looked like a businessman. When he produced a card bearing the words, J.F.Goodfellow, Import, Export Agent he was sure he was right. He called the Admiral and was surprised when he was told to send the man up. Had he but known. He was talking to the Head of MI.5, the counter terrorist sector of the British Government, Colonel Mark Philpot. Both men had been friends for almost twenty-five years and met quite often for the odd round of golf. They greeted each other amicably. Philpot opened his briefcase and pushed a file across to Pervis. He waited until the Admiral read it through. When he had finished he handed it back. It was a dossier on a man named George Reilly, known member of an Irish Republican terrorist group, wanted by the police of both countries. The photograph of the man on the ladder matched the one on the file. The Admiral waited for Philpot to speak. He put the file back in his briefcase snapping the lock shut.

"Now George, you see what we have here, one known terrorist and several more people whom we can safely assume are associates of his, one ship, one dead Greek, some kind of fight and the ship ends up in Gadaffi country, what does it sound like to you?

"You don't have to be a genius to imagine what's on that ship, it has to be arms and the destination has to be Ireland. Mark, it has to be stopped, God knows there's enough carnage going on there without more stuff getting in, have you notified the Irish police yet."

"No, I think we'll play our cards close to our chest on this one for the time being, I suggest you send that submarine of yours to keep watch on the ship and when it moves to follow it until we can make sure of its final destination. I'll decide later what action to take. Bye the way are you free for a game on Saturday?"

Pervis consulted his diary while assuring Philpot that he had already sent orders to the Gadfly.

"Saturday morning Mark, we can have lunch afterwards."

Philpot stood up and adjusted his bowler.

"Right then, George, Saturday morning, Good day then, I had better be getting back."

Pervis walked him down to the main door. The Security Guard checked him out and wondered afresh what a man like him had been doing with the Admiral.

The Christopher Columbus was brought into the port of Benghazi naval section and tied up at the quay. An ambulance was waiting and the injured O'Shea was taken to a military hospital for treatment. The one eyed man in the ragged clothes sitting on the harbour wall hauled in his fishing line and removed the fish from the hook. He dropped it into the basket at his feet. Gathering up his bits and pieces he made his way to one of the poorer areas a short distance away where he lived in a small room. He let himself in and locked the door. Taking up a loose floorboard he took out a small transmitter. On the hour he transmitted in code the following message in Russian.

'Ship Christopher Columbus brought here to day under naval escort.'

He replaced the radio and covered the hole in the floor. A hundred miles away on what looked to all appearances to be a Russian fisheries ship the message was picked up and relayed to Moscow. It was one of the reports on Colonel Ivan Gudenuv's desk when he came in next morning.

Gudenuv was not in the best of form when he arrived at his Moscow Headquarters on that particular morning. The previous evening his wife and himself had entertained some colleagues and their wives. The vodka had flowed freely and this morning the Colonel's head felt as if a steam hammer was pounding his forehead. His secretary a large buxom woman of forty dropped the sheaf of reports on his desk and retreated. Gudenuv wearily picked them up and started to go through them. The report from Libya sent a shiver up his spine. What was the ship doing there? What had happened? It was imperative that it be got moving again as soon as possible. The whole of the Red Shamrock operation depended on it getting to Ireland on time. Besides who else had seen it arrive. If the Americans or the British got news of it the whole plan could be in jeopardy. He quickly drafted urgent instructions in code to the Embassy in Libya to ask Gadaffi to help the ship and its crew on their way as a matter of urgency. A full report on what had happened was to be sent to him immediately. Somewhere in the back of his mind a tiny voice was telling him that the whole thing was starting to go wrong. Anotal Kirov's face swam before him. He remembered his words after that fateful meeting and his sly grin. He reached for the next file.

Yuri Koniev, who doubled as the Embassy's First Secretary and also KGB.man, had just arrived at the home of his French Algerian mistress whom he had met about a year ago when he received Gudenuv's message. That he had a wife and two daughters in Moscow worried him not a bit. After all a man could not be expected to live like a hermit. Besides it gave him a chance to move around in other circles and listen to the local gossip. The girl was a dancer in one of the hotels, which put on various cultural shows for their visitors. She lived in an apartment block on the edge of the city. They had just returned there and Koniev was looking forward to sharing her bed before he returned to the Embassy. She was at least ten years younger. He loved the golden brown of her body, which was beautifully proportioned. As she went to prepare some coffee he rang the Embassy to see if anything was happening. They told him of Gudenuv's message and instructed him to get back there immediately. His apologies were greeted by the girl with a torrent of abuse and demands for an explanation. Kissing her hungrily and telling her he would see her tomorrow he left hurriedly for the Embassy. Here he read the full text of the message from Gudenuv. Retiring for a few hours sleep he left orders for an early appointment to be made for him with Colonel Gadaffi.

At twelve-o clock next morning he was explaining to a poker faced Gadaffi about the ship and its crew. Without as much as a flicker the man listened impassively, then muttering something to his interpreter he rose and left. The man turned to Koniev with a smile and said.

"The Great One says it will be as you requested."

He bowed, the meeting was at an end. That night as he relaxed in Naomi's arms he explained to her why he had to leave her so quickly.

137

She plied him with more kisses and nibbled at his ear as he sleepily answered her questions. When he had gone she scribbled a report on a piece of paper and going down to the next floor slipped it under the door of room number five. Later on the man in that room tapped out a radio message which was picked up by an American listening post on the Italian mainland. In due course it found its way onto the desk of Colonel Maurice Curley in Washington.

CHAPTER 16

After the bodies had been removed in a plain black Garda van, Maguire and McQuillen left the forensic men working at the scene and went back to headquarters. Here Maguire sat behind his desk and motioned McQuillen to a chair opposite.

"John, I think we'll keep this quiet for the moment, when the rest of them get back make sure they keep their mouths shut, I don't want the press or the television crowd to get onto it, invoke the official secrets act if you have to. Now what I think we'll do is to drop any reference to Kearns and Grant, just put them as missing persons to the papers, someone might come up with something, It might be difficult with Kearns, according to reports he's changed his appearance, however its worth a try, do it."

On her way to work the following morning Jean McKay stopped to buy the morning papers for the office of Michael McCall. One of her functions was to read them for anything that might be of interest to the T.D. and mark them up for his attention. She had opened the morning mail and made a neat pile in the tray. Then she started on the newspapers. On the second page she saw the photographs of Grant and Kearns. Under the heading, Missing, with a request for persons with information to contact the Gardai. Her heart started pounding. It could not be true. Joe was missing. She knew now she had been right. He had been in some trouble, that phone call, the fact the he had said he was around but could not see her. What had happened to him? She remembered he had told her if anyone asked her about him to say she did not know him.

"Jean, Jean, are you all right Jean?"

McCall had come in and was looking at her curiously. Her voice shook as she replied.

"Yes, yes I'm all right, I just saw something in the paper, that man,

139

Mr. Kearns who came to see you last week, he's missing, its in the paper, do you think we should phone the Gardai?"

McCall picked up the paper and read the notice. He gave her a smile and looked down at her.

"Not at all Jean, what could we tell them, that he was here and I gave him an interview, what good would that be? No, they need more to go on than that. Anyway these fellows have a habit of turning up in the end, no, there's no need for us to get involved."

Picking up the papers he gave her a reassuring smile and went into his own office. Jean found it very hard to concentrate during the rest of the morning. She could not get the thought of Joe out of her mind. The arrival of two men to see McCall brought her back to reality. The one with his left arm in a sling gave her an appraising look and asked for McCall. The other one was grim faced with wide staring eyes, which seemed to bore right through her. When she announced them McCall came out and ushered them into his office. Some time later he called for three cups of coffee. When she brought the tray in and handed the cups around she noticed the blond man had the newspaper on his knee. It was open at the pictures of the missing men. Jean went out and sat at her desk. Her mind was in turmoil. What was that man doing with the paper? Was it just coincidence? It was very strange, It was McCall's paper. Why should a visitor pick it up at all? Unless McCall, had shown it to him. The answer came but she did not want to believe it, McCall had to know something about the disappearance of the two men. No, it was ridiculous, Jean, you are letting your imagination run away with you. That kind of thing only happens in films. There must be some other explanation. She tried to continue with her work but the thoughts kept floating around in her mind. The two men came out about an hour later, Blondie saying goodbye to her with a smile and a wink. McCall came out with them and told her he had dictated some letters for her to go out on the evening post. He scribbled his signature on several pages of notepaper and again emphasised the importance of posting them, and left almost immediately.

She had completed the last letter and was about to switch the machine off when she heard a couple of clicks in her earphones. Then, her own voice announcing the two visitors. McCall's voice welcoming the men and the door closing, then McCall's voice again.

140

"Well is everything all right? How did it go?"

One of the men, she thought it was the blond one's voice.

"Everything's okay. There's nothing there to link us to the place, Joe and Mick cleaned up before they took those two out to Nevin's place."

McCall's voice again.

"Good, bye the way where are the caretaker and his wife, are they out in Nevin's too? Where are they?"

Silence, McCall's voice again.

"I've asked you a question, where are they?"

"We hid them in one of the old stables, no one will find them there, sure your man that owns it won't be back till after we've taken over, then it will be too late, by that time we will have confiscated the property for the state."

He gave a short laugh,

"Or maybe for me for services rendered."

McCall's voice, venomous and angry.

"You bloody fools, what did you have to kill them for, now we have two more missing persons, here look at this mornings papers, they're already looking for Kearns and Grant, if they find those bodies it will start one hell of a rumpus. They should have been taken to Nevin's place, Jesus, how stupid can you get."

Sound of McCall asking her for coffee. Blondie's voice cold and calm.

"They had seen our faces, what else could we do?"

McCall again.

"Do? Your orders were to take over the house not to kill anyone, if we alienate people by killing harmless civilians how do you think we are going to get any support from the population at large?"

A pause as Jean arrives with the coffee. Then Blondie again

"Okay, so it was a mistake, there's nothing we can do about it now, what do you want us to do?"

"I'm not sure if that girl suspects something or not, she was very upset when I came in and found her reading the paper about Kearns and Grant. Wanted to contact the Gardai, I managed to fob her off, as far as I can tell she only met Kearns when he came here to se me, I'll keep an eye on her anyway, you fellows get back to headquarters and I'll contact you later."

The sounds of the men's departure and of Mc'Call closing the door.

Jean switched off the machine and sat there. The colour had drained from her face. By some chance McCall had not switched the recorder off when the men arrived. What she had just heard was kidnapping, murder, and God knows what else. The question was what should she do. If she went to the police they probably would not believe that a prominent figure like McCall was involved in anything like the story she would tell them. The enormity of the situation made her cold and angry. Who would believe her. Sure she had the tape, but to go into a police station with that. They would probably make a note of it and politely send her home.

She removed the tape from the machine and replaced it with a new one. Then she recorded from the original as far as the letters. She put the original tape in her coat pocket and prepared to leave for home. McCall's door seemed to beckon to her, she stood for a moment undecided, then on a sudden impulse went inside. She stood uncertainly looking around the room. The morning paper was still on the desk, the faces of the two missing men looking up at her. There were various papers and files cluttering up the desk. Some urge came over her and she started to look through them, for what, she did not know. Mostly they were on Dail matters and letters from constituents about various matters. Jean pulled open a drawer and went through it but found nothing except a couple of sheets of paper with details of the Government's special meeting at Ballyorney Castle on the Easter weekend. It contained a list of names, some of which were marked with an ' x.' She was engrossed in reading the list when McCall's voice broke in on her.

"So Miss McKay, what have we here? I'm afraid that you must suspect I know more about our missing friends than I'm telling you, well your right."

He had picked up the phone and was dialling a number.

"Get over here as soon as possible, I have a problem I want you to take care of."

He replaced the receiver. Jean said nothing. McCall looked at her steely eyed.

"You realise that I cannot let you go Jean, this is something that you would not understand. I promise that nothing bad will happen to you. If I let you leave here you will only go to the police. I suppose they would find it hard to believe anything you told them but it could still cause problems for us, now sit down and be a good girl."

Jean suddenly made a run for the door. She reached it and was just through but McCall was after her and grabbed at her coat. The material ripped as she tried to pull away. At that moment the front door opened and Blondie caught her with his good arm and crushed her to him.

He smiled into her face.

"Your a pretty little thing, I'll look after you, sure you might even get to like me."

He hugged her close to him. McCall eyed him coldly and said harshly.

"That will do, let her go, she's not going to do anything foolish. Now I'm telling you, nothing is to happen to her, is that clear? Take her out to Nevin's place."

He turned to Jean.

"Go with them Miss McKay, I promise you will not be harmed but please do not cause any trouble or we will have to keep you quiet."

He picked up her handbag and handed it to her.

"Here take this, I'm sure there's things you will need in it, I'm sorry about your coat."

He gestured to the torn pocket, which was hanging down. Blondie put his arm around her and led her out of the office. The other man took up station on her other side and they walked up Wisbeck Street. Blondie had his arm protectively round her shoulder. Jean looked at the people passing by, no one gave them a second glance. On the corner a young Garda huddled in his raincoat and watched the traffic with unconcealed boredom. They reached the car and the other man opened the doors and got behind the wheel. Blondie guided her in to the rear seat and got in beside her and the car moved off. When they reached the Blessington road the light was fading and the rain pelting down. Jean sat silent looking out the window. It was now dark and she could see nothing of the countryside as they swept by. Two hours passed before they drove through the gates of a large country house. After about a mile they stopped at a security gate. The headlights lit up a group of snarling Rothweilers before Blondie pointed something at the gates and they opened. They drove through and the gates closed behind them. The car stopped in front of a set of granite steps leading up to the front door of a large mansion. Jean saw a man in butler's uniform carrying large umbrella come down the steps. Blondie grinned at him.

"Here you are Ned, look after her well, I think she might have taken a shine to me."

Ned was politeness itself.

"Will you come this way please, miss."

He held the umbrella over her as they went up the steps. Inside it was pleasantly warm. Ned took her coat and put it in a small cloakroom off the hall. Then he motioned her to follow him. They entered a room with a blazing fire. The two men sitting in front of it stood up as they entered. One of them, a bearded figure let out a cry.

"Jean, what the hell are you doing here?"

It took her a few seconds to recognise Joe Kearns. She was in his arms before Ned had closed the door. Grant was looking on, a broad grin on his face. Jean was crying.

"O Joe, I was so worried about you, your pictures are in all the papers as missing. I asked Mc'Call to go to the Gardai and tell them you had been there but he would not do it. Then he left me some dictation and on the end of the tape he was talking to these two men. I was looking in his office papers when he caught me and the other two brought me out to here, where is this place?

She clung to him fear written on her face. Joe introduced Grant and explained the whole situation to her. Jean told them about the conversation details on the tape. Grant asked her where the tape was now. Thinking back she remembered putting it in her pocket before going into McCall's office. In the struggle when her coat was torn it must have fallen on the floor. It was probably still there.

144

Grant walked over and stood looking out into the darkness. At the end of the valley he could just discern the white line of the waterfall. Time was running out, they would have to make some attempt to get away from here. The two women were going to be a problem. Joe Kearns and himself would have stood a better chance on their own. The Irishman impressed him. So far he had been quiet and efficient and to a certain extent could look after himself. For a fellow with no military training he was all right, but the girl's were another matter. His thoughts were interrupted by the sound of a Helicopter landing at the rear of the house, doubtless Nevin had returned from the Dail. If he could get to the chopper he could fly them all out. He was not the greatest of pilots but he could handle one after a fashion. Tonight he would make a reconnaissance. Jean and Joe were sitting holding hands and talking. Grant sat down beside them.

"I'm sorry to interrupt children but you do realise that we are in big trouble here. After Jean's capture there's every likelihood that these people will decide that they don't need us around. The longer we're here the less likely we are to stay alive. I think we have to get out of here as soon as possible, that means starting to organise ourselves now."

The door opened and Conor Nevin and Val came into the room. The T.D. came forward a beaming smile on his face.

"A, so this is the beautiful Miss McKay. Welcome my dear I hope your stay here will be a pleasant one, Val here will look after you."

Val Nevin came forward and took her by the hand.

"Jean isn't it? I know you came here with only what you stood up in, come with me we're about the same size, I'll probably be able to find something to fit you."

She took her arm and the two went upstairs. Nevin turned to Kearns and Grant.

"Gentlemen, why so quiet? Are you not enjoying your stay? After all we are not keeping you locked up or anything, believe me, I promise no harm will come to any of you. Now what say we are friends until this thing is over, then you can go. Come let's have a drink"

Going over to a cabinet he opened it up and displayed a miniature bar. Grant walked over and stood beside him a smile on his face.

"Ah, what the hell sir, make mine a bourbon, sure, your looking after us very well, we really have no complaints about our treatment, roughly how long do you think we will be here?"

Nevin selected a bottle and poured a generous glass, he smiled.

"Call me Conor, Harry, and Joe, Isn't it? What will you have Joe?, or did someone tell me you were a teetotaller?"

Joe Kearns decided at that precise moment that he did not like Conor Nevin. Grant gave him a warning look. He forced a grin at the man.

"I'm not quite that bad really, if you can manage it I would like a glass of white wine. But I would like you to know that I feel we are being very well looked after, thank you very much."

Nevin nodded to him smiling and picked up a housephone. They heard him speak to Ned asking for a bottle of white wine from the cellar. Joe mused, Socialist or not this fellow likes to live well. Ned arrived with a bottle of white in an ice bucket and opened it. He poured a glass for Joe and withdrew. The three men chatted for about half an hour before Nevin suggested they go to their room and change for dinner. Joe and Harry were surprised but the TD. smiled broadly and waved them up the stairs. There, to their utter amazement were laid out two dinner jackets, shirt's shoes and trousers. They dressed and went back down stairs to find Nevin similarly attired in the library. He greeted them heartily.

"Gentlemen, now isn't this extremely civilised, the ladies will be down in a moment, ah, here they are now."

The men turned as Val and Jean came down the stairs. The sight took their breath away. Val Nevin was wearing an off the shoulder dark blue dress. Her hair shone under a silver tiara, which threw off slivers of light. Grant could only gasp inwardly at her beauty. Jean McKay was wearing a green dress of some shimmering material and to Joe looked absolutely beautiful. His heart gave a sudden leap as he drank in her beauty. Jean blushed scarlet under his gaze. Nevin took the two girls one on each arm and walked them gaily into the dining room. Grant raised his eyebrows to Joe as they followed.

The scene through the dinner could have been any country house. Guests, being entertained by their host to the best of his ability. Conversation flowed on various subjects. The current situation was studiously avoided.

Val Nevin and Jean seemed to be finding a lot in common thought Joe. Grant was trying to get Nevin to talk about Northern Ireland but the T.D. was parrying his questions with others of his own. Joe thought he's a typical politician, never answer any question directly but stop your opponent with another question. He looked again at Jean. She is absolutely beautiful he thought, if we get out of this mess I'll ask her to marry me. She caught him looking at her and smiled. At least she is more relaxed now. Val Nevin was probably the key to getting out of here. He listened as Nevin went on a tirade against the English Government to which Grant was listening intently.

CHAPTER 17

The first that Jeans mother knew of something being wrong came with a call from the school to say that Joanna had not been collected and was there a problem. Graine McKay was puzzled. It certainly was not like Jean. Perhaps she had been delayed at work, but then surely she would have phoned either the school or herself. Something had to be wrong. The school principal made the suggestion that she would drop the child home. This Graine gratefully accepted and sat down to ponder on Jean's non-appearance. She rang McCall's office. There was no reply. Jean was not there. Graine McKay was not one to panic. There had to be some rational explanation. Perhaps Jean had to go somewhere with McCall and been delayed. Yes that could be it, but Jean was a very responsible person. She surely would have phoned knowing she had to pick up Joanna. The sound of a car brought her to the window. It was the teacher with the child. By eight-o clock there was still no word from Jean and Graine McKay was beginning to feel frightened. She rang the local Garda station and spoke to someone there who told her he would check on the possibility of her being involved in an accident and she gave him a description of Jean. Some time later he rang back to say that as far as could be ascertained she had not been involved any accident. He tried to calm her by telling her that Jean had probably gone off with a friend and would turn up safe and sound. As the night wore on Graine became more and more convinced that something dreadful had happened to her daughter. At eleven thirty she picked up the phone and dialled a number. She waited impatiently as it rang. A woman's voice said hello.

"Maggie? This is Graine, Is John there?, Jean hasn't come home, I'm desperately worried and don't know what to do."

A few seconds later the quiet voice of her brother in law, Detective Inspector John Maguire came on the line. He listened carefully as she told him about Jean. When she told him where she worked his teeth clenched on his pipe stem. He underlined the name in his notebook.

"Graine, has Jean got a boyfriend, or is there anyone she could be with?"

"No John she has no boy friend since the break up, except, no, I don't think he would have anything to do with her not coming home, no, there's no one."

She was crying now, Maguire pressed the point.

"Graine, you mentioned 'he' there, who was that?"

"That was that nice man who helped her and Joanna when they were caught up in that demonstration a couple of weeks ago, Joe Kearns, he's a reporter. He did take her out to dinner one time. A few days ago she had a phone call from him, he said he was going away for a bit and that he would call her again, I know she was a bit worried about him. As a matter of fact I think they had both started to like each other, he's a very nice young man."

Maguire sat still his pen travelling across the page, his brain assimilating the information. Jean knew Joe Kearns and he was missing with Grant. Telling Graine not to worry and to try and get some sleep. He would do everything in his power to find the girl. His wife was already on the way out with a small overnight bag to stay with her sister and lend her some support. Maguire refilled his pipe and sat smoking and making notes until he finally went to bed at one thirty.

———————————

It was two a.m. before Harry Grant left Joe Kearns sleeping soundly and treaded softly down the corridor. Passing Nevin's bedroom he could hear him snoring. He smiled softly. The man had indulged himself in food and wine at dinner. Now he was in a deep sleep of contentment. Grant moved on and found a stairs, which seemed to lead to the roof. Here a glass-panelled door blocked his way. The thin light from his fountain pen torch showed him a control panel fixed to the wall beside the door. Harry studied it for a while. It controlled the four television cameras on the roof and also the alarm system for the rest of the house. He reached for the switch that controlled the cameras, for a moment he hesitated then flicked the switch to off. Silence, he could not believe it. Looking at the rest of the system he thought about switching it off, but that was too simple. Most systems had to be coded out before switching off or the alarm would trip. Grant examined the switches

149

carefully with the aid of the torch. On the wall beside the panel he found it. Someone had scratched into the paintwork, 'key in A.D.2920'. Carefully Harry punched in the letters. Then taking a deep breath he switched the alarm off. He could almost feel the silence. Surprisingly there was only one Yale lock on the door, which opened easily to his touch. Harry walked to the edge of the parapet and looked over. This was the rear of the house. The Helicopter was parked on the grass about two hundred yards away. In the moonlight nothing stirred.

Then near a clump of trees to the right of the machine he saw the glow of a cigarette. There was at least one guard on duty. Moving round to the front parapet Grant viewed the scene below. The Range Rover was parked at the front steps. Here he could see no signs of life. Making his way back inside he spent the next hour examining Nevin's study and desks In one drawer he found a note book containing a list of names and addresses none of which meant anything to him. Behind a painting he found a wall safe. He did not even try to open it. In another desk drawer under some papers he found a loaded Czech automatic pistol. Carefully replacing everything he made his way back and reset the alarm systems. He was making his way back to the bedroom when he sensed something. A whiff of perfume came to him as he turned. Val Nevin was standing at the door to her bedroom. They looked at each other without a word until he walked into the room and closed the door. She was wearing a white silk kimono type dressing gown. She came forward to meet him and he took her in his arms and kissed her. Then he moved a little away from her and undid the cord of the robe, which he slipped off her shoulders and let slide to the floor. She shivered slightly as he led her towards the bed.

Next morning Nevin left early for Dublin. Harry and Joe had breakfast together during which Grant explained about his wanderings around the house during the night. Joe listened eagerly and wondered when they could try for an escape. Grant said that the Helicopter offered the best chance. Perhaps they should try tonight. It seemed as if there was only one man on guard and Grant reckoned he could take care of him. All Joe would have to do was get the two girls to the machine. Grant said he would finalise things later. There was no sign of Val or Jean so the two men went outside and walked around the perimeter fence ignoring the growls of the dogs, which kept pace with them. The weather was cold with a clear blue sky, which foretold an early frost. As they came around to the front of the house the Range Rover could be seen crossing through the security fence They watched as it carried on down the avenue and out of sight. Inside the house was quiet. Ned materialised from somewhere and Grant inquired of him where the ladies were. With something of a smirk the man replied.

"I believe sir they have gone shopping."

Turning on his heel he walked away leaving Grant and Kearns looking at each other. By evening there was no sign of the girls returning. The Helicopter dropped out of the sky at about dusk. Nevin greeted them cordially and in response to Joe's question remarked.

"A yes, the girls, what would we do without them, they've gone shopping you know, I can't tell to when they'll be back, but isn't that just like them, let them loose and they don't know when to stop."

He gave a great chuckle of laughter.

"Sure you'll see them later, yes, you'll definitely see them later, come now we must have dinner."

He put his arms around their shoulders and walked them into the dining room. During the meal he kept up a conversation, punctuated by little bursts of laughter. They had finished eating and were drinking cups of coffee when he turned to Grant and looked at him with a grin.

"Now Harry, tell me, what do you think of Val?"

Grant froze in his seat. Joe Kearns darted a quick look at him. Nevin went on grinning at him.

"Come on Harry, we're all men of the world here, what do you think of my wife?"

He's playing Grant like an angler plays a fish, thought Joe. Grants mind was working overtime. He must know. He's got to know, but how? Stall him play him along.

"She's a very beautiful woman sir, very beautiful indeed."

Nevin smiled at him.

"Yes she is isn't she, much younger than me Harry, by about twenty years as a matter of fact, would you say she's happy here Harry?"

Grant took his time in replying.

"I really couldn't say, she seems happy enough to me."

Nevin shook his head, still smiling.

"I don't think so Harry, she feels she's lost here, I'm too old for her, she needs a younger man, someone like yourself. Come on and we'll go and meet them."

He rose and all three made their way to the front of the house where the Range Rover was waiting with Ned at the wheel. As soon as they were aboard he drove off. The T.D. hummed a tune as they drove. He seemed to be in very high spirits. Sometime later they entered the gates of what looked like a mining complex. There was a lot of activity going on with men unloading boxes and crates from two huge lorries. They drove by and stopped beside a modern bungalow. Inside, an Arab adorned in a black dinner jacket greeted Nevin. He introduced him to Grant and Kearns as Sheikh Mahout Ben Bela. Joe judged him to be about forty-five or fifty. He was tall and his eyes bore a hint of cruelty.

"You are welcome to my humble abode, please come in."

His English was perfect. No doubt he had been educated at Oxford or Cambridge. Nevin embraced him and all four entered into a large room furnished in Arab style. They all sat on cushions while a servant in Arab dress brought them a tray of fruits. The Arab handed Nevin what looked like a list of sorts. He proceeded to read this and a smile of satisfaction spread over his features. He then passed over a suitcase he had been carrying and the two shook hands. Then Nevin got up and left the room. He returned leading his wife Val and Jean McKay by the hand. The girls gave no sign of recognition and smiled a sleepy smile. To Harry and Joe it was obvious they were drugged. Nevin stood them in front of the Arab.

"My dear friend, please accept these little tokens of my appreciation for your help. They will, I'm sure brighten up some of your nights, I'm happy to be able to add them to your collection."

He turned to Grant and Kearns.

"The Sheikh has a collection of most nationalities at home in his Harem. Up to now he did not have any Irish girls so I have decided to help him out."

Joe Kearns felt the blood rush to his head. Nevin was giving a present of the girls to this Arab. He glanced at Grant. The two men moved as one. Kearns was on Nevin before he could move. His foot came up and kicked him in the groin. With a scream of pain he doubled up. Joe caught him a blow to the jaw as he went down on the cushions his lips spurting blood.

Grant had gone for the Arab. The girls were in the way and he brushed them aside. The Sheikh had started to reach for his pocket and managed to draw a small pistol. Grant collided with him as the gun went off. He felt a burning pain in his left lower chest. Then his hands were on the Arab's throat as they fell to the floor. The Arab was trying to break his grip now, he was strong and kept twisting and turning and trying to get his knees against Harry's chest. Grant could feel something wet on his left side. He tightened his grip on the man's throat and squeezed as they had taught him to do at combat school. It seemed to be taking a long time he thought, as the struggles grew weaker. They had told him it would only take thirty seconds. It seemed like a lifetime. He squeezed harder, there was a red mist now in front of his eyes. He gave a final squeeze and collapsed over the body. Joe Kearns stood up and looked at Nevin writhing on the floor. He went over to Grant and turned him over. There was a large red stain spreading down the bottom left of his shirt. He picked up the Arabs gun. A sound behind him made him turn. The Arab servant was coming at him with a long knife raised in his right hand. Almost without thinking Joe pointed the gun and pulled the trigger. A bullet tore into the man's chest. He fired again as the man's momentum carried him forward to fall across the body of his master. The two girls were huddled in a corner of the room still wearing those silly smiles. He bent down beside Grant and opened his shirt. The small hole under was pumping out little globules of blood. Wiping it clean Joe made a plug from a piece of shirt and plugged the hole as best he could. He bound up the lot with part of the Arab servant's sash.

Joe realised that he had to get the American to a hospital or he would probably die. The girls would be of no help until the effects of the drug wore off. Nevin was still lying moaning on the floor. Joe cautiously pulled back the curtain. The Range Rover was parked opposite. He could see the figure of Ned reading something in the cab by the light of the powerful arc lamps, which lit up the area. No one seemed to have heard the shots or the struggle. He went back to the kitchen and soaked a towel in icy cold water and went back to the girls. He wet their faces until they seemed to be more awake. In the kitchen he made some strong coffee and made them drink. After that they were able to talk to him although a bit drowsy still. He told Val to fetch Ned with the Range Rover over to the door. Pulling Nevin to his feet he put the gun to his head.

"Now Mr. Bloody TD. We're going out of here. One wrong move, and your dead. Is that clear?"

The man nodded. Val came back and told Joe that Ned was outside. Ned had turned the Rover and parked it. As he came through the door Kearns hit him behind the ear with the gun and he went down as if poleaxed. Giving the gun to Val he told her.

"Keep that on Nevin, if he moves just pull the trigger, I'm going to get Harry into the car."

With some help from Jean he managed to get the American across his shoulders and out to the car, He laid him across one of the back seats and then went back for the girls and Nevin. He put the T.D. in the front passenger seat and the girls in the rear. Giving the gun to Val he told her to keep the man covered and shoot if necessary. Then he got behind the wheel.

"Come on Nevin which way to the nearest hospital? Left or right?"

The man gestured with his right hand and muttered something through his smashed lips.

"Okay, we'll try a right turn, it has to lead somewhere."

They were approaching the front gate now and a man was standing at the red and white barrier pole watching them. Joe flashed the lights at him and he moved to raise the pole, saluting them as they passed through and accelerated down a straight country road. After about two miles they were going down hill with mountains on either side. On the near side the road dropped away to the valley below. Joe could see lights twinkling like stars in the darkness.

When Michael McCall reached his office at about ten-o clock he had to avoid two men in a tent like structure outside the front door. Behind them, was a van with the logo of the Telephone Company on it. The

154

men were examining wires in the cavity. As he opened the door of his office two more men in overalls approached him.

"Excuse me sir, may we come in? We are checking out all the phone lines around here, there have been several complaints."

McCall glanced at his watch, the man held out an ID card. McCall glanced at it.

"Come in but make it quick, I have to be out of here by eleven."

One of the men went into the main office while the other picked up the phone on what was Jean McKay's desk. In Mc'Call's office the man connected a meter to the phone and dialled a number. He spoke to someone and replaced the receiver. After a few moments it rang and he spoke again. Turning to McCall he said.

"That seems to be okay, what kind of trouble were you having sir?"

McCall looked at him blankly.

"I didn't know we were having any trouble, are you sure you have the right number?"

The young man consulted a list.

"According to this someone reported that this phone was getting a lot of wrong numbers, I think you'll find it's all right now, if you have any more trouble let us know. Do you have a secretary or anyone that might use the phone more than your-self? Maybe she could tell us more about it, when would we get her here?"

McCall replied irritably.

"I have a girl but she's off work for a few days, I'm not sure when she will be back, I'll ask her about it when I see her again."

The man gathered up his tools and called to his mate.

"Everything all right out here Johnny? I can't find anything wrong, We had better go and let this gentleman get on, sorry to have bothered you sir, thank you very much."

McCall nodded and showed them out. On the pavement the men held a conversation with the two in the hole which was hurriedly covered in and the tent removed. All four departed in the telephone van. It soon arrived at the underground garage where Joe Kearns had been taught

155

to shoot. There the two men made their way to Detective Inspector John Maguire's office. Seeing the grins on their faces, he took the pipe out of his mouth.

"All right, you fellows look as if your horse had won the Derby, what have you got?"

The younger of the two took a tape from his pocket and put it on the desk.

"I found this on the floor of the front office where the girl worked. There was also traces of cloth, That could have come from a coat, there was nothing else."

The other man broke in.

"There was a newspaper there in McCall's office, it was open at the picture of Grant and Kearns. When I asked him about a secretary he said she had a few days off."

Maguire had already loaded the cassette into a player. All three listened as it played. The Inspector sucked at his pipe and blew out a cloud of smoke. As the tape wound on the picture was becoming clearer. Grant Kearns and his niece were being held by McCall. The man was up to his neck in this conspiracy. He was one of the leaders or perhaps the leader. They were being held at Nevin's place. Where was that? And who was Nevin? The only one of that name to come to Maguire's mind was that ex Minister. Could it be possible? Was he in the plot too, Maguire picked up the phone and dialled. As he waited for the connection he asked.

"How would you fellows like a Helicopter ride?"

When they reached the military airfield at Baldonnell the helicopter was already waiting. After a few words with the Commandant the machine took off and headed for the dark blue line of the Wicklow Mountains. The pilot and his crewman chatted as they flew. Maguire, a large map of the area spread on his knees tried to look for landmarks. He asked the pilot if he knew the countryside well and he replied that he flew over it so often he knew every hill and valley. Maguire described where he wanted to go and a few minutes later they swept over a valley with a large house at one end and a waterfall at the other. The pilot explained that when Nevin was Minister of Defence he regularly used to fly him on occasions. Taking the machine down low they could see the dogs in the perimeter guard track. There did not seem to be any other sign of life. One of Maguire's men who, was looking through binoculars remarked.

"There's a bloke down there in the trees to the left of the house with a rifle or a shotgun."

The pilot flew up the valley as far as the waterfall and swept round in a circle. As they passed the house again Maguire could see the man. He was beside one of the large beech trees and was trying to keep out of sight. Another man came out of a building and looked up at them as they passed. The winchman had been taking photographs during their passes and when they landed back at Baldonnell he left to have them developed. In the meantime Maguire was talking to the Captain in charge of a group of Special Force Commandos who were trained in anti terrorist warfare. The men were moving around checking their equipment. Maguire and the Captain planned the attack. They would go in at daybreak using microlight aircraft to get over the mountains and glide down to land around the house. Maguire and his men would come in at the same time from the main entrance. The Detective Inspector and his men were entertained by the Commandant before getting a few hours sleep in preparation for an early start to be in position at Nevin's house when the aircraft arrived.

CHAPTER 18

George Reilly awoke to the sounds of footsteps coming down the corridor. He nudged Fergus Doyle as a key turned in the lock. A man dressed in military uniform came in. Reilly guessed he held the rank of Captain. He saluted the two men.

"Gentlemen, let me apologise for your stay here. Please come with me, I'm sure you realise that we had to know if you were who you said you were. On behalf of the Libyan people and our leader Colonel Gadaffi, I welcome you to Libya."

He ushered them out and along a corridor up to ground floor level. They were the taken by car to what looked like a large private house in a quite suburb. Here the Captain showed them to a huge bedroom where new clothes were laid out on the two beds.

"Please help yourselves gentlemen, if you want anything you have only to press this bell, the staff here will look after your every wish. By the way your companion is in hospital and has been attended to, he is making a good recovery and will be up and around again soon. The remains of your other two comrades are being looked after. We are having them embalmed so you can take them back to Ireland, or perhaps you wish for them to be buried here?

He looked at both of them, a question on his face. Reilly thought quickly. They had to be brought home, after all they had died for Ireland and that country was always loving of its martyrs, also it would be good policy after the take-over to have a couple of hero's.

"I, think we will take them home with us Captain, I'm sure their relatives there would like to know they were buried near them so as they could visit their graves, thank you very much for all you are doing for us."

The Captain saluted and left. Fergus Doyle was opening doors and called to Reilly.

"George, I'm going to soak myself, I feel like a tramp, come and look at this,"

He disappeared into a bathroom that was large by any standard. Afterwards the two men went downstairs to be met by Francis Coughlin. She was looking absolutely stunning in a light blue suit and white hat. Reilly caught his breath, she certainly did not look like the person with the gun blowing away the young Sicilian on the ship. That, the Captain was captivated by her, was very evident as he chatted away in his faultless English. She turned as the men came forward.

"George, Fergus, I'm so glad to see you, the Captain here was just telling me he did a couple of years at Trinity College, he knows Dublin like the back of his hand."

The man acknowledged this with a smile and guided them to a room where a meal had been prepared. Afterwards he bade them good night and gave them his telephone number in case they should require him at any time. They were sitting around chatting and drinking iced coke when Francis spoke.

"George I've sent a message to Dublin about what happened, we will probably get a reply tomorrow, I think we should move on from here as soon as possible, Don't you think so?"

Reilly looked at her sharply, She doesn't waste any time he thought, I'm supposed to be in charge of this operation and here she is taking over, aloud he said.

"Yes, I suppose your right Francis, the Captain is arranging for the bodies of McConville and Tynan to go back with us. It wouldn't be fair to leave them here, but what about O'Shea? Will he be fit enough to come with us, the Captain said he was much better."

Fergus Doyle stood up and walked across to the window.

"There's no way we can leave him here, no matter what happens I'm not going home without him."

George looked at Francis, for a moment a dark shadow of anger crossed her face. She looked at Doyle.

"May I remind you that this ship has to get to Ireland at least a week before the take-over, otherwise we will never get the stuff distributed. If you want to be Court Martialed, go ahead and stay here, anyway the matter may not arise, O'Shea is a tough one. He'll most likely be up and around when we go to see him in the morning."

Doyle grimaced at Reilly from across the room. Next morning at the hospital they did find O'Shea up and about, his arm in a sling. He was in chirpy form and greeted them with the question.

"When are we getting out of here, I'm fed up, there's nothing to drink only coke and water and the only one that speaks English is that Captain and one of the doctors."

The girl glanced at Reilly.

"There George, didn't I tell you he was a tough one."

Turning to O'Shea she said.

"Get your things and come back to the house with us John, I'm sure we will be sailing within the next twenty four hours, is that not so George?"

She appealed to Reilly, who merely nodded. Afterwards in their room the three men sat together while the girl left to find out if there was any word from Dublin. Fergus Doyle spoke first.

"George, who is in charge here? I thought you were, but her ladyship seems to have decided that she is running things. I might as well tell you that I don't like it one little bit."

George got up and walked slowly around the room. O'Shea looked at Doyle his face anxious.

"You know George we are with you all the way, you were made commander of this operation in Russia, I don't want to be bossed by a woman."

Without turning his head Reilly replied.

"Thanks lads, but you know who she is. We have no alternative only to carry out her orders. She certainly seems to have taken over. So far she is the only one that has direct contact, I haven't even been asked for a report, yes it looks as if she is in charge now, let's see what happens when she comes back."

He walked out of the room and sat on the balcony.

Joe Kearns kept the Range Rover moving as fast as he dared on the narrow road. At the bottom of the hill the road levelled out into a dark tunnel of trees. They swept through a sleeping village, no lights showed in any of the houses. A few miles later the headlights picked out a blue Garda car parked at an angle towards the centre of the road. In the centre stood a red luminous sign, which read, Stop, Garda Checkpoint. As Joe drew to a halt a Garda with a torch came forward. Kearns leaned out the window.

"We have a seriously injured man her, Garda, he needs urgent medical attention, we also have to get in touch with Detective Inspector John Maguire of Special Branch."

The Garda looked at him with some suspicion. His companion moved forward and looked into the Range Rover, shining his torch onto the huddled figure in the back seat. He took in the bloodstained jacket and pale face. His torch ran over the other people and focused on Nevin, he uttered an oath.

"Jesus, its Mr.Nevin the T.D. What the hell happened to you sir? Are you alright?"

Nevin spoke through swollen lips.

"No Garda I'm not all right, these people have tried to kidnap my wife and myself, they have tried to kill a friend of mine who tried to stop them and assaulted me. Lucky he was able to shoot that one. I am ordering you to arrest this man immediately, my wife and I will return home and contact you in the morning."

"The Garda looked from Nevin to Kearns, who had taken the gun from Val Nevin when they stopped. The Garda shone his torch around, seeing the gun he said.

"I think you had better let me have that sir and then we will all go to the station, we'll sort the whole lot out there, as it is this other man needs medical attention."

He turned to his companion.

"Frank call in for an ambulance and a doctor to meet us."

He turned to Kearns.

"If the women would go in the car sir, I'll travel with you in this vehicle."

There was a storm of protest from Nevin, which the Garda ignored.

Val and Jean transferred to the police car. When they arrived at the station some twenty minutes later an ambulance and a doctor were waiting. After Grant's wound had been examined and dressed, he was driven off to hospital. Inside, Nevin and Joe Kearns and the girls were taken into an office. Here, they were joined by a Sergeant. He was a big man and by his accent came from somewhere in West Cork. He looked at the four. His eyes settled on Nevin, by now the other two Gardai had vanished again.

"You seem to have been in the wars sir, I think we will get the doctor to have a look at you, in the meantime could we have some names and addresses, I know you Mr. Nevin and your good lady, Could I have your name sir?"

He addressed Joe, who gave him his name and occupation and asked again for John Maguire. The sergeant pretended not to hear and continued writing on a large foolscap page. He then turned to Jean and asked her particulars. It was here that Joe interrupted, asking for the use of a phone. With a wave of his hand the Sergeant indicated one on the desk. Joe dialled his emergency number, spoke his name and started to explain his position. He got no further when the Sergeants hand snapped down on the cradle breaking the connection. The man's face was crimson with rage, his eyes bored into Joe's.

"That's not allowed friend, your not going to alert your friends to try and spring you from here that easy, you just sit there now or I'll have to lock you up."

At that, Nevin who had been tidied up, broke in.

"That's right Sergeant, these people are criminals of the worst type. Look at the state of me, Could my wife and I not go home and come here in the morning and make my statement, I'm sure my wife would like to get to bed, as you can see she's most upset by the whole thing."

Val, who had not uttered a word since they had been taken into the station, turned on him with a look of scorn.

"There's no way I would ever set foot in your house again, you lying bastard, after what you tried to do to that girl and myself, only for Joe and poor Mr.Grant we would have ended up as that Arab's playthings."

She glared at him from across the room. Nevin looked at the Sergeant and spread his hands.

162

"You see Sergeant, my wife seems to be in some kind of shock or something, she's even starting to imagine things, perhaps if I could get her home and have our own doctor look at her I could come back here tomorrow, after all I am a T.D. and ex Minister, surely I'm entitled to some consideration?"

The Sergeant looked doubtfully at the little group.

"Well I suppose it couldn't do much harm, can you be here at eleven o clock to morrow morning."

Nevin was about to reply when the phone rang on the desk. The Sergeant picked it up. As he listened his face went pale. He looked at Joe Kearns and answered into the mouthpiece. His replies were punctuated by, 'Yes Sirs and No Sirs'. He replaced the receiver slowly. Then looking at Joe he paused for a moment before addressing him.

"Mr. Kearns, I have been told that I'm to cooperate with you in every possible way, I apologise for any inconvenience I've caused. Just tell me what to do, there's a lot more to this than I realised."

Kearns could not believe his luck. Somehow his call had been traced. Thank God for modern electronics. He stood up. Nevin who had been listening suddenly made a run for the door. Joe was after him in a flash and caught him as he tried to get through. From outside one of the other Garda came in and held the still struggling Nevin. Joe turned to the Sergeant.

"First, everything that went on here tonight is top secret, no one is to be told anything, is that clear? Nevin is to be held here until collected by someone from your Special Branch. I'll make arrangements for that. Next I want to go back to the house we escaped from, I'll take one of your men with me, then if you can arrange some accommodation for these two girls so as they can get some sleep until they too are picked up, that will be all for now."

He went to the desk and dialled his number again giving details of what he was about to do and where the girls and Nevin were. Then he turned to the Sergeant again.

"Can you find out about Harry Grant, what's his condition now?"

The Sergeant nodded and picked up the phone. He spoke for a few minutes. Then said to Joe.

163

"Your friend is all right, he's lost a lot of blood but the bullet has been removed and he's sleeping."

Joe looked across at Val and saw her eyes light up. He took Jeans hands in his.

"Jean love, someone will be here to collect you both later, rest assured you will be in the best of hands. I have to go now but I'll see you again as soon as possible, this whole thing will sort itself out before long."

She clung to him and turned a tearstained face to his.

"Oh Joe, I don't understand what's happening anymore, just look after yourself, I couldn't bear it if anything happened to you, I love you."

He kissed her and held her at arm's length.

"Well now isn't that the limit, sure I love you too, so I won't let anything happen to me but I have to go now and I will be back to you as soon as a I can."

He gave her another hug and nodded to the Garda who was watching with an embarrassed grin on his face. The Sergeant had vanished with Nevin some time earlier.

The first light of dawn was breaking as Joe swung the Range Rover through the gates at the entrance to the mining complex. The security guard, no doubt recognising the vehicle swung the barrier up. He looked curiously at them as they drove through. Up at the house the lights were still blazing. The two men went up to the door and rang the bell. After a few minutes they heard fumbling with bolts and locks and it opened. A small man of about sixty peered out at them. Joe had never seen him before. In a broad Dublin accent he asked.

"Yes gents what's up?"

Joe pulled out his press card and flashed it in front of his eyes.

"I'm Detective Sergeant Kearns and this is Garda Kelly, we had a report that there was some kind of fight here last night, may we have a look inside?"

The man hesitated before opening the door wider.

"Nothing happened here last night, sure I would have known about it, the boss is away at the moment, come on in."

164

Inside the whole scene had changed. The house was now furnished like any ordinary Irish house. Of the Arabic fittings there was no sign. They walked around, Joe looking for signs of the scuffle. There was none, the Arab's body must have been removed and disposed of, in all probability into one of the mineshafts. They went outside and stood for a bit watching the activity around the place. Joe turned to his companion.

"Tell me, do you know where Nevin's house is from here?"

The Garda nodded.

"It's about five miles from here up in the mountains, will I drive?"

Joe nodded and with a jerk the Garda let in the clutch.

Detective Inspector Maguire was dozing in the front seat of a black unmarked Garda car a few hundred yards from the front gates of Nevin's house when he received news of Grant and Joe Kearns's escape. When told that his niece was safe he breathed a sigh of relief. Some of his men were already on the way from Dublin to bring them back. The T.D. Nevin was in custody. He wondered how many more high up officials was mixed up in the unfolding plot. His thoughts were broken by a distant humming like a swarm of bees as out of the brightening sky came the first dots of the Microlight aircraft. They swept down towards the house and Maguire raised an arm and waved his own men forward. At the security fence the dogs made no sound. They had fallen to the drugged pieces of meat, thrown over the fence earlier in the night by some of Maguire's men. The gates were a formidable obstacle but Maguire had thought of that. An army Sergeant and a sapper had travelled with them. They ran forward and placed a couple of charges against the locks. Seconds later there was a small explosion which blew them off. The Sergeant swung them open. The Inspector and his men arrived at the house to find the commandos had rounded up three men, one of whom was Ned. The Captain came over to Maguire and saluted.

"These are all we have found at the moment we're still searching the house and the outbuildings, so far we haven't fired a shot."

He sounded rather disappointed. Maguire told him to put a guard on the gate and let no one enter. He then went into the house where his men were searching through every room. Wandering from room to room he looked at each in turn. Certainly these politicians liked to live well. Maguire remembered back a few years when Nevin was a young county counsellor. He had certainly come a long way since that. The Inspector idly wondered how he had accumulated such wealth as was apparent here in such a short few years. Looking out on the front lawn, it had started to rain. The three men were standing against the police car, their legs spread, American style, their hands on the roof. Three soldiers, now wearing ponchos to keep off the rain, trained their guns on them. Maguire shrugged, let them soak up some rain before the questions, it might encourage them to talk a bit quicker.

Down the hall he found himself in what was Nevin's bedroom. There were at least ten suits in the large walk in wardrobe. Opening drawers revealed shirts and shoes of various colours and types. There was a desk in the window alcove. In one of the drawers he found the Czech automatic which Grant had discovered earlier. In another he found a cardboard box. Inside were bundles of one hundred-dollar notes. At a rough count they came to about ten thousand dollars. Another bundle consisted of Russian Roubles. He was keeping his options open, thought Maguire. Hearing a car engine he went to the window. A Range Rover had driven up and a soldier was talking to the driver. Maguire swore under his breath, he had given instructions that nobody was to be allowed in. He hurried downstairs, if it were one of those smart reporters he would have him held until this was all over. If news of this got out now there would be hell to pay. When he came out on the steps he saw a uniformed Garda was behind the wheel. There was a man in the passenger seat who jumped out. He had a short growth of beard. There was dried blood on his face and clothes, which were torn in places. There was a large bruise under his right eye. He ran up the steps.

"Inspector Maguire? My name is Joe Kearns, could we have a talk?"

Maguire looked at him with a faint smile, so this was the fellow that young Jean had been seeing.

"Mr. Kearns, Joe, how did you know we were here? By the way have you looked in a mirror lately, you could do with a bit of a clean up."

Joe explained what had happened to Grant and himself and how they had escaped last night. When he had finished the Inspector asked him about Jean and if she was all right. Seeing Joe looking at him curiously, he explained that he was her Uncle. Then he told Joe to go upstairs and tidy up. Some of the soldiers were cooking breakfast and the smell of bacon and eggs made Joe realise how hungry he was. It had certainly been a hective twenty-four hours. He had killed a man, seen another man killed and his friend Grant wounded. He himself had fought like a madman, driven like a lunatic and survived. As he shaved off his beard he looked at himself in the mirror and told himself, Kearns old son this is getting rough. Downstairs he sat with Maguire and wolfed down his first meal since last night. Outside he could see the three standing at the car in the rain. He looked inquiringly at Maguire who went on eating his breakfast. Joe motioned to the window.

"Inspector, those fellows will get pneumonia if they're out there much longer, particularly the older one, His name is Ned he was here when we came, he was also at the house last night when we escaped, that's how he got the cut on his head."

Maguire downed his tea with evident satisfaction before replying.

"Joe, son, we're only trying to soften them up a bit before we ask them a few questions, it won't do them a bit of harm. In case you don't know, your friend Ned is a killer. He acts as hitman. We know of at least six victims he has murdered. One of his favourite methods is to travel by public transport, follow his victim. Shoot him in the head with a silenced gun then return the same way. The other two beauties are also known killers, it was those two that roughed up your landlady."

He lit up his pipe and blew out a cloud of smoke.

"We can't touch them, we've got nothing on them that will stand up in court, so they laugh at us and carry on, I can tell you that we will get very little out of them, so this is nothing to what they gave their victims. Yes, what is it Tom?"

One of his men had come in carrying two guns laid on a piece of plywood and covered with a piece of plastic.

"We found these down in the stables Chief, one of them is Russian automatic, those people in the house on the Blessington road were shot with a Russian automatic."

Maguire looked at the weapons.

"Okay. Tom leave them there, go and have some breakfast, the fingerprint boys will be here soon and we'll see what they can tell us, after that its up to ballistics."

He stood up and called for one of his men to bring in Ned. The sodden figure that shambled into the room was a sorry sight. Maguire sat looking at him for fully three minutes before speaking.

"Well Ned, so we've got you at last, do you know who this is?

He indicated Joe. Ned ignored him. Maguire went on.

"Your in big trouble this time Ned, Mr.Kearns here has told me about the goings on here for the last few days and last night, what have you got to say about that?"

Ned's face was a mask of fury.

"I've got nothing to say to you Maguire, nothing happened here the last few days, Kearns can tell you anything he likes, as for last night, I was here all the time."

Just then another member of the search team came in carrying a small revolver with a silencer attached hanging on a pencil through the trigger guard. He gently laid it on the table.

"We found this under the floor in his room, Chief."

He nodded towards Ned who turned his face away and gazed out of the window. Maguire stuck his pencil through the guard and dangled the gun.

"So that's it Ned, you get up close to your man put the gun to his neck and pop its all over."

He turned to Joe.

"You see Mr.Kearns, what happens is the bullet enters through the nape of the neck in an upward direction and blows away the front of the skull. Of course Ned here always files a cross on the point of the bullet so that it makes a bigger hole as it exits. The victim is usually dead in seconds, A sweet fellow is our Ned."

He told the detective to take Ned up to his room and get him into some dry clothes and then bring in the other two. When the two men came in they stood insolently in front of Maguire. The blonde one looked at Joe, his eyes were like those of a dead fish but his mouth was smiling.

"So you got us Maguire, very smart the Microlights, and you, we should have killed you Kearns, you interfering bastard."

The other one said nothing, Maguire puffed at his pipe.

"Now Sean don't be like that, we caught you fair and square, you're not going to get out of this one, we are going to pin those murders in Tallagh on you."

He saw the man's face flicker.

"O yes we found the bodies, no doubt the bullets from those guns will match with the ones from the bodies, this time you are probably going away for about twenty-five years."

He blew smoke towards the ceiling. Joe thought he heard a movement at the door and turned his head. The other man suddenly flung himself at the table and grabbed for the guns. He flung one to Sean Mahon and pointed the other at the Inspector and Kearns. Mahon grinned at Maguire.

"I could kill you now you old bastard, but I need you to get us out of here. Now we're going to walk to that squad car, then you Kearns are going to drive us out of here, I'll have this gun at Maguire's head, any tricks and he gets it, understood."

Maguire stood up.

"Better do as he says Joe."

The two walked in front of the guns to the door where Maguire called to his men outside.

"They've got us covered here don't do anything rash, start the engine of the squad car and open the doors, put your weapons down on the ground."

Slowly the little party moved out and down the steps. Mahon keeping the gun pressed against Maguire's head, the other man swung his gun in an arc walking backwards. They reached the car and Mahon motioned Joe inside behind the wheel. At the same time Maguire flung himself on the ground. There was a burst of gunfire, the other man bucked as if kicked by a mule, gave three or four steps and fell to the ground. Mahon, his face distorted with rage and hate had spun round and fired a couple of shots. Maguire with surprising agility for a man of his age was trying to roll under the car. Mahon swung his pistol toward him. Joe Kearns pushed the car door at him with all his might. It caught Mahon on the side, the force pushing him out into the driveway. Another burst of gunfire caught him in the chest and he danced around in the roadway for three or four steps before collapsing in a heap. John McQuillen came cautiously out from behind some bushes and crossed the driveway, his Uzi hanging at arm's length, then picking up the men's weapons, white faced, came over to where Maguire was dusting himself down. A couple of soldiers came over and threw ponchos over the bodies. No one spoke, Joe was still sitting in the car. Maguire reached in and turned off the engine, he caught Joe's arm and guided him out. The rest of the men stood around in little groups.

Inside the house Maguire was talking quietly to McQuillen who was drinking some of Nevin's whiskey. Joe went across to them and sat down.

"John you saved our lives out there, only for you the Inspector and myself might not have seen another day, thanks very much."

McQuillen looked at him and then at Maguire, who gave a nod. McQuillen downed his whiskey and looked at Joe again. He stood up gave a short laugh and walked out. Joe started after him but Maguire caught his arm and with a shake of his head said.

"Not now Joe, not now."

Some time later a military ambulance arrived and another team of detectives who photographed the scene and took statements from witnesses. Joe was excluded from this. The bodies were then put on board and driven off.

Joe moved around the house with Maguire as the search continued. He told Maguire everything that had happened to him from the beginning except about the Taoiseach. The Inspector listened impassively as they wandered from room to room. So far nothing more incriminating had been found and Maguire was wearing a puzzled look. He walked outside, Kearns following. Standing in front of the house he gazed at the facade, sucking his pipe and trailing a cloud of blue smoke. Suddenly he turned to Joe.

"Come on lad, I think I see something."

They went back upstairs to Nevin's Room. The Inspector went straight to the large walk in wardrobe. Opening the door he stood for a moment. Then he pushed the clothes to one end of the rail and gave a grunt of satisfaction. Set in the corner was the outline of a door. It opened to his touch letting them into another room which was an office of sorts. Kearns and Maguire moved to a large writing desk and started to open drawers. The first one revealed a large desk diary, which he opened and started to read through. Joe looking over his shoulder saw it contained pages of names and addresses, with notes and numbers alongside. Maguire slapped it down on the desk. He turned to Joe triumph gleaming in his eyes.

"We've got them Joe, this is it, lots of names and addresses, come on we must get back to Dublin."

CHAPTER 19

George Reilly awoke to the sound of a tap on his door. He lay still for a moment and glanced at his watch, it was three a.m. He opened the door to find Fergus Doyle grinning at him.

"Come on George, her ladyship is downstairs, we're sailing in an hour, according to her we have got to get the ship off the Irish coast a week before Easter."

Reilly looked at him grimfaced.

"So she has taken over completely has she? Well, let's hope she knows what she's doing or we are all going to end up very dead."

In the car taking them to the port there was a stony silence. Francis told them of her conversation with the men in Dublin. When no one made any comments she stayed silent until they reached the ship. Reilly noticed that the tractors had been removed and were standing on the quay. All evidence of the fight had been removed. The fuel tanks had been filled and the two coffins loaded for their return to Ireland. They moved out of the harbour under the expert guidance of the Libyan pilot whom they dropped at the mouth of the river. Then with a grey dawn starting to brighten they set course for Gibraltar. In the Gadfly the radar operator picked up the movement almost as soon as they had left the harbour. Pritchard ordered the submarine up to periscope depth to check that it was the same ship. The freighter passed within a quarter of a mile of them, Pritchard could easily read the name on her stern. There was a man leaning over the rail. The Captain felt that he was watching them. He saw the man straighten up and toss the end of a cigarette into the water. The periscope slid down and the Gadfly took up a following course some two miles astern. George Reilly walked thoughtfully back to the bridge, He was sure he had seen something as he smoked a lone cigarette. It was a flash of light, or something reflecting the sun's rays, the first of the early morning, he wondered vaguely what it could have been. Sitting down at the table he started to plot his course towards the distant Irish coast.

In Washington Maurice Curley had been going through the report from their agent in Benghazi. He studied the photographs of the ship taken by satellite spy in the sky cameras and marvelled again at the clarity of them. He wonderd out loud if there was any news of Grant. Then picking up the red telephone he rang the President.

Detective Inspector John Maguire had no sooner reached his office with Joe Kearns when, he received a message telling him that Nevin had hung himself in his cell. He immediately gave orders for the body to be brought back to the family home and a statement to be issued later to the press that the death had taken place after a family row. It was now four o clock and the news would be released in time for the following mornings papers.

In Moscow Ivan Gudenuv was sending out final instructions to the various ships which were to take part in the operation.

The largest of these was the Volograd. This was a fisheries factory vessel of twenty five thousand tons. It bristled with sophisticated sonic and radar equipment. Now it was loading six hundred troops and their equipment in a Baltic port before starting out on its journey to be off the West Coast of Ireland by the end of the month. Gudenuv then read the latest report from Bengazi. The arms ship had left on the morning tide. With any look at all the ship would be off the Irish coast by the twenty sixth of March. This should give plenty of time for the stuff to be unloaded and delivered around the country. So far everything seemed to be going according to plan. He ran over the various reports again. A feeling of unease gripped him, what if the whole thing did go wrong? No, everything was going as he had planned. Apart from that clash with the Mafia off Sicily which had delayed the ship for four days. There had been no reports of any-thing being suspected by the opposition. In England the strikes and unrest had started and as expected some troops had been brought home from Northern Ireland. There, the Irish Freedom Movement had ceased all activities. Dublin was paralysed by a transport strike, which was meant to last until the take-over. During the coming week the electrical unions were coming out to join their colleagues in a gesture of solidarity. This would ensure total chaos on that particular weekend. The Colonel sat for a moment longer. Then he locked the papers in his office safe. Donning his greatcoat he went down to his car and ordered the driver to take him to the military airfield where the Tubeluv aircraft which he used, was kept. Here he found his personal pilot and instructed him to always have the plane ready for immediate take off as he might need to use it in a hurry. This done, he drove to his apartment. Olga was in the kitchen preparing the evening meal. She called to him.

"Ivan, is that you? I've invited mother and father over, they'll be here in about half an hour, how did the day go?

She came out of the kitchen and kissed him on the cheek, her hands white with flour. At forty she was still a beautiful woman with a mass of blonde hair and if she was a trifle plump he loved her all the more for it. He took off his coat and followed her into the kitchen.

"It smells delicious, it will be nice to see your parents again, they haven't been here for some time."

Olga gave him a smile.

"As a matter of fact, Father said he wanted to talk to you, something about some job you were doing."

Gudenuv felt a tinge of fear. What did Ishinskey want to talk about. He had always enjoyed excellent relations with his in law's, they regarded him as a son. His thoughts were interrupted by the sound of the door bell. Olga shouted.

"There they are, let them in please."

After dinner they sat around chatting and drinking wine and vodka. The Colonel could contain himself no longer. Looking his father in law directly in the eye he said.

"Olga tells me there is something you wish to discuss with me."

The older man sipped his vodka in silence for a moment, then stood up.

"Let's go into the other room."

The men excused themselves and moved into the Colonel's study. The Minister turned to his son in law.

"This plan for the take-over of Ireland, how is it going? What's happening, there's talk floating around, is everything under control?"

Gudenuv looked at him warily.

"Yes father, everything is going as planned at the moment, the arms ship will be off the Irish coast about a week before the event."

The older man stared into space.

"I was talking to Serge Albninov, he came in from Dublin yesterday, It appears there have been happenings there which could upset this coup of yours, I don't wish to alarm you but there's talk of an American student and an Irish reporter being missing. Serge thinks the American is C.I.A. It appears that he visited some of our Irish Comrades, told them he was doing research into the situation in Northern Ireland. Then a few days later these two were caught at the window of a house where a Irish Freedom Movement meeting was going on and were taken prisoner. After that Serge could find out nothing more. He thinks they may have been shot, the Irish Special Branch are all over the place trying to find them, he goes back tomorrow and if there is anything further he will contact you direct."

Gudenuv stroked his chin thoughtfully.

"There's not much we can do now only wait, we can't stop, everything is moving, by the weekend of the thirty-first of March all our ships will be in position, our Irish friends will go ahead as planned. We can succeed, we will succeed."

"I hope for your sake your right."

Said the older man straightening up a picture on the wall,

"There will be hell to pay if it goes wrong."

In silence the two walked back and rejoined the women.

When Michael McCall turned on his radio before getting out of bed the news reader brought him to full awakeness. The words bored into his brain.

"The ex Minister of Defence, Conor Nevin has committed suicide by

175

hanging himself at his home. The authorities are trying to contact his wife."

There followed a short report on his life in the Dail. He sat there thinking, what the hell could have happened? Where were Meehan and Farrell, what had happened to the American and Kearns, then there was the girl. He picked up the phone from the bedside table and dialled. When the connection was made he spoke sharply.

"Get over here as quickly as you can, I need you in a hurry"

A short time later a small green van drew up at the house. The man who got out slowly and rang the front door bell was Jack Monaghan. If Harry Grant could see him he would have recognised the silent one from his first meeting in the White Leprechaun. McCall let him in and closed the door, turning angrily.

"Have you heard any news this morning, Nevin's gone and hanged himself, there's no word of the other two idiots or Grant or Kearns, I don't know what's happening, get yourself out there, see if you can find out anything."

Monaghan picked a piece of toast off McCall's plate.

"That's the first I've heard about this, all I know is that they were supposed to get rid of Kearns and Grant last night, I know that Nevin was giving the women to one of our Arab friends."

He gave a short laugh.

"It seems things didn't work out right."

McCall's eyes blazed.

"The man was a bloody fool, we're better off without him, go on get out there and see if you can find out anything, get back here as soon as you can, if I'm not here I'll be at headquarters, is that clear?"

Monaghan nodded and left. McCall drove out of the house at nine thirty. A hundred yards down the road a battered Ford Transit pulled out from the kerb and joined the line of traffic, two cars behind him. The Transit tailed him until he pulled into the car park of the Ambassador hotel some six miles north of the city. In the bar four men awaited him greetings were exchanged and they all went upstairs to a room on the sixth floor There around a table began a meeting of the inner council of the Irish Freedom Movement.

At the head of the table sat McCall, flanked on his left by the man known as John or Johnny Coughlin. On his right sat Tim O Mahony, who looked after arms and ammunition and stores. By his side was Johnny McGrath who was in charge of transport. Beside Coughlin sat James Reddin, who was overall commander of the Dublin army section. The first thing they discussed was the death of Nevin. McCall told them he had already sent Monaghan to find out all he could about what had happened. He expected him back in a couple of hours. Coughlin reported that the arms ship had left Benghazi and would be here in plenty of time. The Russian ships were taking up positions around the coast and the Trade delegation would arrive on the Thursday before the Government meeting. Everything else was ready. The ship would be unloaded at night at a deserted pier, which was used by ships loading ballast for export. The activity would blend in with normal procedure. The whole operation would be carried out openly with the men disguised as Irish army personnel with lorries and Land Rovers painted in Army colours. The pier was situated about two miles from the centre of the town along a deserted shoreline. No one would pay the least attention as ships came and went all the time.

In London Colonel Mark Philpot sat at his desk reading the latest report from Gadfly. By tonight the ship would be passing through the Straights of Gibraltar and out into the Atlantic. There was no doubt in his mind that it was destined for the Irish Republic. Gadfly would shadow her all the way. At present speed it would take another week at least for it to get there. He would wait a few days more before getting in touch with his counterpart in Dublin. Then there were strikes all over and serious rioting was beginning to develop nightly in all the major cities in England. There seemed to be a pattern to the troubles. Events were happening with a regularity that seemed to be more of a coincidence. It certainly had the police tied up all over the country. The army was on stand by but had not been used as yet. Philpot gave a shrug, if it came to the push he would order Gadfly to sink the ship. This could be done at night, it could be put down to another unfortunate accident at sea. A phonecall to his old friend Pervis would be all that was needed. It would save a lot of trouble and lives in Ireland. He put on his bowler and coat and walked the short distance to number ten Downing Street.

The Prime minister sat opposite him and listened as he outlined the situation to her. She broke in on him once or twice to ask a specific question. When he had finished she rose and looked at a large wall map of Western Europe. She traced the course of the ship from Gibraltar to the Irish coast. Turning to him she pointed to the Northwest coast of Scotland.

"I have a report from the Air Force that there are quite a few large Russian fishing vessels moving around that area. According to our pilots none of them have been seen to be actually fishing, is there some tie up with your arms ship, I wonder, keep a close eye on the situation. I'll be available at any time if you want me, in the meantime do whatever you think necessary, I will instruct the R.A.F. to carry out more surveillance flights, I, think this could be the beginning of something big, Thank you for coming."

She shook his hand and showed him out. He knew now that he had been given almost unlimited powers by the lady in No 10 ten. She would back him in any decision he made. Back in his office he called one of his men to report to him. About an hour later there was a knock at the door and a tall wellbuilt man with a slight limp came in. Jeremy Carter was ex S.A.S. and parachute regiment. Aged thirty-five, he had the bearing of a professional soldier. He had served in the fourth paras in Belfast in the seventies a young Lieutenant until a sniper's bullet nearly ended his life. It had finished his army career. Now he worked for M.I.5. Philpot was now sending him to Dublin disguised as a business man in an attempt to find out what if anything was going on there. Reports from Belfast said it was quiet and had been so for the past five or six weeks. The Embassy in Dublin had noticed nothing out of the ordinary in its weekly reports, but you could not beat the man on the ground, He turned to Carter and began to brief him on his assignment.

The Christopher Columbus passed through the Straits of Gibraltar during the night of the twenty second of March and struck out northward, parallel with the Spanish coast and about six miles off shore. For the past three days George Reilly had avoided Francis Coughlin, only speaking to her when spoken to and cutting short any meetings he had with her. Now he handed the wheel over to John O'Shea who was more or less fully recovered from his wound.

"That's your course John, keep about six miles out from the coast until we hit Biscay after that comes the good part."

O'Shea gave him a grin.

"Sure a few more days George and we'll be toasting good old Arthur."

George grinned back at him, O'Shea certainly pined for the national Irish drink. Some people were easily pleased he thought as he went back to his cabin. When he entered Francis was sitting on his bunk. She gave him a smile.

"Hello George, can we have a talk?"

He nodded and she went on.

"I know you think I'm taking over command from you but that's not true. With all that fuss with the Libyans, I thought that if I could get hold of my father things would be sorted out quickly and they were. He has complete trust in you and told me not to get in the way, he says that if anyone can get this ship home its you. I just want to tell you that I will not interfere in anything again, you're the Commander from now on, okay?

George looked at her in silence. She looked at him anxiously. He reached out and caught her hands.

"Then I give the orders Francis."

She stood up.

"Yes George, I suppose so."

"Then here's one for you. Lock the door."

Detective Inspector Maguire was feeling so tired now that he could scarcely stand. He phoned Jean's mother to tell her the girl was all right. Then he sent both girls under the supervision of a female Garda Sergeant to Peggy Noone's Guesthouse with orders to stay there until he contacted them again. Jean argued that she wanted to go home but Maguire told her that she could still be in danger and appealed to Joe

179

to tell her why. Kearns asked her to listen to the Inspector and she acceded. He was feeling very tired and was somewhat grey in the face. A car was sent for and the girls left.

"Joe, I'm going home to get a few hours sleep, I suggest you do the same, if you go with Sean here he will show you to a room, I'll see you in the morning, good night."

Kearns followed the young Garda to a bedroom where a rather large set of pyjamas lay on the cover.

"There you are sir, sleep well if there's anything you want, just ring."

He indicated a bell over the bed and left. Joe sat on the edge for a moment. Then went into the bathroom and had a shower and a shave. Everything he needed was there. He put on the pyjamas and climbed into bed. He was asleep in an instant.

After he awoke next morning he went in search of Maguire whom he found in the canteen eating breakfast, he pointed a chair opposite.

"Morning Joseph, did you sleep well, what about some breakfast?"

He indicated a counter at the end of the room.

"Over there and grab a tray, get whatever you want its on the house"

Kearns was surprised at the Inspectors easy manner. The country was facing God knows what and here was the Head of Special Branch casually eating breakfast. He collected a meal and sat down. Maguire pushed a newspaper across. Between sips of tea he smiled at Joe.

"That should stir things up a bit, they won't know what's happening, it might start them running about a bit."

Joe glanced at the headlines, which told the story of Nevin's suicide. He looked up at the Inspector across the table.

"Inspector, what did you find in that note book, was there anything about the coup? Date's or times or anything?"

Maguire shook his head.

"Names and addresses in plenty, some short notes which mean nothing to us at this stage, one with a date which says, 'Col' arrives between March the twenty-fifth and thirty-first.

He took the book out of his pocket, turning over the pages.

"This entry here is interesting, it is the holiday weekend, the first to the third of April. It just says, 'Meeting at Ballyorney Castle.' but it is heavily underlined. I think that is where this coup will be attempted. The whole Government will be at a weekend meeting in the Castle, if they were going to try something that would be the time and the place, and didn't your friend, One Arm, tell you that something was going to happen at the end of March or beginning of April."

He handed the book across to Joe, who glanced through it, he felt himself starting to tingle. This had to be the answer. Maguire was right they were going to try for a coup over the Easter weekend, yet the other two dates in March were mentioned and who was 'Col', yet it would seem very foolish to try anything at the castle where security would be at its height. He handed the book back to Maguire who got up from the table.

"Come on Joe we have been summoned to a meeting with some very important people."

No words were spoken on the short journey, which Kearns discovered when the car swept down a ramp into an underground carpark was Dail Eireann. They were brought up to the Taoiseach's private office. Here behind his desk sat the man himself flanked by the Commissioner and the army Commandant who were at the first meeting with Joe.

CHAPTER 20

The Taoiseach welcomed them.

"Good day Inspector, good day Mr. Kearns, thank you for coming, I believe you have something to tell us, sit down please."

Maguire opened his notebook and gave a resume of events up to and including the last twenty-four hours. Joe noticed that he did not mention Michael McCall. He left out all references to him, including the fact that he had captured Kearns and Grant. When he had finished the Taoiseach looked at both men.

"Tell me Inspector, have you any knowledge at all of exact dates and times or where this thing is to take place?"

Maguire looked at the Taoiseach blankly and to Joe's amazement told him.

"At this moment sir I have no knowledge of anything, I had hoped to find out something by questioning Nevin but his suicide precluded that, we're still trying to find out who the rest of his accomplices are."

The Army Commandant looked at Maguire, a superior smile on his face.

"Really Inspector, do you mean to tell us that after all that, including searching the mans house you still have not found anything which will tell us what's happening."

Maguire turned sleepy eyes on him.

"I'm afraid that's correct Commandant."

The Garda Commissioner broke in.

"John, may I remind you that this is the twenty fifth of March, these rumours say that whoever is going to happen will take place at the end of the month, time is running out, what do we do now?"

Maguire was about to answer when the Taoiseach's secretary entered and handed the Inspector a note. He read the contents and stuffed it into his pocket. Standing up he said.

"Taoiseach, Gentlemen, may I tell you that as a result of this message we may learn a bit more about the situation, I'm afraid I must ask you to bear with me, as soon as I have more news I will be in touch with you direct Taoiseach."

Fitzgibbon stood up and shook hands with both men.

"Thank you Inspector and you Mr. Kearns, I appreciate your bravery in all this, rest assured it will not be forgotten, you were very lucky not to have been killed or seriously injured, thank you again."

In the car Maguire sucked at his pipe.

"Joe, I suppose you're wondering why I didn't tell them everything in there. Well it's like this, I only told them the truth, we really don't know what's going on, besides, who can you trust, I'll tell you something, that army Commandant is one of the names on Nevin's list."

Joe glanced at him. He was puffing away, looking out of the car window. Kearns said nothing. Outside the crowds were walking around, driving cars, sitting in buses, getting on with their lives, unaware that things were building up to a climax, of what? Maguire leaned across to the driver.

"Take us out to the airport Sean."

He looked at Kearns.

"We have to meet someone, this whole thing is getting more interesting by the minute."

At the airport the car was driven around to the cargo area. There standing on the tarmac was an executive jet. The car drove straight out to beside the steps where two uniformed Customs Officers waited. Maguire got out and went up the steps, Joe following. Inside the plane a man stepped forward and reached for the Inspectors hand.

"John Maguire, so, we meet face to face at last, I'm Maurice Curley, C.I.A., glad to meet you."

Maguire shook his hand warmly.

"Welcome to Ireland Maurice, or as they say in Irish, Cead Mile Failte, a hundred thousand welcomes, did you have a good trip?"

The American nodded and called to the pilot and another man.

"You fellows get down to the Embassy and sort things out there, I'll be along later, they'll fix us up with somewhere to stay, preferably close by, I'm going with the Inspector here okay?"

The taller of the two turned to him.

"How do we get there chief? Will we take a taxi?"

Curley thought for a moment.

"No, hire a car, we might need it later."

Maguire interjected.

"Sure there's no need for that Maurice, I've taken care of it, one of our lads will be here shortly, as a matter of fact here he is now."

He indicated a red saloon car, which had just arrived with John McQuillen at the wheel.

"John there will look after your lads and take them out to Ballsbridge. We'll go back to my office and on the way I'll put you in the picture."

On the way he introduced Joe to the American and told him of the recent events leading up to the wounding of Grant. When he described Joe's part, Curley looked at him with interest. He didn't interrupt Maguire, who carefully avoided giving him all the details. Later in Maguire's office Curley opened his briefcase and took out a file. He looked at it for a moment then without a word handed it to Maguire. Joe could see it contained photographs as well as typewritten pages. The Inspector studied them carefully then looked at Curley, who gave a grim smile.

"John those pictures were taken a few days ago by one of our satellites. They show a ship in the port of Bengazi. Our agent there reported that there were four Irish people on board, one of them was a girl, one of the men was wounded and treated in hospital. In one of the pictures you can see some tractors which were unloaded standing on the quay. We know that the ship sailed three days ago. We think it is carrying arms and ammunition and is heading for here."

He paused.

"We also got a garbled report some time ago that three Irishmen were leaving Moscow for home. The end of the message said, 'Something big', after that our man went off the air, we can assume that he was nabbed by the K.G.B., we didn't hear from him again."

Maguire handed the file over to Joe who started to study it carefully. He marvelled at the clarity of the photos. They had been taken from about one hundred miles up. It was fantastic, he could see the row of tractors and the figures of men on the quay side. What a pity they were all taken almost directly overhead or they might have been able to read the name of the ship. Maguire was asking Curley if he had the name. Without a word he reached into his briefcase and passed a sheet of paper to the Inspector whose face lit up. He passed the paper over to Joe.

"The ships name is the Christopher Columbus Joe, it looks as if that note in our friends diary is the same, Col. is the name of the ship, that's what's arriving on the twenty fourth or the twenty fifth, that bloody ship, the one thing we don't know is where? We are going to have to work fast, do you think you could contact your friend, what do you call him? One Arm."

Joe was thinking fast, One Arm would not be too keen to even speak to him. The big problem would be to find his man. Every Irish Freedom Army man in Dublin was looking for him, Joe Kearns, and he certainly did not want anything to happen to One Arm. He knew only too well what their method was in dealing with anyone who betrayed them. A mock trial and then a bullet in the back of the head. Yet he would have to try.

"I'll give it a shot Inspector, that's all I can do, If I do find him and he comes up with the information, can I offer him a deal of some sort?

Maguire blew a cloud of smoke towards the ceiling.

"We'll look after him Joe, If you find him and he talks, bring him back here, it's probably the best place for him."

When Joe Kearns left the Garda Headquarters some time later his own mother would not have recognised him. He wore a long overcoat, which was tattered and faded and streaked with dirt. A greasy cap was pulled down over his face, which was a dirty shade of grey. A wine bottle protruded from his pocket. He hobbled along in a pair of old boots several sizes too large, muttering to himself, he weaved a crazy path along the pavement much to the annoyance of passers-by. At the end of Harcourt Street he almost bumped into Ken McGuiness, the sub editor of his old paper. He muttered a string of curses and moved on. In a shop window he could see McGuiness standing looking after him.

Making his way towards the Coombe he turned into a narrow street which led into a small square of little houses. Here on the corner lived the man he was seeking. There were a couple of boys of school age playing football in the centre, their bags making imitation goal posts. They paid little attention to him as he made his way around the corner to the lane, which ran at the back of the houses. He opened the latch on the back gate of One Arm's house, letting himself into the tiny back yard. Then he knocked gently on the back door of the house. Inside he could hear a radio or a television set. He knocked again, there was the sound of shuffling feet. A thick voice said.

"Shove off and leave me alone you rotten bastards, leave me alone."

Joe put his head to the door and called softly.

"Frank, Frank, it's me Joe, Joe Kearns, open the door."

There was silence. Then the sound of bolts being withdrawn. Slowly the door opened, Frank O Brien stood in the opening. Joe gave a gasp. His face was a swollen mass. Two bloodshot eyes blinked at him from purple bruises He mumbled through puffed lips.

"Joe? Is it really you, Jesus they're looking everywhere for you, your a dead man, what the hell is going on, look at what they did to me, they were looking to know if I had seen you, come in quick, you can't stay here, you know that."

He led the way into a tiny kitchen and drew the curtains. Joe sat on a chair. One Arm struggled to light a cigarette opposite him.

"Frank, I'm sorry they did this to you, I've been lucky myself, I was very near being killed, but that's another story, If I live long enough I might even tell you about it someday but at the moment there is something more important. We know that a ship is about to arrive here in the next three or four days. The one thing we don't know is where they are going to land the arms and stuff that's aboard. Is there any chance, you might

186

know something about it? I can tell you now you will be protected, as a matter of fact I can take you somewhere now if you wish."

Frank O Brien blew smoke through his nostrils.

"Joe you know these boys, if they want to get me there's no hiding place, particularly when I'm like this."

He indicated his missing right arm.

"No matter where I go. I stand out like a sore thumb. Anyway I don't know where your ship is going to come in, I'm not circulating in the crowd any more since I spoke to you a couple of months ago when Jem was killed, I had seen no one until those fellows came around two nights ago looking for you."

Joe felt disappointment welling up inside him, he had been sure that O'Brien would have known where the ship would come in. Even if he did know he was not going to tell. From the state of his face you could not blame him. It was dark now outside. The two men sat at the table, the tip of the cigarette a red eye in the gloom. Joe broke the silence.

"Frank, I think you should come along with me, you'll be safer, there's no point in staying here, your friends might come back, next time you might not be so lucky."

O'Brien stood up and walked out to the front room. He peered out into the square. Joe had followed him looking over his shoulder. Outside there was no sign of life.

"Okay. Joe, I'll do as you say, I'll just get a few things.'"

He pulled down the blinds and switched on the light. Picking up a canvas bag he went upstairs. When he came down he said to Joe.

"We'll leave the lights on and go out the back gate."

As they rounded the corner Joe heard a noise. He cautiously moved his head around the corner. Two figures were knocking on One Arm's door. Joe moved back, his fingers on his lips to O'Brien. In the light of the street lamp the man's face was wracked with sheer terror. The two men knocked harder. They looked around. One of them watched while the other gave a heave at the door, which opened with a sharp crack. The two were inside in a flash and out again as quick, walking briskly towards the entrance to the square. Joe turned to O'Brien.

"Is there another way out of here Frank?"

O'Brien nodded and led the way back towards the lane at the rear. Along the wall there was a gap which led across a patch of waste ground. When they crossed this they came out into the Coombe. They made their way in silence across to the corner of Stephens Green, turning right into Harcourt Street and Garda Headquarters at the other end. They were almost halfway there when Joe saw the car. It was coming fast and as close to the footpath as it could get because of parked cars. As it approached he saw the passenger window come down and the barrel of a gun appeared. He shouted to O'Brien to get down and threw himself on the pavement as a hail of bullets swept towards them. O'Brien gave a cry and slumped down on some steps at the entrance to a block of offices. Joe rushed over to him. A stream of blood was coming from his mouth and he was breathing great rasping breaths. He tried to catch at Joe's coat with his one good hand and slipped back coughing Joe bent down to him and caught his hand, a gush of blood came from his mouth.

"See, I told you they, get me Joe, nearly got you too, listen, Ballingeary, the Jetty that's where."

The rest was indistinct, the breathing stopped and his head lolled to one side. Joe looked around, several more people had been hit and were lying around some being helped by others who had gathered. With siren blaring a squad car arrived and the crew jumped out. Two ambulances came to a stop and some first aid people came from nowhere. Joe viewed the scene of carnage with a sick feeling before making his way to Garda Headquarters. At the entrance the Garda on duty stepped in front of him and asked

"And where do you think you are going?"

Joe, suddenly realising his unkempt appearance stopped short.

"Get hold of Inspector Maguire, Special Branch, tell him its Joe Kearns."

He sagged against the wall as the man doubtfully picked up the phone, almost immediately he waved Joe on.

"Straight across to that building over there, sir, the Inspector is waiting for you."

Maguire met him in the foyer and without a word took him by the arm and into an office.

"Joe, I've just been getting a report on the shooting, your friend is dead, so are three more, one a young girl of sixteen, your lucky not to have been hit yourself, tell me did you find out anything?"

By this time Kearns was feeling sick and angry and the shock and horror of the last fifteen or twenty minutes was eating into him. Those bastards did not care who they killed. Innocent people meant nothing to them, he heard Maguire's voice as if in a dream.

"Yes, Inspector before he died Frank mentioned something about Ballingeary and a jetty, I think it must be there they mean to bring in the ship, does it ring any bells?

Maguire nodded.

"There was a case last winter when a couple of men were fishing on the pier there one night when some fellows arrived and told them for their health's sake to shove off home. We wouldn't have known anything about it only one of our fellows heard some talk in a pub. It's a good place for an operation like that but the logistics of it makes the mind boggle. They would need quite a few lorries and a lot of men to sort out something like that, but it certainly is a good place for it as it is so isolated."

He continued.

"I think we will say that you were killed tonight with your friend Joe, it might make them a bit more careless and give you a chance to find out a bit more."

He pressed a bell on the desk.

"Here, go with Sean and get cleaned up and change your clothes. Then maybe you would go down to Ballingeary and see if you can find out if anything is happening down there, you can get a car from the pool, Sean will see to that for you, watch out, you know now what these people are like.

Joe left a short time later in an old grey Escort. His first stop was the Guest House in Baggot street. Peggy Noone opened the door to him.

"Yes, what can I do for you? If its a room your after I'm afraid there is none."

Joe shook his head.

"No it's not that, I would like to see Miss Jean McKay please if I may."

Peggy Noone looked at him cautiously.

"I'm afraid Miss McKay is not here, she got some bad news and left here to find out more about it, I don't know when she will be back."

Joe realised that Jean had probably seen a news flash on television and heard of the deaths of O'Brien and himself, damm he should have phoned her. Maguire would explain the full story to her. He muttered.

"Thank you very much, I'm sorry to have bothered you."

Peggy Noone watched him as he drove out before going into her office and phoning Special Branch to report the visit.

In Maguire's office, McQuillen and the Inspector were comparing notes. McQuillen asked if they should send more men down to Ballingeary. Maguire shook his head.

"What ever chance Joe Kearns has, if we go galloping in down there we would stand out like sore thumbs, no John we'll have to wait until the last minute before we move. Besides when Curley gets here I'm going to ask him to plot the course of the ship by satellite, you know they have that station in the factory down in Kildare. They should be able to tell us the exact course and speed of the ship every hour. Once we have that we can calculate the exact time it will dock at Ballingeary. Now lets see what our friend McCall was up to today."

He picked up the report on the McCall visit to the hotel and noted the names of his companions at the meeting and said to McQuillen.

"I wonder if anyone turned up at Nevin's house today making enquiries."

The other phone was ringing and Maguire picked it up. It was from one of his men stationed at the airport to tell him about the arrival of Jeremy Carter. The man had been met at the airport by an official of the British Embassy. In the lobby they had held an animated conversation. Afterwards they then drove away in a diplomatic car. They had

190

gone first to the Embassy before the man booked into a small hotel near the railway station in Amien Street.

McQuillen meantime had been talking to the one of the Gardai left on duty at Nevin's house. He told him that some reporters had been there during the day but had left when told there was no one in the house. One was a bit more persistent than the others and kept asking questions. He particularly asked how many people were in the house at the time and if so where could they be contacted. McQuillen asked for a description of this man and wrote it down. He read it out to Maguire who nodded.

"That's our man John, at least now we have a description, see if we can put a name to it. It also looks as if M.I.5. may have joined us, I wonder what they are doing here?

His musings were interrupted by the arrival of Jean McKay, Val Nevin and the female Garda who spoke to Maguire.

"Inspector, we heard the news on the radio about the shooting, Jean is distraught, she insisted on coming over, I couldn't stop her"

The Inspector came around the desk and took his niece in his arms, she was crying and between sobs asked him.

"Uncle John, tell me its not true, Joe isn't dead, tell me o please tell me."

A fit of sobbing shook her body. Maguire gently led her to a chair and sat her down. His mind revolted at what he was going to tell the girl. She was his niece and very much in love with Kearns, but he could not jeopardise the investigation. Then there was always the possibility that Joe might yet meet his end by some other means before this whole thing was over. With a look at McQuillen he put his arm around the girls shoulder.

"I'm sorry Jean, very sorry but its true, they didn't have a chance, the news got to R.T.E. almost before I had heard it myself, I was just going over myself to tell you what had happened."

She just sat there, tears streaming down her cheeks, not saying a word and staring at the wall. Val Nevin came over and took her in her arms. Maguire gratefully stepped aside. McQuillen had left and returned with cups of tea one of which he offered the girl. She took it mechanically. The Garda Sergeant turned to The Inspector.

"Sir, don't you think that Jean would be better off at home with her mother and the child."

Maguire hesitated for just a moment.

"Yes Mary, I suppose you are right, get my wife on the phone she's already there and tell her what's happening, then take Jean home. Mrs. Nevin can go with her if she wishes, there's plenty of room for you all out there. I'll check with you later."

They were interrupted by the arrival of Maurice Curley who looked curiously at the girls as they left. He looked at Maguire.

"I, see you've been having some excitement since I saw you last. Is that the same Joe you introduced me to earlier?"

The Inspector waved him to a seat.

"Yes Maurice but he's not dead, we put out that story to confuse the enemy as they say, that girl will never forgive me when she finds out that I lied to her, may God forgive me. Tell me have you been to see Grant? I hear he's recovering at an alarming rate."

Curley grinned.

"We build them tough in the States John, he's very well as a matter of fact he might get out of hospital to night, he's been so arguementive about it they might just throw him out. The bullet just missed his lung, but only just. Say I'm glad your man is okay. Harry was telling me about him, for a newspaper reporter, he's all right. Only for him Harry would be dead."

Maguire gave him a sly grin.

"We're fairly tough here too Maurice, now tell me what's the total information on that ship, we know that its going to come in at a place about forty miles south of here called Ballingeary. What I would like to know is how much stuff is on board and its exact moment of arrival. We then might be able to get the whole lot of them together."

Curley nodded.

"From what we know up to the present, from our satellite picture and working on the size of the vessel we think it could have up to five hundred tons aboard. There are positively four people on board, three men and a woman. Our man in Benghazi says there was a fight with

192

the Mafia somewhere off Sicily and the Captain and Mate were killed along with all of the Italians. Two more Irish were killed as well. Their bodies are on board. That's it up to the present."

Maguire then gave Curley all his information then told him of the arrival of the Britisher earlier in the evening. Curley gave a low whistle.

"I wonder do they know something we don't. It would be interesting to talk to our friend, what do you think?"

Maguire was filling his pipe. He nodded to McQuillen who got up and left to organise the pick up of Jeremy Carter. Blowing out smoke he looked at his watch.

"It's eleven o clock Maurice I'm going home to bed. I suppose you have transport."

As Curley nodded Maguire went on.

"We will have our English friend here in the morning, say about eight, that's a reasonable time. McQuillen's gone to arrange it so I'll see you here in the morning. Good night Maurice."

The American, non-plussed, followed the Inspector out without a word.

Joe Kearns arrived at the cottage near Ballingeary and let himself in. It had remained undisturbed since he had left for Dublin. Tomorrow he would check out the pier. It might prove very interesting. He wondered if he should ring Jean and decided against it. No doubt Maguire would have told her by now that he was alive and well. He went into the kitchen, made some sandwiches and settled down to a mug of tea. He thought again about One Arm and the carnage and resolved there and then to to do his utmost to stop the men who were trying to take over the country. Maybe he would have a bit of luck tomorrow.

CHAPTER 21

On the Christopher Columbus George Reilly checked the course again as they crept up the Portuguese coast. At their present speed they would be off the Irish coast on the night of the twenty fifth of March. He had already decided they would take a direct line from the Spanish coast to the Tusker Rock off the South East of Ireland. There he would open his sealed orders. Fergus Doyle interrupted him.

"George, there's something puzzling me. Yesterday I was playing around with the radar when I noticed a blip. It seemed to be behind us. I thought it was another ship and went on deck with the glasses but after ten minutes of searching saw nothing. When I went back it still showed on the radar. Then it disappeared, a few minutes ago I checked again and there it was, still behind us. Maybe you would like to see for yourself."

The men went down to the radar set and Doyle pointed out the blip to Reilly who watched it for a time.

"That's strange Fergus, can you tell how far away it is or how large?"

Doyle gestured helplessly.

"This set is not the greatest. The rangefinder says it's about two miles behind us. There's no way I could tell the size. I'll keep a watch and if it gets any closer I'll call you."

Reilly watched the screen for some moments more.

"Right I'm going up to have a look. If its still there and I don't see anything we'll change course in an hour's time and see if it follows us. If it does we will have to try and find out what it is, providing of course it's not a fault in the set."

Going back to his cabin he collected a pair of powerful binoculars. He climbed up to the roof of the superstructure and scanned the seas behind the freighter without seeing anything. On the shore side he could see mountains and sandy beaches. A train of goods wagons moved across his line of vision. After another look behind the ship he climbed down.

The girl was waiting for him.

"What were you looking at George?"

"I was just admiring the scenery Francis, nothing special."

They leant against the side and watched the water churning back from the propellers. A bunch of seagulls positioned off the stern were wheeling and diving. Doyle appeared at their side.

"Sorry to bother you but the bad news is I've just picked up a gale warning for the area ahead. It's a Westerly force seven, gusting to storm force eight. I only hope this old tub can take it, I've heard that these Biscay storms can be very rough."

Reilly swore and looked up at the sky. This was all they needed. What should he do now, put in for shelter or risk it and keep going. It could take six or eight hours for the storm to blow itself out. The three of them were totally inexperienced in handling a ship in rough weather. True O'Shea and Doyle had worked on fishing trawlers off Ireland's West Coast but this was different, damn, there was nothing else for it except to try for a port and sit out the storm. Here again they would be taking a chance. George supposed that they would have a visit from Customs officers. They would try to bluff their way through. After all they were not unloading anything. Francis gave him a nudge.

"What will we do George? I don't fancy the prospect of a storm in this old bucket, do you think we can find a safe harbour?"

He looked at her for a moment, his brow knotted.

"I don't think we have a choice, we have no real sea experience, I'll go and have a look to see where we can go in."

In the bridge room he checked their position. The nearest place was Oporto, which was to have been their port of call to unload the tractors. About two hours would get them there just before dark. Giving Doyle instructions he went back out on deck. The wind had certainly freshened now and dark clouds were chasing across the sky. He felt the first drops of rain. The sea was capping the waves with white foamy crests and the ship was starting to bounce. Going back inside he tried to raise Oporto on the radio. After a while He made contact with an English speaking Portuguese who gave him instructions to approach the mouth of the river and await a pilot. About an hour later they sighted the lights of the port in the gathering dusk. Reilly thought grimly that they were getting there just in time. Gusts of wind were catching the ship and Doyle was doing very well to keep it going in a reasonably straight line. At the mouth of the river they dropped anchor and waited. Some time later a launch approached and the pilot came aboard and took the ship into the port, tying up at a wharf behind a grey coloured warship flying the British Ensign. Doyle shut down the engines and looked at Reilly.

"That's a bloody good one George, we're right behind a British destroyer, if they only knew what we have on board, ironic isn't it."

He gave a laugh and turned to John O'Shea who had come up from the engine room. Reilly told them to get a meal organised and they would all then have a good rest. The storm should have passed by morning according to the forecast so maybe they could leave early. As the Portuguese pilot was leaving two Customs Officers arrived. Reilly met them at the top of the gangway. One of them addressed him in perfect English.

"Good evening Captain, I'm afraid we must check your cargo manifest and the ship. Its just routine, we understand you are just here to shelter and that none of your crew will be going ashore."

Reilly nodded and handed them the cargo list. The Officer glanced through it and said.

"I see, farm machinery, may we have a look please?"

At that moment Francis appeared, she bid the men good evening and with a smile asked.

"Would you gentlemen like to join us in a glass of wine on the bridge when you've finished your inspection?"

The two men were looking at her with appreciation. The older one took of his cap and bowed.

"Madam that would be very nice thank you."

They moved off, Reilly leading the way. The men gave cursory glances at the packing cases plainly marked farm machinery and returned to the bridge where they drank some wine and left. It was raining solid sheets now and the ship was rising and falling with the waves, which were being pushed up the river by the wind and tide. The storm was building up, The wind whistling through the derricks and rattling them in their sockets. Reilly thought grimly, they were in the safest place. They would not have lasted the night at sea in that storm. A call from Francis announced the meal was ready and he went into the diner with the others.

Some time later the submarine Gadfly crept up the river and anchored beside the grey mass of the destroyer.

Michael McCall had not had a good day. He had returned from the meeting with the Inner Council to find Jack Monaghan sitting in his favourite armchair and drinking his whiskey. When he told McCall that he had not found out anything they did not know already he nearly exploded with rage. He paced up and down while the man in the chair calmly drank the rest of the whiskey, stood up, and spoke.

"I've sent two of the lads to find One Arm, they should be able to find out something about your man Kearns from him. Then if we can find him we'll find out what happened at Nevin's place. My guess is that Maguire has got the lads in custody and that Kearns and the American are free. If he gets them to talk the whole thing will go up in smoke. There's no sign of Ned either, they must have him as well."

McCall paced up and down clenching and unclenching his fists.

"We can't stop now, the ship is on its way and will be here around the twenty fifth. Everything is ready the men the trucks, everything. We've got to find out what's happening."

Monaghan poured himself another glass of whiskey. He tossed it around in the glass before answering.

"If they have got them they will be holding them in Harcourt Street. That's where Special Branch operates. There just might be a chance that I could get in there."

McCall looked at him doubtfully.

"Good God man you wouldn't have a chance, they would pick you up for sure."

197

Monaghan sipped his whiskey thoughtfully, his eyes faraway.

"There's only one way. Maybe I could get in, as a member of the civilian staff. I used to know a fellow who worked for the catering crowd who runs the canteen, if I could see him I might just do it."

The phone rang on the desk opposite and McCall picked up. As Monaghan watched his face turned a shade of purple before he raged into the mouthpiece.

"You stupid bloody fools, I gave orders there was to be no violence there was no necessity for that, it was stupid, stupid. Where are you now. Right, get back to headquarters and stay there. I'll sort this out later"

He turned, slammed down the receiver and turned, furiously to Monaghan.

"Those two bloody fools of yours, they found One Arm allright. He was with some one else, they think it might have been Kearns. They were heading down Harcourt Street, towards Garda Headquarters. What did the bloody fools do, they shot them up. They think, only think, mark you that they killed the two of them. Is there any end to this stupidity. Maguire and his men will have a field day, the Government will go berserk, turn on that television we might just get some news."

Monaghan turned the knob and the screen lit up. The announcer, grim faced, was describing the carnage. When McCall heard that five were dead and four more injured, he threw his hands in the air. Two of the dead had been identified as Joseph Kearns and Frank O Brien. The names of the others were being withheld until relatives had been informed. The Taoiseach came on and condemned the atrocity and said that the perpetrators would be hunted down. Monahan switched the set off and stood up.

"I'm going down there. This might be the chance we've been waiting for there will be a lot of confusion down there tonight."

McCall turned to him.

"You could be right, I'll come with you. At least I will be recognised as a sympathetic TD. I'll try to get an interview with one of the Inspector's, that might get us into the building. After that we can work out our own salvation."

When they reached Harcourt Street it was cordoned off. At the barrier a Garda on duty recognised him and after a few words they were let through. At the scene of the shooting lights had been rigged and the place was being searched for empty cartridge cases and other clues. Pools of blood marked the spot where the bodies had lain. McCall surveyed the scene for some time, being given the story by a plain clothes Sergeant. Al the time he muttered,

"Terrible, terrible, something will have to be done about all this."

McCall thanked the Sergeant and they made their way to Garda Headquarters where he would tried to get to the Commissioner who was at a meeting of Senior officers. As they turned into the gateway a car slowed to let them pass. McCall glanced at it as it went by. In the back seat he recognised Jean McKay. She was dabbing at her eyes with a white handkerchief. Beside her was Val Nevin. McCall caught Monaghan's arm.

"Did you see who was in that car, no, of course not, you would not have recognised her. That was Jean McKay, my secretary, I knew she must have fallen for Kearns. He must be dead all right otherwise what would she be doing here, Jack you go and get a car and watch for them coming out, find out where she goes, they can only come out one way, down that street there."

He indicated the road opposite.

"I'll go on in and see what I can find out."

Monaghan crossed the road and took up his position on the pavement. About ten minutes later a Toyota Carina drew up almost opposite him and the driver parked and locked it. Carrying his briefcase he entered the apartment block some distance away. A light went on in one of the top windows and the blinds were drawn. Monaghan crossed the road and taking a bunch of keys from his pocket started on the lock of the Carina The fourth one he tried opened the door and he slipped inside. He tried the key in the ignition and the engine started, switching it off he settled down to wait.

Inside the Garda building McCall eventually got to speak to a Superintendent Murray who was dealing with the press. He tried to question him about the events leading up to the attack. The Superintendent was adept at parrying questions both from the press and McCall and ended the session after agreeing with McCall that it was disgraceful that citizens of Dublin were no longer safe on the streets. McCall had failed to learn anything further. From what he could gather the Special Branch had no idea who was responsible. His request for a meeting with Detective Inspector Maguire was met with a blank refusal, being told that he was too busy to see anyone. McCall then left and went to the White Leprauchen to talk to the two assassins. Some time afterwards Jean Mc Kay, Val Nevin, and the Garda escort left for Sandymount. No one noticed the Red Toyota move away from the kerb and follow the unmarked Garda car.

Colonel Mark Philpot was dining at his club when his buzzer went. Excusing himself he withdrew to a private room where he received the following message from his office. It was from Gadfly.

"Target in port to ride out storm. Have joined them. Await instructions. Pritchard."

Philpot went back to his table and finished his meal. He then left by taxi for his office where he dictated orders to Pritchard to place limpet mines on the ship's hull, which could be detonated by radio signal. If at all possible he was to find out the exact nature of the ships cargo and its final destination.

In the port of Oporto the storm was at its height. Huge waves rolled up the estuary raising the ships on their chains some eight to ten feet at a time. On board Columbus Reilly and the others lay in their bunks sleeping. In the Gadfly Pritchard read Philpot's message and swore. On a night like this to try to plant explosives would be next to impossible. It would be best to wait and see if the weather calmed down before attempting to do the job. He sent for two crewmen who were experts in underwater demolition and asked them to prepare the mines and be ready to slip over the side and plant them when the opportunity came. After some thought he decided to have a chat with the Customs people. He was lucky to find the office only a short distance away. Here he explained to a poker faced Senior Officer what his mission was and about his suspicions that the ship contained arms. At least, Pritchard thought, the man understands English. The Officer picked up a phone and spoke rapidly in Portuguese with sidelong glances at Pritchard. He put the instrument down and dialled another number.

A short time later two Custom Officials came in and spoke to him. He in turn pointed to Pritchard and spoke in English.

"Captain these are the men who checked the ship when it arrived. They tell me its carrying farm machinery according to the manifest. The crates are also stamped farm machinery. They were down in the holds and did not notice anything out of the ordinary."

Pritchard nodded and asked.

"Where do the papers say they came from."

One of the men replied.

"The papers say they came from Trieste."

Pritchard thanked them and wondered on his way back if there was any chance of getting into the ships hold. Back in Gadfly he set his alarm for o two hours and turned in for a few hours sleep.

CHAPTER 22

At seven-o clock on the morning of the twenty sixth of March, John Mc Quillen and another man entered the Railway hotel. He asked for the number of Jeremy Carter's room and was told number twenty-five. McQuillen knocked on the door. Silence, he knocked again. A sleepy voice answered.

"Yes, what is it?"

"Mr Carter this is the police, will you open the door please?"

The door opened and McQuillen found himself looking at a tall slim man who gazed at him with mocking blue eyes.

"Mr Carter, will you get dressed please and come with us."

Carter smiled and gestured for them to enter.

"Gentlemen, I'm hardly in a position to refuse your request now, am I? I'll just be a moment or two, you don't mind if I have a quick shower and a shave? I suppose breakfast is out of the question, no, I thought so."

This was in reply to a shake of McQuillens head. When they arrived at the Garda building, Maguire and Curley were waiting. Carter looked at them curiously as he entered. Maguire indicated a chair to him and he sat down.

"Mr.Carter, I'm Detective Inspector Maguire, this is Colonel Maurice Curley of the American C.I.A. We have a good idea of who you are and why you're here. I called you in this morning because we are in the middle of a crisis of sorts. We know you are probably M.I.5. Now it looks as if we all know something, which would be of assistance to the others, What I want to know if you will tell us why you are here and what they know in London. You are M.I.5. Are you not?

Carter nodded.

"Inspector I have no idea what's happening, I was just told to get over here and find out as much as I could about what is going on. I do know my boss would not have sent me unless he knew something. What I would suggest is that I could get in touch with him and perhaps he could come over here and talk with you".

Maguire looked at Curley, who nodded. Maguire asked.

"How soon can you contact him?"

Carter looked at his watch.

"I can get him now if I can use a phone."

Maguire pushed the instrument across to him and he dialled a number.

"Good morning sir, Carter here. It's about that order. The head people here would like to discuss the matter personally with you. Can you get here as soon as possible? They say it is imperative that the whole deal is clarified within the next few hours. You will come this morning, good, I'll meet you at the airport, Thank you Sir."

Carter put down the phone and told Maguire.

"He will be here about eleven thirty Inspector."

Maguire looked at Curley with satisfaction. He then gave Carter a run down on the whole situation and the impending arrival of the ship. Carter then left with McQuillen to get some breakfast and go to the airport to meet Colonel Mark Philpot. After they had left Maguire turned to Curley.

"Well Maurice, what do you think of that. At least we know the British know something. Now about this ship maybe they know something about it that we don't.

Maguire struck a match and sucked at his pipe. He pressed a bell on his desk and ordered a car. Looking at Curley he gave him a smile.

"I think I'd like to have a look at your place down in Kildare Maurice, your old satellite tracking station should be able to tell us something."

Curley gave a burst of laughter.

"John, you old so and so how long have you known?"

Maguire winked.

"Since it first started up Maurice, since it first started up. Come on, I want to be back for our English friends arrival."

When they reached the factory in Kildare, Curley introduced Maguire to a rather embarrassed Manager. They then went to the section where the tracking of the spy satellites was carried out. Maguire was fascinated by what he saw. There was a full report on the progress of the ship from the time it had left Libya. Including photographs of the vessel at sea. The fact that the ship had docked in Oporto the previous evening had been noted. The Inspector asked why and was told it was due to the heavy storm in the area. Maguire was impressed and asked the operator.

"Do you think you could keep a special watch on that ship and follow its course. We think its heading for Ballingeary. If you could plot its exact time of arrival it would be of great help to us."

The man nodded and looked at Curley who told him to pass on all information direct to Maguire's office.

When they got back to Dublin they found Carter and Colonel Mark Philpot awaiting them. After introductions all round Maguire explained the situation giving the American and Irish positions. Philpot listened in silence until they had finished. He then explained why he had sent Carter to Dublin. From his briefcase he produced photographs of the crew of the Columbus as taken from the submarine. Maguire instantly recognised George Reilly and the other two He also identified the girl as Francis Coughlin remarking that she was an ardent Revolutionary and Marxist. Philpot looked at the others.

"The question is, gentlemen, how do we find out exactly what is going to take place on that weekend and how do we stop it?"

Maguire reached for the phone.

"I'm going to question the man we arrested a couple of days ago, we have left him alone for a few days and have been feeding him a drug which may let him answer our questions."

He gave an order and a few moments later a Garda arrived with a rather quiet Ned. If Joe Kearns could have seen him he would have been surprised. Ned was not the aggressive man he had seen in Nevin's house. His movements were slow and he seemed in a daze.

Maguire nodded to the Garda who put the man sitting on a chair.

"Well Ned and how are they treating you? Is everything all right?"

Maguire asked. The man seemed to think for a moment before replying.

"Yes Mr Maguire everything's fine."

Maguire studied him for a moment.

"Ned, you were telling me about this ship that's coming in shortly and what's going to happen on the holiday weekend, now, what's going on at all Ned?"

Beads of sweat started to form on the man's forehead and his hands clenched and unclenched. He slowly shook his head from side to side.

"Don't know, don't know what's going to happen, don't know, don't know."

He kept shaking his head from side to side. Maguire spoke gently to him.

"Now Ned that's not what you told me yesterday. You said that you and your friends were going to be allright after the March April weekend. Tell me Ned is Michael McCall one of the leaders? I think he is"

The man gave a sudden start at the mention of McCall's name. Maguire went on.

"We know that McCall is the leader Ned and that you know what's going on. Be sensible and tell us, it will be all the better for yourself I promise."

Ned looked at them, his eyes blinking. When he spoke his voice was a whisper.

"All I know Mr Maguire is that they are going to take over the Government, as God's my Judge that's it, they're going to do it, believe me, if they find out I've told you anything they'll kill me for sure."

Maguire nodded to the Garda who took Ned out. He turned to the others.

"That gentlemen is it. We know what's going to happen. We don't know all the people involved at the moment. I think that the place for this is certainly the Government meeting at Ballyorney Castle on the holiday weekend. Every precaution will be taken. I don't need to tell you that these people are left wing and probably backed by Russia. It would be disastrous if this country were to become another Cuba. Do I make myself clear?"

Philpot was polishing his glasses. He put them on and looked at Maguire.

"Inspector, before I left London I had a meeting with the PM. She has had a report from the Royal Air Force of several large Russian factory ships moving out into the Atlantic. I think we should arrange for a twenty four-hour surveillance. When I get back I'll see to it."

Curley broke in.

I'll get our boys on the job. There's no way this coup can be allowed to happen. I'm going to see the President and talk to him about the situation. I hope you all realise we are on the verge of world war three here."

The three men looked at each other in silence. Maguire was first to speak.

"Let's hope that Joe Kearns can find out something in Ballingeary. I can't make a move until they do. We're tailing McCall and a few more but so far we have nothing to go on except those recordings of his conversation with those men about Grant and Kearns. All I can say is for us all to keep in touch and work together until this thing is resolved."

All three shook hands before dispersing.

Joe left the cottage near Ballingeary and drove down to the town's harbour area. He skirted the piers where the fishing trawlers were unloading their catch and turned on to a road, which led through the sand dunes towards a fairly high rocky promintory which jutted out into the sea. In the distance he could see quarry workings. There was a high wire fence stretching across the road and disappearing through the sand dunes and the rocky breakwater in the direction of the beach. Near the entrance he turned into a car park which was bounded by huge boulders piled on top of each other. He parked the car and climbed up the rock wall. In the distance he could see the jetty jutting out into the sea. Climbing back down he walked towards the gate into the complex. A large notice stating that it was private property told him admittance was for business only. Two large lorries carrying loads of aggregate passed him heading for the mountain of stuff at the end of a conveyor belt leading out to the pier.

He walked on. There was no one in sight. In the distance a loading shovel with a bulldozer blade was pushing more stones into another mound. Joe had just reached the entrance to the jetty when a young man wearing a baseball cap and greasy overalls stepped out of a shed in front of him and stood waiting for his approach. Joe gave him a smile.

"Morning, not a bad day."

The man looked at him, unsmiling.

"You shouldn't be in here, this is private property, did you want something?"

"I just wanted to have a look at the pier, someone told me it was a great place to fish from, is that right?"

The man glowered at him.

"Sometimes they fish there at night but it hasn't been very good lately, anyway no one is supposed to be in there at all. Its too dangerous we lock the gates at night now so you would have to park your car and walk there with all your gear. I don't think it would be worth your while at all."

Joe gave him another smile.

"Thanks very much anyhow. I suppose your right, it would hardly be worth all the trouble."

He started back towards the gates feeling the man's eyes following him.

Back at the cottage he searched around and found a fishing rod, reel and some black waterproof rain gear. In a bag on a shelf in the garage he found weights and hooks. All this he placed in the boot of the car. In the house the freezer provided a couple of Mackerel which he could use for bait and provide an excuse if he was stopped.

At two a.m. in Oporto harbour Pritchard was awakened by his alarm. The two demolition men were waiting in their wet suits. By now the storm had abated but outside the rain was coming down in sheets. Pritchard gave them their instructions about the planting of the mines before slipping over the side with them. He approached the ship from the stern and made his way to the bow anchor chain, which he clambered up and landed on the deck. He ducked down behind the front derrick. The stern superstructure was in total darkness except for a light burning in the bridge room. Pritchard made his way stealthily towards the stern. There was no sign of life. He found a door and opened it slowly stepping into a corridor. A flight of stairs ran downwards towards the holds. To his right were four doors leading into cabins, which he took to be, crew quarters. He moved down the stairs towards the storage area. At the bottom he was in total darkness. Taking a small torch from his bag he opened a door and stepped into the hold. Closing the door behind him he slipped the catch on and switched on the lights.

Crates of all shapes and sizes were stacked floor to ceiling all labelled farm machinery. Making his way along he found a side passage where boxes about a Metre long were stacked. Taking a short steel bar from his belt he slipped it under one of the lids and heaved upwards. The wood splintered and opened a little. He adjusted the bar and got better leverage and the lid came off. Pritchard reached in and removed something wrapped in oilproof paper. When he unwrapped it there was no mistaken it for what it was, was, an AK47 Kalashnikof rifle known to terrorists the world over as the Widow Maker. Carefully he replaced the weapon and put back the lid pressing the nails back with the bar. Now he knew for certain what the cargo was and where it was going. Philpot would be pleased.

Pritchard put off the lights and slowly opened the door. He started up the stairs and had almost reached the top when he heard a movement above him. Shrinking down he looked upwards as a figure moved across the passageway and out on to the deck. Very slowly he took out his automatic from its waterproof holster and moved cautiously towards the door, which was slightly ajar. Peering through the gap he could just see someone standing against the rail looking towards the lights of the city. In the beam from the lighthouse he saw that it was a girl. She was only about six feet away and blocking his path to the bows. Something seemed to be attracting her attention as she was now leaning over the side looking down at the water. Pritchard saw his chance and pushing the door open he slipped through and down the steps to the deck below. He had almost reached the anchor chain when he heard a crack and felt something hit him in the left arm and he stumbled to his knees. At the same time he heard a shout. The girl was shooting at him. What's more she had hit him in the arm. Regaining his feet he climbed over the side and dropped like a stone to the water narrowly missing the anchor chain on the way down. He hit the water and went under. As he surfaced a light was being played on the water from above. Pritchard hugged the side of the ship and treaded water. Then he moved slowly along the hull and past the stern. Coming on a line of steel steps leading to the quay he climbed up to the top. Using a line of railway wagons for cover he made his way back to Gadfly.

A doctor from the destroyer dressed his wounded arm. The bullet had plowed a furrow in the fleshy part of his shoulder. Another half inch and it would have struck bone. The two frogmen reported that they had attached the mines to the hull of the ship. A message was sent to Philpot in London and relayed to him as he breakfasted in the Embassy in Dublin.

O'Shea bursting into his cabin shouting awakened George Reilly.

"George, get up, there's shooting outside, come on."

Reilly pulled his pants on and a jacket and went outside. The wind had almost died but it was still raining. In the light from the masthead which had been switched on he could see Francis Couglin, gun in hand looking over the side into the water. Reilly and O'Shea rushed towards her, Reilly grabbing the gun and shoving it under his jacket.

"Francis, what the hell is going on? Did you fire those shots? What the hell are you trying to do, get us all arrested, if anyone has seen or heard anything we could be in big trouble."

She turned towards them.

"There was someone on the ship. I saw him near here and shot at him. He jumped over the side, I didn't get a good look at him, he seemed to be wearing black oilskins or something."

Reilly shone his torch around the deck. O'Shea leaned over the side. Along the quay nothing stirred. The rain beat steadily down. Reilly looked at the girl.

"Are you sure you saw someone Francis, it's very easy to make a mistake in the dark and weather like this."

She looked at him with scorn.

"I'm telling you I saw someone, he was here at this spot and he jumped into the water, I'm not that stupid that I don't know when I'm looking at a man or a shadow."

She brushed past them and back to her cabin. O'Shea came back after looking round all the decks and asked Reilly.

"What do you think George? Did she see someone?"

Reilly walked around the deck his eyes darting here and there.

"I don't know, if she did see someone who was he? Maybe he was just a common thief, after all it is dockland. Go and see what the forecast is we'll get something to eat and see how soon we can get out of here. As soon as its light I want to be sailing down this river, pilot or no pilot, do you think we could get out to sea on our own?

O'Shea gave a grin.

"Get Fergus and tell her ladyship to rustle up some grub. It'll be light in about two hours and we'll be on our way."

Reilly went below and checked the ship. Nowhere could he find anything amiss until he got to the hold. In the passageway between the cases he found some small pools of water, proof positive that someone had been there recently. Climbing back to the wheelhouse he gave orders for immediate sailing. A little later at first light O'Shea swung the bows around and started slowly down river. In the bows Reilly kept watch with binoculars and hand held radio for the marker buoys. They reached the mouth of the estuary without incident and set a Westerly course for the distant Irish coast.

Joe Kearns left the cottage about eight-o clock and drove down to the car park at the entrance to the complex. There were two cars already there and a number of men were dressing in oilskins and assembling fishing rods. The gates were closed and locked although there were lights around some of the buildings in the distance. Joe donned his gear and taking his rod followed the others over the gates. The pier area was in total darkness except for the lights of the fishermen. Kearns let them get some distance ahead before setting up his rod between two pillars and leaning it on the rail. He waited for the others to get settled into their positions before he moved back towards the buildings. To his left a wall of boulders formed a breakwater for the pier. The first building he came to was where the conversation with the young man had taken place that morning. It was in total darkness. Joe tried the door but it was padlocked. Moving to the next building he saw a broken window. Pulling himself up he climbed inside. It seemed to be filled with a couple of large dumper trucks. He shone his torch around, shading the light with his hand. The front doors contained a small wicket with a Yale lock. Slipping the catch he stepped out and pulled it behind him and walked towards the concrete pillars of the loading terminal. He had almost reached them when he heard a sound as if a sliding door was been opened. Slipping behind a large rock he peered into the darkness. Low voices could be heard approaching and two shadows passed by about two metres away. The sound of a car engine was heard as the machine headed towards the main gates. Joe moved in the direction the men had come. In front of him he could barely see the cliff face towering upwards in the darkness. In the distance headlights lit up the sky as the men drove towards Ballingeary. Joe felt the rockface, which was wet and cold with water seeping down it. His foot caught in something and he fell forward putting out his hands to save himself from the cliff face. Something moved and he heard a slight noise. He pushed against the rock and felt it move. Joe pushed harder and the rockface moved on oiled rollers. He slipped inside and closed the door behind him Switching on his torch he found himself in a huge cavern hewn out of the rock. In front of him stretching back into the cave were six big identical eight wheeled lorries painted in Irish army grey complete with company numbers and insignia. Along the wall on racks hung a line of Irish army uniforms, complete even down to the boots. Behind the lorries were three Land Rovers, which were usually used as escorts with army convoys. Joe whistled through his teeth. So this was how they would move the arms around the country. What better way to get through garda checkpoints. No one would query an army convoy moving openly around the country. It was brilliant. These people were one jump ahead. He moved further back into the cavern.

It was obvious that there must have been more shipments of arms because more boxes were stacked back there. He found sleeping quarters and cooking facilities as well as a portable shower and toilet unit. There was a high powered radio with an antenna stretching up the wall towards the roof. A line of steel steps fixed into the rock went up alongside. From the current of cold air he deduced there was another entrance from above. Joe had seen enough. He made his way back to the entrance. The door moved easily back, and he slipped outside closing it behind him. Making his way to the pier he collected his fishing gear and drove back to the cottage. On the phone to Maguire he told him what he had found. The Inspector told Joe that the ship had left Oporto and at present speed and course would probably arrive at Ballingeary on Saturday night about midnight.

CHAPTER 23

During the day Maguire met again with the American and the Englishman and discussed the situation. Philpot told him about the planting of the mines and the search of the ship and confirmed its cargo. The Russian ships were under surveillance and an American aircraft carrier had been ordered from the Mediterranean along with a couple of destroyers to patrol off the Southern Irish cost. The Inspector was sure everything was covered. He could do nothing more until the others made their move. Then he would have to move fast himself. The arms ship was the key. They could destroy it before it arrived, or wait until it unloaded and follow the trail then quietly arrest everyone involved. He had already sent McQuillen and a crew to check out the Castle and the search had revealed nothing. Maguire was sure he was right. The assassination of the Government would take place there. It had to be there, on that weekend. Kearns had mentioned gas. How were they going to get it into the place. They would know that security would be intense. If he arrested McCall now the only charge he could pin on him would be conspiracy and maybe the kidnapping of Grant and the others. There was too much at stake. Better let the whole thing run its course. He went home to get some sleep.

McCall meantime had received word from Jack Monaghan about Jean McKay and Val Nevin. He wondered how much information the Special Branch had learned from the girls. Kearns at least was dead. So far there had been no moves against him self. He wondered why, they must be playing a waiting game. A little insurance might not go astray. Monaghan would be ringing him for more instructions in an hour. If they could seize the girls and hold them until the coup was over it might stop Maguire from doing anything further. He would personally see that no harm came to them. There should be very little loss of life in the forthcoming coup.

When Monaghan rang he gave him directions about the girls and told him that he had already sent three men and a large van to meet him. The girls were to be taken to Ballingeary and held there. It was three a.m. before Monaghan made his move. He had waited until he was sure all in the house would be fast asleep. Monaghan and two of the others made their way to the back of the building where they found a basement window. It was short work with a penknife on the rotting wood before the pane of glass was removed and one of the men went inside. He opened the back door and let the others in. They crept upstairs, Monaghan with a chloroform bottle and pad in his hand. The first bedroom they found was Jean's mother who was sleeping soundly. Monaghan gently closed the door. In the next room Val Nevin was asleep her dark hair spread around the pillow. Monaghan advanced and poured some of the liquid onto the pad and gently placed it over her nose and mouth and she went limp. In the next room was Jean McKay. It was all over in a couple of minutes. The girls were wrapped in bedclothes and brought out to the van. Monaghan picked up articles of clothing and stuffing them into a bag brought them out to the van. The whole job had taken just fifteen minutes. They drove to a disused factory where they waited for daybreak and the morning traffic. Monaghan reasoned that it would be safer travelling in daylight and less likely to be stopped by Garda roadblocks. He would send the men with the girls to Ballingeary emphasise that they were to come to no harm. They were to be treated with the utmost courtesy at all times. The van reached Ballingeary at about nine thirty. At about the same time an envelope was handed in to Garda Headquarters for Detective Inspector John Maguire.

On board the Columbus George Reilly opened his sealed orders and read through them carefully. The orders were brief. He was to bring the ship as far as the Tusker rock. There he would put out the call sign. They would be answered and then guided into the jetty at Ballingeary by radio. When the ship berthed it would be unloaded and then taken out to deep water and scuttled. The crew would then proceed to Dublin to assist in the coup. Reilly carefully burnt the papers and went up to the bridge where O'Shea was watching the wheel, which was fixed on a course towards the Irish coast. Reilly plotted a new course to Rosslare and the Tusker and from there to Ballingeary. He calculated the ship's speed and distance. At present speed they should be in Ballingeary at about midnight to morrow night. He told O Shea who threw his arms to Heaven.

"George, I can't wait to get off this old tub, you know we've been aboard far too long, I could do with a bit of action."

Reilly nodded and thinking deeply walked outside to the rail. There was a fair sea running and the ship was dipping its bows in the grey waters. O'Shea is right, he thought, I'm getting pretty fed up myself. There's nothing as monotonous as a bloody ship and four people in the middle of the ocean. A couple of miles behind them the radar operator in the Gadfly watched the blip on his screen and made another note on his report sheet. Pritchard lay in his bunk and thought about the girl who had nearly ended his career. Lucky for him that the bullet had hit the fleshy part of his arm. It smarted a bit under the dressing but on the whole he had not fared too bad. He fell asleep thinking about the face of the girl who had tried to kill him.

John Maguire arriving at Special Branch Headquarters at about nine a.m. on Saturday morning he had slept badly and had a mild headache. His nose was stuffed and wondered if he was going down with flu. In the lift up to his office he caught up with John McQuillen and they both entered the office together. There was an envelope on the desk with his name on it, which he opened. The words blurred before his eyes as he read them twice. Without a word he handed it to McQuillen who read it and his face went white. He read it again, aloud.

"We have Miss McKay and Mrs. Nevin. It is up to you to protect them. They will be quite safe as long as our plans are not interfered with. Their lives are in your hands."

Maguire sagged in his chair. He read the note again. For once he was at a loss for words. McQuillen grabbed a phone and dialled the McKay house. Presently a child's voice answered sleepily.

"Hello"

McQuillen spoke softly to the child.

"Hello Joanna, could you get Sergeant Kathleen for me please, tell her its urgent."

The child answered yes and he heard the phone being put down. A minute which felt like an hour elapsed before he heard the Sergeants voice.

215

"This is McQuillen here Special Branch, will you go now and check if Mrs. Nevin and Miss McKay are all right, don't ask any questions just do it, I'll hang on."

He heard a strangled gasp and the line went dead. She was back on almost immediately.

"They're both gone, the bedclothes and everything, it looks as if they were taken during the night. I found a pice of cotton wool and a bottle on the floor it smells of chloroform, what will I do?

McQuillen looked to Maguire as he spoke.

"Do nothing we will be there shortly."

He hit the cradle and dialled again for a car. On the road McQuillen drove like a madman until Maguire who by now had recovered somewhat muttered to him.

"Slow down John, better get there in one piece than not at all. There's no rush really the bastards are long gone."

McQuillen grunted and spat out of the window.

"We should have expected this, it was bloody stupid of us, we should never have left them without a proper guard."

Maguire sucked at his pipe and gazed out at a row of small cottages as they swept by.

"It's me they're after John, they must know that Jean is my niece. They think it will stop me keeping after them, it also means that we have them worried. That bloody ship will be arriving to night, they're not taking any chances that we might know about, this is a warning, its hands off or the girls die and believe me they are quite capable of doing just that. What we can do about it I don't know, I suppose we will just have to play it by ear."

He lapsed into silence and a few minutes later the car stopped in the driveway of the house. The Sergeant, looking flustered came to meet them. She addressed Maguire.

"Morning sir, I must apologise for this, I didn't hear a thing, they came in through the basement window and went out through the front door. The mother is not awake yet and the child doesn't know."

She led them into the house. In the hall they met Mrs. McKay in her dressing gown an inquiring look on her face. Maguire led her into the sitting room. McQuillen and the Sergeant went up to the bedrooms. Here he noted the missing bedclothes. There was no sign of a struggle. He was shown the pad and the bottle and confirmed it was chloroform. The two men hurried out. Afterwards when they got back to HQ. The Inspector sat behind his desk and lit up his pipe. McQuillen phoned around looking for any information about any unusual activity during the night but the surveillance teams reported that their charges had all retired at between eleven and midnight and not left their homes during the night. Maguire was worried. The safety of the girls was paramount, yet he could not relax his efforts. Young Jean had certainly being through enough these last few days without this latest episode.

He reached for the phone and called Maurice Curley asking him to come over. Then he got on to Philpot at the British Embassy and asked him the same. When the men got there they were accompanied by Carter and to Maguire's surprise Harry Grant. The Inspector told them of the latest kidnapping. Curley looked into space and Philpot looked serious. Curley spoke first.

"John with all due respect about the girls this is something too big. We can't let them get away with taking over the country."

Philpot reminded them. The ship could be destroyed at any moment. All he had to do was give orders to the Gadfly's Captain. Grant wanted to know all the details of the girls kidnapping and McQuillen took him to one side and briefed him and Carter. Curley suggested they arrest McCall. Maguire shook his head.

"I think at this stage we really can't do that, beside I want the whole lot of those bastards. The only thing we have against him is that tape. Arrest him and the others carry on, no, if we get the lot it will be the answer to our prayers. Don't forget they don't know how much we know, they don't know your here and they don't know the Colonel's submarine is tracking the ship. We have to play this very carefully. Now the ship will arrive tonight. I think we will just follow the trails to their destinations and then pick up everyone we can. I will ask the technical boys if they have anything we could fix to the trucks to guide us when they leave."

Grant broke in to Curley.

"Did you bring any of those darts we used in Germany that time we followed those Russian Agents."

Curley nodded, he explained to the others.

"These are small darts which can be shot into the woodwork or similar, they send out a radio signal, we can follow them with a monitor and locate them anywhere, lucky I brought them along."

He opened his briefcase and took out a packet. Inside were six objects, which looked like small bullets of twenty-two calibre except that they had a very pointed front like an ordinary dart. Grant looked at Carter across the table.

"They also contain a deadly poison which can kill in thirty seconds if you happen to need it."

He took the dart and pointed to the top where there were two lines and an arrow.

"You just twist that to make your selection, blue for the radio, red for the poison and bingo you're in business."

He put it back in the packet and looking at Curley said.

"I suppose I had better go down to Ballingeary and find Joe, It looks as if its going to be a long night."

Curley nodded and turned to Maguire. It might be a good thing if Colonel Philpot's man went down there as well, he could be a help to Joe and Harry."

Maguire nodded and looked at the Colonel who answered.

"Yes, yes, of course, there's no problem there, you will go with Harry, Jeremy."

The Inspector then took an envelope from a drawer in his desk.

"Gentlemen, I think the time has come for me to resign as Head of Special Branch. I'm appointing John McQuillen here as my acting successor. I feel that this will be a signal to the subversives that I have no further interest in the situation. It will make their position as regards the girls a bit pointless, they might even let them go, I will leave the country this evening."

He spoke to McQuillen.

"John, you make arrangements to have the news put in all the papers and on television."

McQuillen made to protest but Maguire waved him to silence. He continued.

"When Harry and Mr. Carter get to Ballingeary the three of you should be able to get those darts on to the lorries when the ship comes in. Remember, try not to get into any trouble, Joe Kearns says they are going to use trucks painted in Irish army colours. Try and get any information back here to John. He will look after things at this end. Now gentlemen, I will say goodbye and be on my way, thank you for all your help."

He stood up and shook hands with all of them before donning his coat and leaving his letter of resignation on the desk. Later, on the first of the evening papers and on television there was the announcement of the sudden resignation of Detective Inspector Maguire and photographs in the later editions of him and his wife embarking at Dublin Airport for a holiday in the Bahamas. On the six p.m. news they were shown on television. Michael McCall watched the news as he grabbed a meal before his departure to Ballingeary. It angered him to think that Maguire had thrown down the gauntlet leaving him with the two girls. On the other hand he had at a single stroke removed the most experienced counter espionage Detective in the twenty-six counties from the scene. He felt a glow of satisfaction surge through him. Maguire could not suspect anything out of the ordinary or he would not have resigned. McCall felt that it must have been on the cards for some time. He finished his meal with evident satisfaction and went out to his car to drive to Ballingeary.

Following John McQuillen's instructions Grant and Carter arrived at the cottage where Joe Kearns was staying at about seven p.m. that Saturday evening. Joe welcomed them and was delighted to see his friend looking so fit. He told them about the subversive's hideaway. Grant told him about the kidnapping and Maguire's resignation. Joe could not understand why Maguire had resigned and worried about what was happening to Jean. Grant urged him to forget everything for the moment. The big thing was the arrival of the ship. He had brought some equipment with him and proceeded to distribute it to the others. Each man had a black one piece overall with several large pockets. A packet of ten darts and a small compressed air gun along with an automatic pistol in a waterproof pouch followed. Joe already had his gun in one of his pockets. Grant insisted he take the automatic as well. They drove down to the harbour and parked near the deserted trawler pier. Then they blackened their faces and moved around to the beach where they started to make their way on foot towards the complex and the pier where the ship would berth.

The night was cold with a soft rain falling but before they had covered half distance they were sweating. A short time later they climbed the bank of boulders to have a look. They were almost directly in line with the gates and the fence. Grant reached into his haversack and produced what looked like ordinary sun glasses. When they put them on they could see almost perfectly. They were special infra red lenses.

A car drove up and they could see two men who had been sitting in a small van move forward to meet the vehicle, which stopped. The gates were opened and the car went through. Retracing their steps they followed the beach until they came to the rocky breakwater. When they climbed this they were inside the compound beside the road leading to the jetty. There was no sign of life in or near the pier. Joe led them around to the building from where he had entered through the cliff face. The car was parked close to the wall but what caught their eye were the six huge lorries which were now lined up nose to tail in the darkness. Grant nudged the others and pointed to the trucks. The darts were fired into the canvas hoods. The sound of engines signalled the arrival of six more trucks with men dressed in army uniforms and a command Land Rover with pennants flying. The men made their way to the cliff face and disappeared inside. Grant went forward with more darts. The three then withdrew to the hut Joe had found on his first visit to await the arrival of the vessel.

On the Columbus that evening off the Tusker rock Reilly started to send out his signal. He wondered what would happen now. The Irish navy patrolled these waters and there was also air surveillance. They had been broadcasting every quarter of an hour for over an hour when O'Shea came to him elation on his face.

"George, come on they're on the radio, they want to talk to you."

Both men rushed to the radio room. George took the mike in his hand and O'Shea pressed send, Reilly called.

"Sweep calling home come in please."

The reply came swiftly.

"Sweep proceed to destination you will be met on arrival. Unload half cargo and receive further instructions, out."

Reilly looked at O'Shea.

"What the hell do they mean, are they telling me to sail this bloody ship further, I want to get off this thing, I'm fed up to the teeth with this bloody ship."

O'Shea grinned at him.

"Let's get there first George, then we can argue with them afterwards."

Reilly muttered something incomprehensible and stormed out. Francis Coughlin watched him go a frown on her face. She had heard the conversation in the radio room and ducked out of the way as Reilly came out. It was not like him. His nerves must be beginning to fray. She would have to keep an eye on him. He also seemed to be avoiding her again lately. She went in to talk to O'Shea. Reilly was up in the bows. It was cold with raindrops hitting off his face, a feeling of total dejection had settled on him over the last few days. Something was telling him that the whole business was going horribly wrong. He could not shake the feeling off. Yet he knew there was nothing he could do about it. He leaned against the rail and wondered what the bloody hell he was doing there at all.

It was one a.m. when the ship finally docked at the jetty in Ballingeary. It had been the easiest thing in the world to steer the freighter alongside and tie up. Unloading started immediately by about thirty men in army fatigues and under arc lamps, which had been switched on. The whole scene was like a genuine Irish Army Operation with armed sentries positioned at the pier entrances and Officers in Land Rovers overseeing the operations. George Reilly and the others were taken to the cavern. Here, they were showered with congratulated by the others. McCall and the girl's father thanked him for getting the ship through and then called him to one side.

"George, I want you to take the ship with the rest of the cargo around to the Westcoast. The rest of the stuff will be landed there. Afterwards you can sink it. There is a small harbour at Inishmela. It's deep enough to accommodate the ship. You can be there by Wednesday night. Also we have two prisoners for you, female, they are to be treated with the utmost courtesy and no harm is to come to them, understood?"

Reilly nodded. McCall went on.

"You can leave here as soon as the lorries are filled. When you finish with the ship make your way to Dublin with the others. I will meet you there. You have done a great job and will be suitably rewarded when we take over. We are going to need men like your self and the lads. Now go and have something to eat and a rest, we will call you when we're ready."

Outside Joe Kearns and the others had seen the ship arrive and the whole place come to life. They were fascinated by the speed of the operation, Two lorries being loaded at the same time. Grant wondered if he could get into the cavern and said he would try to get nearer the entrance. Carter would wait in the hut and Joe would try to get on board the ship and find out more about it. It was easy to climb out of the window and use the rocks for cover He made his way through the boulders until he was at the pier. The whole area was bare of any cover and to get to the jetty he would have to travel another two hundred yards. Joe climbed down to the water's edge under the pier. It was built of concrete beams and pilings without a hand grip anywhere. Then something caught his eye. A baulk of timber was floating in the water. He reached out and managed to move it towards him. The lid of a paint tin seemed to be right for a paddle. He straddled the log, wincing at the cold of the water and slowly paddled from post to post until he reached the end of the pier, and floated down to the ship.

CHAPTER 24

He bumped along the steel side of the ship towards the stern. All the activity was towards the front of the vessel where the covers were off the holds and the crates were being swung up by the derricks onto the lorries. Joe found a steel ladder on one of the pier upright's which was nearly in line with the stern. He climbed up to the top. His legs were nearly numb from the water, his hands barely able to cling to the steel rungs. Sliding over on to the concrete he ducked behind a pillar. A rope, of about two inches thick ran from the stern to a bollard on the quay. He thought of climbing along it and discarded the idea. His body was so cold now it would just not respond to anything like that. About five yards away a gangplank led to the deck. He watched for about ten minutes. No one seemed to be looking his way. The nearest man was about forty yards away. Dropping down on his stomach he inched his way forward to the gangplank and crept along it on to the deck. In front of him was an open door, which he entered. He could hear the sound of the generators down below and went cautiously down the steel steps. At the bottom he found himself in the engine room. The heat hit him as he entered. It was then he realised how wet and cold he was. He stripped of his clothes and hung them across the pipes leading from the boilers. He found a pair of trousers and a couple of tee shirts hanging on a makeshift line. Someone else used the place as a drying room. Putting on the trousers and a tee shirt he went on a tour of the cabins. All had been occupied one by a woman. He went up to the bridge and watched the scene below. Suddenly all movement ceased. The men stood looking towards the hold. The derrick came slowly up from the hold. On the platform were two coffins draped in the tricolour. The men stood and came to attention as they cleared the ship and were reverently placed aboard one of the lorries, the men saluting before resuming work. Joe wondered who they were and what had happened to them. He made his way back to the engine room and changed back into his now dry clothes.

Climbing back up to the bridge he watched as the last lorry was loaded.

It drove from the pier to join the other two beside the hut where they had left Carter. As Joe watched he saw Carter leave the hut and climb into the last lorry. Almost casually it seemed, some men surrounded the vehicle and a man dressed as an officer came forward with a revolver in his hand and went to the tailboard. Carter appeared and climbed down. With his hands in the air he was marched toward the cavern. The lorries with their escorts drove off towards the town and the main Dublin, Wexford road.

Joe found himself alone on the ship. There was nothing he could do for Carter, unless Grant could do something. It was the man's own fault, why had he not stayed where he was? He hoped he would be able to hold out. The, Irish Freedom Army were not noted for being gentle with anyone found spying on them. He decided to have a look down in the hold. There were still stacks of crates left. One had fallen and burst. It had contained Russian sub machine guns and these were strewn around the floor. Joe wondered if there were more lorries coming. He looked at his watch. It was still working and told him that it was now three a.m. Dawn would be about six. It did not leave much time if they were to unload the rest of the stuff. He made his way back to the deck. Most of the lights were out now. He was considering making a break for it along the pier when he saw a figure with a rifle walking where it joined the land and discarded the idea. Climbing back down the ladder he tried to find the log. It had disappeared, probably drifted off with the tide he decided. Without it he could not get back underneath the pier. If he could swim it would have been different. Joe climbed back up the ladder. He had just time to drop on the deck as he heard someone approaching along the pier. When he raised his head over the rail he could see a little group approaching. Two girls walked in front with another covering them with a gun from behind.

Then came three men with a fourth whose hands seemed to be tied behind his back. Joe looked around for somewhere to hide. There was a lifeboat fixed to its davits and covered with a tarpaulin nearby. He had just time to climb into it and pull the cover over him when the group reached the gangplank and started to come aboard. Joe raised his head and watched from under the cover. As they came up onto the deck one of the girl's anorak hoods fell back to reveal the face of Jean McKay. Joe dropped back down into the lifeboat. The other girl had to be Val Nevin. They had brought the girls here. No need to ask. The man had to be Carter. He raised himself up again and watched them

224

disappear through the open door. One of the men had gone directly to the stern and thrown off the rope. He then went to the bows and did the same with the front one. Joe felt the ship tremble and start to move. The bows moved away from the jetty and turned out to sea, until it was travelling Southwards. The ship had gone about three miles when the night sky behind them reddened with a massive explosion. A white flash lit up the night and a few moments later the shock wave hit them rocking the ship. The men and girl rushed onto the deck and looked back at the red glow, punctuated by smaller explosions. Joe could have reached out and touched them. The girl was gripping the rail with both hands.

"Jesus Christ, my fathers back there, we'll have to go back, turn the bloody ship around."

The tall man caught her by both arms.

"Francis we can't go back, it doesn't matter what's happened we can't go back."

He turned to the other two.

"Turn off all unnecessary lights. John, get as much speed out of her as you can, although at this hour I don't think we will have been noticed."

He held on to the girl, who struggled to free herself.

"Let me go George, let me go, it was that English bastard that did it, he must have planted a bomb, I'll kill him, God knows how many are dead back there."

She was kicking wildly to free herself. Joe watched, as the man George tried to calm her. Eventually he slapped her across the face.

"Stop it Francis, your making an idiot of yourself, calm down, we'll question your man later on. Come on now go and lie down or something, it's been a long night."

She broke away from him and went towards the cabins. Joe waited for about ten minutes before moving. He was feeling cold again and realised he would have to get inside into the heat. Joe could see the man at the wheel, he had his back to him. Of the others there was no sign. He had slipped out of the lifeboat and down the steel ladder to the deck. There was a door in front of him, which he opened and found himself in a passageway. What looked like three cabins, was to his left.

He tried a handle. It was locked, as were the other two. A row of steps led downwards. He followed them and found himself in the engine room. A man was reading gauges on a panel. Ducking low below the glass panel he crept past and found another door. This opened into a small storeroom with a jumble of ropes paint cans and bits of canvas lying around the floor. Choosing a corner he wrapped himself in a piece of canvas and tried to sleep.

When Grant left the hut he made his way through the rocks until he was as close to the opening into the cavern as possible. There was constant coming and going and everywhere was lit up by the arc lamps. He waited for an opportunity to try for an entry. Hearing the commotion he saw the capture of Carter who was taken in to the cavern. The last of the trucks departed and most of the arc lamps were extinguished. Then the door in the cliff face opened and a group of people emerged. Grant recognised Val Nevin and Jean McKay instantly. Carter was between two men. They all went towards the ship. Three other figures stepped into a car and drove off towards Ballingeary. The lights had all been extinguished now and there was just a soft blue glow coming from the opening. Grant moved closer and looked around the corner of the door. A short distance away a man was tinkering under the bonnet of a Land Rover. He could see two more men further in who were moving what looked like ammunition boxes. Just then the man at the engine looked up and spotted him, making a grab for a Kalashnikov rifle lying against the mudguard. Grant's bullet got there first and the man spun round. As he fell he caught the bonnet prop and the lid came down with an almighty crash. The other two made a grab for weapons and Harry fired at them. He must have hit one of the boxes because there was an explosion and a ball of dust and flame came towards him. He was lifted off his feet and thrown through the air. For what seemed like an age he flew until he landed with a thump on something soft and slid downwards, ending up in a small pool of water. His lungs felt as if he was drowning. It seemed no air was getting into them. He gasped and sucked until he started breathing again. Painfully he staggered to his feet and promptly fell over again. His breathing was coming in ragged gasps and his legs were like jelly. He lay against the bank of grit, which had undoubtedly saved his life and tried to get his strength back. After awhile he staggered off in the direction of the beach reeling from side to side like a drunken man. It would not be long before the explosion brought local Garda to investigate. In the darkness it had seemed to Harry that the whole cliff face had slid down from the top and buried the entrance. Between the rocks he rested for an hour before making his way back to the car. Breaking the side window with the butt of his gun he hot wired the ignition and managed to drive back to the cottage. He collapsed on to a bed and into a dreamless deep sleep.

Someone was beating a drum and shouting in his ear. It took him some time to realise the banging was on the door and the shouting from the same place. Opening his eyes he sat up and immediately his head swam. A voice was calling.

"Joe, Joe Kearns are you there? Open the door."

Grant staggered forward and opened the door to John McQuillen and two more plain clothes Gardai. McQuillen took one look at him and swore softly.

"Are you all right Harry? You look all in, where are the others?"

Grant went into the bathroom and splashed cold water on his face before answering. He looked in the mirror and was shocked at his own appearance. His eyes were sunk in their sockets and he was covered in fine grey dust. His face was a mass of small scratches and his hair caked with dried mud. McQuillen watched him closely as he emerged and flopped into a chair.

"They have Carter and the girls on board the ship, I don't know where Joe got to, he might be on board as well. I was trying to have a look at the cavern when they spotted me. I fired at them and must have hit one of the ammo boxes and the whole place went up. I just about made it back here, the bang blew me about twenty metres back from the entrance into a heap of fine grit, only for that I was dead."

McQuillen asked him about the girls and Grant told him they seemed all right when he had seen them being brought to the ship. They drove back to the area of the explosion. There was surprisingly little damage. In the daylight all that could be seen was a wall of broken rock covering the entrance to the cavern. McQuillan told Grant that they would be putting out a story that the explosion occurred in an electrical transformer station. There was still no sign of Joe Kearns. McQuillan dropped a worn out Grant off at the American Embassy before driving back to HQ. When he entered the office he got another shock. Behind the desk was Detective Inspector John Maguire, a trail of smoke curling up from his pipe.

"Morning John, sorry to surprise you like this but I had to throw them off and try to protect the girls. This thing is far too big and I want to be in at the finish, you will keep on with the job, I'll be keeping out of sight, what's the latest?"

McQuillen could hardly restrain his delight at Maguire's return. He gave him his report on the night's happenings. All the lorries were being followed and surveillance teams were being set up where ever they unloaded. The Inspector told him to go home and rest. He himself would go out to the Castle and take up residence there until they could discover more, McQuillen could contact him there.

McCall learned of the explosion at Ballingeary when he awoke after sleeping until noon on that Sunday morning. He wondered what had happened. When he had left everything was quite normal. Looking at the television pictures he could see that the cliff face had collapsed. Everything including the three men must be underneath the tons of rock. The camera showed the twisted remains of an electricity pole and beside it the remains of a large shed. The report said it was the transformer house which had blown up. There appeared to be only one uniformed Garda on duty. It looked as if the authorities had no real interest in the place. There was no mention of the ship or anything about other activity. This gave him a degree of satisfaction. He checked his watch. All the stuff should be delivered by Monday evening at the latest. Everything seemed to be going according to plan. By this time next week he would be the new leader of the country. Only six more days to go. When the Goverment sat down to dinner next Saturday night they would all be dead inside ten minutes. By Monday Ireland would have been declared a thirty-two county Socialist Republic. He wondered how the public would react, well if there was any trouble he would be prepared to execute some of the objectors in public. That would stop the rot.

McCall drove to the Russian Embassy, aware that his car was being photographed automatically as it entered the gates by the hidden Garda camera across the road. He was greeted by the K.G.B, man in charge of espionage operations in Ireland. They discussed the forthcoming take over and McCall was assured that every thing from the Russians side was in operation. The first of the five hundred so called businessmen would arrive at Shannon on Wednesday morning. All would be in the country by Thursday evening. The ships were allready in position off the Northwest coast. Colonel Gudenuv had been in touch with him earlier. The riots and strikes were being stepped up in England from to morrow morning. After two weeks of rioting in various English cities three thousand soldiers had been brought back from Belfast. Northern Ireland had been enjoying its quietest period for years during the last two months. McCall and the K.G.B. man toasted each other with vodka.

Then the KGB man reached under his desk and produced a small leather case. He opened it up and placed it in front of McCall. Inside fastened to the side were two narrow red cylinders about ten inches long and two inches in diameter. They looked like two fire extinguishers. The Colonel took one out and handed it to McCall.

"These my friend are yours, you just turn the knob clockwise to release the gas. It is effective immediately. One breath, and your dead. Do not forget to wear the special gas mask. After ten minutes open all the windows and it will disperse. It should be all over within twenty minutes. Its completely odourless so one must be very careful."

He handed the cylinder to McCall who took it gingerly. It felt cold and deadly in his hand. He thought of the men it would kill and shuddered slightly. This was for Ireland and its people, not for himself. They were fools anyway. You could not rule a country satisfactorily by democratic means. There had to be discipline. People could not be allowed to do what they liked, and those capitalist pigs, all they were interested in was making money. Well, after next week they would find things different. He handed the cylinder back to the Colonel who strapped it back in its case and handed the thing to McCall.

In the car he placed it in the boot under a pile of newspapers before driving back to his house. On the way he stopped at a public call box and rang Jack Monaghan. He asked him to meet him at his office at eight. The Special Branch man, following him at a discreet distance made a note in his diary before continuing to follow him to his residence. McCall watched him in his mirror and smiled to himself.

At seven thirty Monaghen let himself into the office and sat in darkness. When McCall arrived and handed over the case Monaghan snapped it open and checked the contents. He took the special gas mask in his hand and tried it on. McCall told him to wait at least fifteen minutes before he left the building after he himself had gone. It was Monaghan's job to get the gas into the Castle and assassinate the Government en masse.

After Monaghan left McCall's office he took a bus to Inchicore where he went into a public house and ordered a pint, taking it over to a corner seat where he could watch the door. He had almost given up hope when the man he wanted to see came through the door. He was about forty years of age and dressed in a donkey jacket faded blue jeans and a cap set at a rakish angle, which gave him a shifty appearance. Monaghan raised a hand in greeting and the man came over.

"Jack Monaghan, you're a sight for sore eyes, where have you been hiding, I haven't seen you for years."

He stuck out his hand. Monaghan gripped it briefly.

"Hello Mick, how are things with you? How are May and the kids? Are you still working for that building crowd?"

Monaghan already knew the answer to that. He had checked up on Mick O'Toole before coming to his local to accidentally bump into him, he continued.

"Anyway before you say anything, what are you having?"

O'Toole's face lit up with a grin.

"I'll have a pint thanks Jack, everyone's fine, the kids are eating me out of house and home and costing me a fortune in school and clothes, we never seem to have a penny these days."

He paused as Monaghan went to the bar and brought back two pints, wlhich he put on the table. There was silence as both men drank deeply. O Toole wiped his mouth with the back of his hand.

"Yeah I'm still driving for that oul Get, I often think I'd be better off on the dole, I just seem to work and work and get nowhere.

Monaghan sipped his beer.

"Where are you working now Mick?"

O Toole glanced around.

"We're working down at Ballyorney Castle at the moment, getting it ready for some Government meeting next weekend, you want to see the place out there, its crawling with Special Branch and soldiers, there's three checkpoints between the main gates and the house itself, we all have special passes, look."

He rummaged for his wallet and took out a pass, which he handed to Monaghan. On it was a description of the man and his photograph. It bore a seal and a dated signature of the Superintendent of O Toole's local Garda station. Monaghan turned it over in his hand.

"That's interesting Mick, tell me do they check your load as well as yourself."

O'Toole nodded, having another swig at his drink.

"You're checked in on a form at the gate and given a numbered card. Your own pass is put through a machine. When you go out they take the card off you, put it in a machine and then wave you out."

Monaghan went to the bar and brought back another pint and put in front of the man.

"Drink up Mick, tell me more about this meeting, are they really all that fussy? It must be very important."

O Toole nodded.

"I'm telling you, no one gets in or out. There are army patrols around the grounds and outside. All the other entrances are closed, everything comes through the main gates."

Monaghan sat and looked at his pint. Now O Toole's pass was in his pocket. He hoped the man would not miss it.

O'Toole was speaking again.

"What about you Jack, where are you living now? It must be three years since we last met."

"O I've been around, up and down the country, I'm living with my sister out in Donnybrook at the moment, are you still living in the same place?"

Mick O Toole downed the rest of his beer.

"Yes, I'm still in the same old shack and lucky to be there at all I suppose."

They talked until closing time. Monaghan bought him some more pints and it was a very unsteady Mick O Toole who bade him good night and made for home.

CHAPTER 25

Monaghan hailed a passing taxi and told the driver to take him to Dun Laoghaire. He got out in George's street and walked towards the harbour. Turning right into a narrow street of small houses he went halfway down until he found the one he was looking for. It was in total darkness. He rang the bell, three short rings and waited. A light came on in the hallway and the door slowly opened framing a figure. He was tall and wore a tasselled cap on his head. His face was lean with a goatee beard and a sardonic gaze. He looked Monaghan up and down.

"Well, and what do you want at this time of night, I was just going to bed."

Monaghan brushed past him into the hallway and the man closed the door behind him. He took the identity card from his pocket and waved it under the man's nose.

"I want this copied with my photograph on it and I want it done now, tonight, is that possible?

Greybeard took it without a word and walked down the hall into a room strewn with various pieces of photographic equipment. He picked up a magnifying glass and studied the card carefully under a powerful lamp. After a while he threw the card down on the table.

"I can make one of these which will pass a cursory examination but it won't fool the computer, there is a magnetic strip in the original which I cannot duplicate. If anyone puts my card into a machine it will alarm straightaway."

The man looked at Monaghan, who swore fluently.

"All right, make me one, how long will it take?"

Greybeard led him to room with the remains of a flickering coal fire and

"Wait there, I'll call you when it's ready."

He disappeared and Monaghan took off his coat and sat down. Some two hours later the man came back and held out two cards. Monaghan took them and then at the man, who smiled. The forgery looked identical. He nodded his approval and asked cryptically.

"How much?"

Greybeard pursed his lips and smiled thinly.

"Five hundred? The late hour and in a hurry."

Monaghan took out his wallet. He counted twenty tenpound notes onto the table. Picking up his overcoat he put it on. Without a word he walked out closing the front door behind him. He walked to the taxi rank beside the church and knocked on the window of a dozing driver who took him to Mick O'Toole's house. He slipped the original card through the letterbox while the cab waited, after which he was driven home to the flat he rented in a quiet side street. By the time he fell asleep he had completed his plan for getting into the Castle.

When Joe Kearns awoke he was cold and hungry. He had not had any food since before he had left the cottage yesterday. His watch had stopped, probably from the ducking it had received when he was trying to get to the ship. From the vibration he knew it was still moving. Opening the door a fraction he peered out. There was no sign of life. Moving out he made his way towards the engine room where he had seen the man the night before. It was empty. A twenty-four hour clock on the wall told him that it was o ten hours on Sunday morning. He found another passageway. The smell of cooking made him hungry. There was a small galley further on with something cooking in a pot on the hotplate and plates with bread and cheese and meat on them. He quickly grabbed some bread and meat and made off to find somewhere to eat. The safest place was probably the room where he had spent the night. When he had finished he set out to find the girls. Making his way towards the stairs leading to the next deck he ascended cautiously. At the top he could hear voices. He moved slowly forward. There was a door to his right, which was slightly open. He put his eye to the gap. Inside three figures were visible at a table. In the centre was the girl terrorist flanked on her left by the tall man whom Joe thought was the leader and on her right the man he had seen in the engine room. In front of them tied to a chair sat Jeremy Carter. His face was bloody from a cut over his eye and he looked dazed. It seemed as if he was being questioned about his actions back in Ballingeary. Another man stood behind his chair. The girl addressed Carter. Her voice had a cutting edge to it.

"You have been tried by a military court of the Irish Freedom Army. You have refused to identify yourself. We know you are a member of Crown forces. Therefore it is the sentence of this court that for crimes against the Irish people you are hereby sentenced to death, that is all."

Carter looked at her dully, his lips moved.

"I've committed no crime against any Irish person, if you people ever get to running Ireland then God help the Irish."

The man behind the chair hit him a blow across the face causing the chair to topple over. The girl stood up.

"Bring him outside, we will carry out the sentence now."

The man went forward and released Carter from the chair and started towards the door. The girl made to follow when the other man called from where he sat.

"Wait a minute, there will be no execution while I'm in command, all right he's guilty of something but he should be held until he can be brought before the Council, lock him in his cabin and stick a plaster on that cut."

The girl turned on him her eyes blazing in cold fury. She was shouting at him.

"There's no way George, he's guilty as hell, he killed my father and the others back there, he's going to die now, if I have to do it myself."

She pulled an automatic from her jacket. Carter shrunk between the two men. George sat behind the table but now he had a Colt pistol in hand, pointing at the girl

"Drop it Francis, I don't want to use this thing but if I have to I will."

His voice had a steely ring to it. The girl turned and looked at him her face contorted with contempt. She was breathing heavily and her face was white. In a flash she turned and fired at Carter. The bullet caught him in the forehead and blew the back of his head off as it exited spanging off the steel wall like an angry wasp. The ricochet caught Fergus Doyle in the neck severing the carthoid artery. A spurt of blood jetted across the room and he fell across Carter on the floor. George Reilly dashed forward and cradled Doyle's head in his arms.

"Fergus Jesus Fergus, I never thought it would end like this."

The tears were running down his face. John O'Shea was staring at the scene as if in a trance. His hand went into his jacket and came out holding his gun. He swung it round at the girl, a sobbing snarl coming from his lips.

"You bloody bitch, you've killed Fergus, bitch, bitch, bitch."

He got no further. A bullet from her automatic caught him between the eyes and he fell across George Reilly who pushed him aside and stood up. His face was grim, his clothes soaked with blood, he fired as he turned hitting the girl in the chest twice. A look of surprise came over her face as she slid down the wall into a sitting position. She looked at Reilly whispering with her dying breaths.

"Why George? Why?"

Before her head fell to one side and she stopped breathing. Reilly put the gun down and went across to her. He ran his bloodstained hand through her hair, then sat down on a seat. Joe Kearns watched the scene with horror. It had taken four minutes and four people were dead. The man at the table seemed to be in shock. He wondered if he should try to talk to him. There must not be anyone else on board or they would have been here by now. He felt in his pocket for the gun. Pushing the door open he went in. Pointing the weapon at the man he knew as George he said.

"Put your hands up please and move out of there."

Joe kept him covered as he rose and moved wearily towards the door, he asked.

"Are there any more men on board?

The other shook his head. Joe backed carefully along the passageway until he came to a door with a key in the lock. He motioned to the man and he moved inside. Joe locked the door before starting to look for the girls. After knocking on several doors he finally got an answer.

Going back to the room of carnage he spotted a bunch of keys. Back at the door he found one that opened the lock. Jean McKay was standing in front of him staring. She moved back to the far wall, her hand to her mouth. Val Nevin lay on a bunk her eyes wide with fear. Joe stood in the opening.

"Hello girls, are you all right?"

Jean rushed forward into his arms.

"Joe, O Joe, we thought you were dead, it was on television, they said you had been killed in Harcourt street, O Joe."

Tears were running down her face as she clung to him.

"What were those shots, where are those men and that horrible woman. She told us we would be shot if we gave them any trouble, are you alone Joe or are others with you?"

"I'm afraid there's only me Jean, the others and the girl are all dead, no I didn't do it they had a fight among themselves, their leader is locked in a cabin at the moment. Come along up to the bridge, I'll have to try and contact someone. This ship is still moving and I don't know how to stop it."

On the bridge Joe went to the radio room. He looked at the panel in front of him. It seemed reasonably simple. There was an on/off switch and a dial. A microphone with a switch on it stood on the bench. He flicked the switch to 'on' and took the mike in his hand. Taking a deep breath he pressed the switch on the handset.

"Mayday, Mayday, Mayday, is there anyone out there? Mayday, Mayday,"

Joe flicked the switch back to receive. He repeated the message several times, turning the dial left and right.

On board the Gadfly the radar operator had tracked the ship since it had left Ballingeary. They were now about a mile astern of her. She was on a Southerly course at about ten knots. His relief came on and he went aft in search of something to eat. It had been a monotonous watch. His relief checked the plot and then settled down to find some music on the radio. As he turned the knobs he heard Kearns Mayday message. He turned the knob and the voice became clearer. They must be close to the ship in trouble. He called Pritchard and they listened for a time to the voice. Pritchard told him to answer.

"Hello Mayday, we read you, what is your position and name of ship, are you sinking?"

The voice coming back was definitely Irish.

"Hello, hello, we're not sinking, the ships name is the Christopher Columbus, we are heading South with no crew and I know nothing about how to steer or stop this thing, please help us."

Pritchard thought quickly. The Mayday was coming from the Columbus. What had happened? Why, was there only one man on board and obviously not a sailor by what he had said. He gave orders to surface to periscope depth. Yes there she was about a mile ahead. Going back to the radio he took the microphone.

"Hello Mayday, What's your name? Joe, Good, now Joe I'm going to give you some instructions, first on the bridge you will find the telegraph, I want you to put the lever to stop, then you will find a red button somewhere nearby, press it and the engines will stop. We will be with you shortly. Are you clear on that Joe?"

Kearns told him he was. He was sweating profusely and felt that he had been lucky to make contact so quickly. On the bridge he went looking for the engine telegraph. He moved the lever to stop and felt the ship start to slow. Then he spotted the red button. He pressed it and the engines stopped. Joe found a pair of binoculars and scanned the seas around the ship but could see no other vessel. A short time later Val Nevin called him to say she could hear shouts. Looking over the side he saw a rubber boat with six men in it. He dropped a rope ladder which was lying on the deck and the men climbed aboard. Each was carrying an automatic rifle and all were dressed in Naval uniform. Joe realised they were British Navy. The officer came forward and Joe spoke to him.

"I'm delighted to see you fellows, I just didn't know what we were going to do, tell me, can you contact the Irish authorities. I have a special number here if you have radio telephone."

Pritchard nodded and told him he was from a British submarine. He asked about the crew and Joe told him what had happened. Pritchard then told him they had been shadowing the ship since it left Libya.

Then he left to go to the scene of the carnage. When he came back he was noncommittal and left to report to London and Dublin. The sub had by then come alongside where some more men climbed aboard. Pritchard came back and said that the ship would be brought into the Irish Naval centre at Hawlboline in Cork. The English crew soon had the ship moving and Joe and the girls had a meal of sorts from the galley. Afterwards he took some food down to the man in the cabin. George Reilly was lying on his bunk still in his blood-soaked clothes. Joe asked him if he had any others and would he, like to have a wash. He was rewarded with a grateful look and a muttered,' thanks'. He left to make arrangements with Pritchard.

It was three A.M. on Monday when the ship finally docked in the Base at Hawlboline. The English sailors were given a meal by their Irish counterparts before returning to the submarine clutching various bottles. Joe and the girls were hustled to a car for the drive to Dublin. The last he saw of Reilly was of him being led away in handcuffs by a naval officer and two armed ratings. In the warmth of the car the girls were soon asleep. Joe tried to make conversation with the driver but his answers were non committal and after a while he gave up, contenting himself with watching the road and the darkened towns and villages as they swept through them. They reached Ballyorney Castle at seven AM. The guards took only a quick glance at the car before waving then on. They must have been told to expect them. On the way up the long avenue Joe noticed more Gardai and army spread throughout the woods and fields on either side. They had picked up an escort of a Land Rover with four armed soldiers on board which, stayed with them until they stopped at the main entrance. Inside, they were welcomed by a Superintendent in full uniform. He showed them to their rooms. After telling them to call if they should require anything he withdrew.

When Joe Kearns awoke he showered and shaved. He found a suitcase with some of his own clothes in it and wondered who had organised that. He went downstairs and met a Garda at the bottom who directed him to a door marked library. He knocked and entered. In front of him was the figure of Maguire, with the familiar haze of blue smoke around him.

"A, there you are Joe, I hear you've been at it again, rescuing maidens in distress and capturing boats and things, tell me about it".

Joe told him what had happened at Ballingeary and about the killing of Carter and the others. Maguire listened nodding his head here and there, not interrupting until he had finished. Then he tapped his pipe on his heel and spoke to no one in particular.

"Well we have the ship and one prisoner, he'll be here shortly and I'll ask him a few questions. The arms dumps have all been marked and we are ready to seize them. You know Joe that its here they plan to kill the Government and stage the coup. We have searched the place high up and low down and found absolutely nothing. To my mind it has to happen on Saturday, probably when they are all together in one room. What is the most likely time? I suppose at dinner, possibly. But the one thing I can't figure out is how? That is the big question, how are they going to get in here to do the job? The final schedule for the weekend will not be issued until Friday evening at the earliest so until then we go on working in the dark."

The sound of a Helicopter brought them both to the window. The machine landed on the grass in front of the castle and two men got out with Uzis at the ready. Another two men followed one handcuffed to the other. The little party came into the castle and into the library. To Joe's surprise the Inspector greeted the man like an old friend.

"Well now George, its been a long time, take those things off of him."

He instructed the escort. Reilly rubbed his wrists and nodded.

"Thanks Inspector, It's been a rough few days,"

Maguire studied the man in front of him. There was an air of total dejection about him. He seemed to be still in some form of shock. His eyes were fixed at some distant point on the ceiling. This was not a like the old George Reilly. The man turned and stared out of the window. The Inspector struck a match and applied it to his pipe.

"Are you going to tell me George what you've been up to for the last three years since you vanished out of that courthouse. That was a neat one, that was George."

Reilly turned slowly towards him. Their eyes met for a moment then he glanced away.

"If I told you you wouldn't believe me Inspector, anyway its all been for nothing, The whole God damn thing was for nothing, They're all

240

dead, you have the ship, Jesus I had to shoot the girl myself or she would have killed me too."

His voice was a whisper and his body shook with sobs. He went on.

"All those years wasted, for what? You know they are going to try for a coup this weekend."

Maguire took the pipe from his mouth.

"We know there's something in the wind George, maybe you would like to tell us more about it."

Reilly looked at him sharply.

"You know better than that Inspector, I wouldn't tell you even If I did know. My job was to get that ship here, after that we were to report for further instructions, you know the rest."

He looked at the Inspector and then out of the window again. Maguire signalled to the Special Branch man who had brought him in.

"George I'm sorry to see you under these circumstances, I'm sending you back to HQ. If you reconsider you can tell somebody there you want to speak with me, think about it, you might save some lives."

His man led Reilly away and Maguire turned to Joe.

"You know I can't help feeling sorry for him, he's not the worst of them I've met, no, not by a long shot."

Michael McCall received a report about the arrival of the ship at Hawlboline before eight-o clock on that Monday morning. The local man in the area described the scene and told him that he had seen two women and a man leave with another man being taken off in handcuffs. When McCall asked if there were any others. He was puzzled when told no. The capture of the ship was a blow. It meant that the West of the country would be short of vital arms and ammunition. The two women had to be the McKay girl and Val Nevin, the man had to be the Englishman. He wondered who the prisoner was and what had become of the others, and Coughlin's daughter, where was she? No use worrying about it now, he would have to go ahead with the plan. Everything was ready. All that was required was the elimination of the Government. By Sunday morning all positions would be consolidated and his new Government would have called on the Russians for assistance. He wondered about the reaction of Britain and America. He did not think they would interfere immediately. First they would call for a meeting of the Security Council of the United Nations. After that the Russians could buy some time. No, he was sure they would not interfere, it all hinged on Saturday night and Jack Monaghan. He had complete faith in Monaghan. The man was a cool professional killer. He had never failed any mission on which he had been sent on. McCall called a meeting for that evening of his new Provisional Government and Monaghan in the White Leprechaun.

The meeting that night was tense. McCall's report of the ship's capture seemed to stun the group. Coughlin was particularly disturbed by the absence of his daughter Francis. Others wondered about the lack of arms in the West and McCall said they were now committed and could not stop. He turned to Jack Monaghan.

"It's all up to you now, The Government must be disposed of by eight o clock on Saturday night, nine at the very latest, are you organised?"

Monaghan told him.

"I have the whole thing worked out. As soon as the job is done I'll call you. I'll be going into the Castle on Saturday morning and fit up the gas cylinders during the day. According to my informant the workmen will be trying to get everything finished by one o clock when they have to vacate. There will be complete chaos there on Saturday morning. All I have to do is get into the dining room for about ten minutes and set the thing up, I'll find some way of staying around until it happens. I will call you by two way radio immediately its over."

McCall looked at the others with rising confidence.

"Gentlemen, there it is, when Jack calls me we move. You all know your jobs. Our men will seize the Television and Radio stations when I get the word so I will be able to broadcast to the nation as soon as I can get there, after that there should be only mopping up. Our Russian friends will assist us from then on. The element of surprise is with us. I can't see any major problems."

There was a murmur of ascent from the table. Monaghan left them talking and went downstairs where he joined the crowd at the bar. He waited until a group were leaving and went out through the door in their midst, noting as he did so a car parked opposite with some men in it. Keeping close to the wall he chatted with one of the group until he got round the next corner. He hopped a bus to Inchicore where he went in to the pub and waited for Mick O'Toole. It was not long before he arrived and saw Monaghan straight away.

"Jack, twice in one week, this is something else, how are things?"

He sat down and Monaghan went to the bar and brought back two pints He put one in front of O'Toole and looked at the man opposite.

"Mick, how would you like to make five hundred pounds?"

O'Toole spluttered into his beer. He put the glass down carefully and looked at Monaghan suspiciously.

"Are you serious Jack, I could certainly do with it, what's the catch?"

Monaghan leant across the table and said softly.

"I want you to get me into the Castle."

O'Toole's face went the colour of putty. He ran his tongue over his lips, there was silence for nearly a minute. Monaghan went on.

"I want to get in there on Saturday morning. Do they search the lorry?"

O'Toole shook his head.

"No, they just have a quick look, they all know me by now so they don't bother, but Jack I can't do it, if I was caught I'll be destroyed, no I can't do it."

He was trembling with fear and his hand shook as he lifted the glass. Monaghan realised he might have to find another way of getting into the Castle. This man would go to pieces if he tried to accompany him in his truck. He smiled across at O'Toole.

"All right Mick, forget I ever mentioned it, I'm sorry for asking, drink up, I have to be going."

The man was visibly relieved. The colour was coming back into his face. He was sipping his beer now with a faraway look in his eyes. He traced a line on the tabletop with his finger.

"I might be able to get you in, it could work."

Monaghan waited until O'Toole continued.

"If you were to hide in the truck before it left the yard, I wouldn't know you were there and if they found you I wouldn't be involved, how is that?"

Monaghan nodded and O'Toole went on.

"I'll make sure there's a canvas cover in the back, you could roll yourself up in that, the chances are that even if they did look in they wouldn't bother lifting it, yes, it could just work."

Monaghan thought so too. He reached for his wallet and took out five twentypound notes and handed them to O'Toole.

"There you are Mick, a down payment, you'll get the rest on Saturday morning, I'll leave it in the cab for you, your right you know it'll work all right, I'm off now, see you Saturday."

He walked away and O'Toole put the money in an inside pocket.

CHAPTER 26

On Tuesday morning Maguire met with Maurice Curley and Colonel Philpot. He briefed them on the current situation. Curley had already arranged for twice daily reports on the Russian ships. They were being shadowed by R.A.F. Nimrod aircraft from Scotland. Philpot told them that other Royal Navy vessels were moving into all effected areas. Curley said that some American warships were on their way from the Mediterranean. The American was now looking very serious, He toyed with his ballpoint pen, doodling on the pad in front of him

"With all due respects gentlemen this thing is getting bigger by the minute, it will have to be stopped. We are on the verge of world war three here. The Russians cannot be allowed to get a foothold in this country, if they do Western Europe is doomed. I will have to notify our President of the seriousness of the situation."

He turned to Philpot.

"Your Government and Nato will have to be advised and put on readiness you will agree."

Philpot was polishing his glasses. He put them on.

"Of course, of course, it goes without saying, but as discreetly as possible, perhaps your President should have a few words with Mr.Gagarin, he might be persuaded to see things in a different light."

Maguire looked at both men. The atmosphere was electric. He himself had been so engrossed in the hunt for the truth that he had not considered the full implications for the rest of Europe of an Irish Socialist Republic. Curley's words had rudely awakened him. The situation was grim indeed. Turning to Curley he said.

"Maurice we can look after the situation here. I think you're right, it is time to talk to your President."

Without another word Curley picked up his briefcase and stood up. He shook hands with both men and left. Philpot turned to Maguire.

"Inspector I would like to thank you for all your help while I was here. I must return to London now and talk to the PM. If I can be of further assistance to you do not hesitate to get in touch, thank you again."

Maguire shook his hand and walked with him to the lift. Here he handed him over to a Special Branch escort to Baldonnell the Irish air force base where a special unmarked R.A.F. plane had flown in to take him and Carter's body back to London.

Joe Kearns walked around the Castle and pondered how anyone was going to get in and wipe out the Government. With the amount of soldiers and police in and around the grounds he considered that it was impossible for anyone to get near the Castle let alone inside. Unless they were going to try the same trick as at Ballingeary and come in as Irish soldiers, or perhaps they were here already, well time would tell. He thought about Jean and how lucky he had been to be on that boat. God knows what would have happened to her if he had not been there. He had a vision of the carnage in the cabin and shuddered. The whole thing was mad. Two soldiers carrying sub machine guns came towards him. They looked about eighteen or nineteen. He nodded and they nodded back. They looked serious. Joe hunched his shoulders and went inside to look for Jean.

At three o clock that afternoon an American Air Force supersonic fighter dropped out of the low cloud onto the runway at Baldonnell air base. It was hurriedly refuelled and checked. It was airborne again within twenty minutes with Maurice Curley squeezed into a cramped seat behind the pilot. He wondered if he could get some sleep on the journey to Washington. When they landed Curley was whisked by Helicopter to the White House where he found the President of the most powerful democracy in the world seated behind his desk. His pet Golden Cocker lay sprawled at his feet and as Curley entered it jumped up and came forward wagging its tail in welcome. Curley bent for a moment and ruffled its ears. The President stood up and reached forward to shake his hand.

"Hello Maurice, I got your message, it must be important for you to fly home in an F.16, I don't think I would relish it myself, sit down and tell me all about it."

Curley lowered himself into a leather chair and gave his report of the plot to take over Ireland. The President listened, asking the odd question and making notes on a pad in front of him. When Curley had finished he stood up and walked over to the window. Here he stood looking out at the expanse of lawn in front of the White House. Finally he turned to Curley.

"Maurice in your opinion can the Irish take care of the situation in their country, we will have to be very discreet here."

"Mr. President they certainly seem to have the thing well in hand at the moment. The Irish Freedom Movement don't know how much the Gardai know and all the head men are being shadowed. Inspector Maguire reckons he can pick them all up at any time. He's very efficient. Mind you, I think the Russians will have to be warned off by our selves. I have the feeling that this whole thing is the work of the head of the terrorist section in Moscow, our old friend Gudenuv, of course it would have to have approval, but you will find that Gagarin will deny all knowledge of it."

"There's no time to bring this to the United Nations Maurice, I can see no alternative only to use the red telephone, however not just yet."

He pressed a bell on his desk and his Secretary of State came in.

"John, call a meeting of heads of military and Government departments for an hour's time, they're already standing by."

He turned again to Curley.

"What steps have you taken militarily Maurice?"

"The satellites are tracking all the ships within a hundred miles of the Irish coast. I ordered the carrier Coral Sea from the Med, it should be somewhere off the South Irish coast by Saturday morning. The British are following some of the Russian ships with their recon planes from Scotland. The biggest problem is the local big names involved however, Maguire will no doubt come up with something there, I wouldn't underestimate him in the least."

The President nodded.

"You know Maurice you can assure him that any assistance he might need from us will be instantly available. I think we should have a couple of transport planes standing by at our English base complete with troops at the ready, we could have them there in a couple of hours. Now you get yourself back there as quickly as possible, you have my complete authority to do whatever is required. If you need it there is a direct line to me at any time, now good luck, try for some sleep on the way back."

Half an hour later they were airborne again the pilot setting a course for Ireland. Curley tried to asleep but found it impossible. They landed at Baldonnell at two a.m. Curley was by this time very groggy from jet lag and lack of sleep. The Commandant suggested politely that he have some rest until morning and offered him a bed in Officer's quarters. Curley who felt like some one with a gigantic hangover gratefully accepted.

Back in Washington, the President's meeting went ahead. The Navy put the Seventh Fleet on partial Alert and diverted some more ships into the Atlantic towards the Irish coast. The Air Force put its A bomb Squadron at Mildon Hall in England on full alert and all leave was cancelled. In Germany all Army personnel and all Officers who could be contacted were asked to return to barracks and stand too. Along the West German frontier discreet orders were filtered down from Nato High Command to be extra vigilant, causing many unanswered questions. Inevitably Russian intelligence gatherers started to note these things and reports began to filter in to Moscow.

Colonel Ivan Gudenuv received some of these reports mid morning Thursday. His immediate answer was to contact his man in the Russian Embassy in Dublin. Talking directly to the K.G.B. man, he inquired if there had been any unusual police or army activity in the Republic. He was assured that everything was normal. Some of the businessmen had already arrived at Shannon and all would be there by nightfall. Otherwise the country seemed to be going about its normal business. The head of Special Branch had resigned and gone on holiday last weekend. Surely he would have stayed on, if anything had been suspected. He had heard some report of a ship being brought into Cork naval base and some people being brought to Dublin in great secrecy, but nothing else, if he heard anything more he would contact Moscow. Gudenuv felt a shiver run through him. Could that have been the arms ship? Impossible, surely the Irish Freedom Movement would have been in touch before this, but then they were so stupid at times, they thought

248

they could do everything themselves. He instructed the K.G.B. man to try and get more information before he put down the phone.

Joe Kearns had spent the last days around the Castle. It was a mixture of joy and boredom. Jean was his companion for a lot of the time, which they spent wandering around the gardens but for the most part they all felt like prisoners. Maguire seemed to be keeping out of the way. Several times Joe had asked for him only to be told that was not available. On Thursday morning he bumped into the man in one of the corridors.

"A Joe, is that yourself, I haven't seen you for a couple of days, I'm still trying to figure out how they're going to take out the Government, we've covered the whole place and still nothing. Have you any ideas? It has to be Saturday and when they are at dinner but we've taken that dining room apart and found nothing, there will be security cameras working from about midday on Saturday, maybe we'll see something on them."

He shook his head. They had reached the dining room now. Joe walked around looking at the vaulted ceiling and the hunting scenes painted on the walls. Down the centre ran a long Walnut table for the full length of the room. High backed chairs stood at attention at each side. At the far end a huge open fireplace contained a fire of logs, set ready to light. It certainly looked innocent enough. He sat down on a chair and tried to imagine how the deed could be carried out. Maguire lit up his pipe and wandered around frowning. Joe's brain was turning all the possibilities. They knew that it was going to be gas, or was it? Perhaps a lone assassin? With a machine gun, or a bomb. It seemed to him that it had to be a one-man job. He was struck by a sudden thought. That the reason nothing had been found so far was that there was nothing to find. The whole event would be on Saturday. It would be then that the assassin would try to enter the Castle and bring his weapon in with him. He stood up and told Maguire his theory. The Inspector listened and scraped out the bowl of his pipe with a penknife.

"You know Joe you could be right, Him or They will come on Saturday, that's when we have to be most vigilant, yes I think that's it."

Joe followed him out and down the long hall. At the entrance they met McQuillen just coming in, he came straight to Maguire.

"Reilly's dead chief, they were moving him back to Portlaois when the car slowed for a junction and he jumped out they called on him to halt but he ran in front of a truck and was killed instantly, it was almost as if he wanted to die."

Maguire just nodded and stared into space. McQuillen looked at Joe and left.

McCall heard the brief news flash on his car radio while stopped at some traffic lights. The announcer broke in on the programme.

"News is coming in that George Reilly who was wanted by Gardai since he escaped from custody three years ago has been killed while trying to escape from a car taking him back to Portlaoise prison."

The music resumed and McCall sat there. Reilly was dead, that left the women and the Englishman from the ship. A fusillade of horns made him start. He let in the clutch sharply and the car jerked forward. Damn, Reilly was a good man, it was a pity to lose him like that, well he would not have talked, he was sure of that, anyhow he knew nothing about the Castle. Monaghan and himself were the only ones who knew the full details and time factors. He wondered again about the rest of Reilly's team.

Jack Monaghan rose at six-o clock on that Saturday morning. He showered and shaved before preparing a breakfast of bacon eggs and sausages. He ate slowly and methodically, enjoying the food, which might have to last him for the rest of the day and into the night. Then he placed the gas cylinders in a leather tool bag wrapped in an old sweater. Alongside he placed an automatic pistol some tools and a roll of insulating tape. His two way radio went in next. He put on an anorak and a cap and looked at himself in the mirror. He looked like any other building worker. Giving the room a last look he stepped out into the street. When he reached the builders yard there was no sign of life. The small door at the side was open. He could see a light in the gate man's hut. Moving forward he slipped inside the gate and walked up the yard, using the pieces of machinery for cover. He need not have worried. The gate man lifted his kettle off the gas ring and poured water on to his tea. His back had been turned when Monaghen slipped by. At the top of the yard Monaghan found the lorry. It was the work of a moment to climb aboard and tuck himself under the large tarpaulin that was lying on the floor. He tried to make himself as comfortable as possible. About fifteen minutes later he heard voices and recognised O'Toole who was talking to the man in the hut. A door opened and the lorry shook as the man climbed into the cab. The engine started and it moved off. About an hour later it stopped again and a voice asked.

"Morning, what have you got?"

"Nothing. I'm here to take stuff away, everything has to be out by one."

"That's right, anyone here after that stays for the week end, so don't be late, here's your pass."

O'Toole laughed.

"Don't worry I'll be out of here in about an hour, do you want to have a look in the back?"

"No go ahead there are two cars behind you, get going."

The lorry moved forward again. Monaghan, grinned to himself, it was so easy. They will never learn. Peering out from under the canvas he could see the Castle up ahead. There was army everywhere. He spotted two camouflaged machine gun posts and several soldiers up trees with rifles with telescopic sights. The truck stopped under a clump of trees at the back of the Castle. Here the builder's material was scattered around amid a confusion of dumper trucks and concrete mixers. O'Toole climbed into the back of the lorry and started to pull the tarpaulin around. He spoke quietly.

"When I say go, slip over the tail and make for the bushes behind the mixer, after that you're on your own."

He fumbled around for a minute or two.

"Now, go, go."

Monaghan jumped down and made for the bushes which was a thick Laurel hedge. Another couple of cars arrived and men got out. They shouted greetings to O'Toole who replied. Then they walked by Monaghan's hiding place and along a path, which led to a door into the Castle. As the last one moved around the corner Monaghan stepped out and followed. As they entered the door he could see they were being checked in by a uniformed Garda who was examining their passes. Monaghan felt his pulse racing. His false disc was in his hand.

He shifted the bag on his shoulder the easier to get to the gun. The Garda glanced along the path towards him. There was no going back. Monaghan approached the man casually.

"Morning, cold this morning."

The man looked at his disc and then to his face, satisfied he handed it back.

"You should have been here all night, then you would know what cold was."

He looked over Monaghan's shoulder.

"Here's my replacement, at bloody long last, go ahead."

He turned away and Monaghan walked into the Castle.

There were men everywhere moving around starting work. Everyone seemed to be hurrying. Monaghan supposed that they had no interest in staying after one o clock and being incarcerated for the weekend. He walked down a long passageway. It ended with two rooms one on either side. According to the plan of the Castle, which he had in his pocket the one on the right was the dining room. Looking through the open door he could see the high backed chairs and the long table. Across the way men were working installing telephones. In the dining room an oldish man in blue overalls was sweeping up dust and shavings. Monaghan walked in and gave him a wave and a smile.

"Morning, busy here this morning, this the dining room then."

The man looked at him gloomily.

"This is it all right, are you with the electricians?"

Monaghan nodded, suddenly seeing the security camera in the corner of the ceiling. The man followed his gaze.

"Great isn't it, they can see everything on those things, they're for the meeting you know, security, they won't be working until we go at one, the Special Branch are going to operate them for the weekend."

Monaghan felt a surge of relief. He took out a packet of cigarettes and offered them. The man took one. Monaghan lit a match and held it. The man lit up.

"Thanks mate, you going to work here?"

"Yes I have to check all the plugs and light switches."

The man blew smoke through his nostrils and lifted the rubbish into a plastic bag.

"I'll be out your way now, I've got to sweep up the rest of the rooms, maybe I'll see you later, thanks for the fag."

Monaghan closed the door behind him as he left and wedged a screwdriver under it. There was another door at the far end of the room. He checked this and found it led to the kitchens. This he wedged as well. Taking a pair of spring clips from his bag he went down under the table. It took about five minutes to screw them to the underneath. Moving about ten feet away he fitted another pair to the wood. Taking the gas cylinders from the bag he pressed them into the clips where they were held firmly. On each of the nozzles he placed a small explosive charge and connected them to a timer made from an ordinary pocket watch. He set it to detonate at eight-o clock and stuck the lot to the wood with quick setting super glue. When the charges exploded they would blow of the nozzles and release the gas which, the Russians had assured McCall was not explosive and completely odourless. All in the room would be dead in seconds. Monaghan rechecked every thing and crawled out from under the table. He looked at his watch, it had taken less than fifteen minutes, good. He unwedged both doors and stepped out into the passageway. It took an almost superhuman effort not to step back into the room. Coming towards him was Detective Inspector Maguire and another man.

Monaghan moved as casually as he could across the way into the other room and dropping his bag on the floor took a screwdriver from his pocket and started to open a light switch. From the corner of his eye he saw the men come into the room and stand looking at the workers. Monaghan busied himself at the switch He had recognised the other man as Joe Kearns. But he was supposed to be dead. How the blaze's was he here? Maguire and the other man were talking as they watched the scene. Two men painting the ceiling seemed to be attracting their attention.

"Hey you, are you an electrician?"

The voice came from behind him. A stocky man in a check cap and with an air of some authority was standing behind him.

CHAPTER 27

Monaghan could only nod.

"Come with me we have a problem with one of the security lights, it was working all right then it stopped, maybe you would have a look at it for us."

Monaghan picked up the bag and followed the man out passing Maguire as he did so. His mind raced. Perhaps outside he could make some excuse and try to get out of the place. His knowledge of electricity was rudimentary to say the least. One thing he did know was that security lights such as were in use at the Castle, were high powered. If he could tell them the bulb was gone he might get away with it. As if to read his thoughts Peak Cap said.

"We've already tried a new bulb and it didn't work, perhaps its not getting any power, anyway you'll be able to sort it out for us."

They rounded a corner where two men were looking into the opened back of the lamp. They looked up expectantly as they approached. Peak Cap gestured.

"It's all right lads this man is going to have a look at it for us."

There was silence as Monaghan moved in and knelt on the grass. He opened the bag and reached inside, his fingers closing on the automatic. Even if he did get it out and shot all three he would never get out of the grounds. He stuffed it inside his jacket. Better try and bluff his way. Taking his screwdriver he confidently started unscrewing the back panel of the lamp. The three men watched in silence. As the last screw came out he made to lift the cover off. There was an almighty blue flash which temporary blinded the watchers. The last thing Monaghan felt was a giant hand picking him up by the chest and flinging him through the air into the Laurel hedge. His body hung there his clothes shredded and smouldering on his lifeless body. The gun fell into the dead leaves under the bush. There was a deadly silence as the others picked themselves up from where they had been thrown. Peak Cap walked over slowly and looked at the thing that a few moments before had been a man. He ran his hand over his face muttering.

"Jesus Christ, Jesus Christ, is he dead?"

One of the others turned and ran, shouting over his shoulder.

"I'll get an ambulance and a doctor."

Joe Kearns and John Maguire heard the shouts and ran towards the commotion. They met the man running up the steps, Maguire catching his arm as he went by.

"What's the trouble, what's up?"

Breathless the man the man replied.

"There's been an accident, I think he's dead, I have to get an ambulance and a doctor."

Maguire grabbed a Garda.

"You phone for a doctor and ambulance, now show us where this happened."

The man brought them to the scene where Maguire took charge and had the area sealed off. Peak Cap, white faced paced up and down. Monaghans body still hung on the hedge. A couple of Special Branch men gently manoeuvred it down onto the grass. A smell like burnt bacon hung in the air. Maguire asked the foreman.

"Who is he? Do you know? His people will have to be notified."

The man shook his head.

"I don't know, he's one of the electricians, I found him in the conference room, you were there at the time Inspector."

Joe was looking at the lamp and where the body had finished up. Something on the ground caught his eye. Bending down he picked it up. It was scorched and discoloured but still distinguishable as an identification disc. He handed it to Maguire who said.

"Well at least we have his name, Michael O'Toole, they'll have his address at the gate."

Just then a doctor arrived and knelt on the grass beside the body. In the distance the sound of an ambulance siren could be heard. After a brief examination he stood up and gestured towards the sound.

"No point in them hurrying, he's as dead as a dodo, he got some dose, I would say he was dead before he hit the hedge, it's a job for the coroner, Take care gentlemen, I'm off now."

Maguire watched him go as the ambulance drove up. The corpse was loaded and driven away. A young Detective Garda was detailed to write up a report and Maguire and Kearns made their way back into the building. It was now twelve o'clock and the workmen were starting to leave. One of the men who had been at the scene of the accident came in with Monaghan's bag.

"Where will I leave this Inspector, it belonged to the dead man."

Joe took it and walked into the room, which Maguire was using as an office. Maguire opened the bag and spilled the contents out on to the desk. A pliers, a small coil of wire a couple of screwdrivers, a two way radio, measuring tape, insulating tape, a ball of what looked like putty some screws and tacks, a hammer and a wire cutter. Maguire and Kearns sat and looked at the objects. Maguire picked up the two way radio and turned it over in his hand.

"Now what would an electrician be doing with a two way radio, but sure, maybe some of them do carry these things these days."

He put it down again and idly pushed at the other bits and pieces. Joe watched in silence, there was something not right here. He knew he was seeing something but did not know what. Then the young detective Garda came in and interrupted his thoughts.

"I've found the man's address Inspector, do you want me to go over there and let them know?"

The Inspector thought for a moment.

"Yes, have your lunch first and get a female Garda to go with you, try and keep it out of the papers at least until tomorrow. See if you can get a positive identification as soon as possible, then get back here, these politicians will be starting to arrive anytime now."

He had barely finished speaking when the sound of a car on the gravel caused Joe to look out of the window. A large black Mercedes had drawn up to the door He could see the Taoiseach, his secretary and the Garda Commissioner alighting. What seemed like a small army, of civil servants were getting out of more cars. Maguire turned to Joe.

"Its started, I only hope we haven't overlooked anything, keep your eyes skinned for anything suspicious, let's hope they try something, this place is sown up so tight that a mouse could not get in or out."

Joe said thoughtfully.

"You know Inspector I can't see them giving up as easy as all that, as sure as God they'll try it, everything points that way, I think I'll go for a walk around."

He met Jean on his way to his room and marvelled at her beauty as she came towards him. Funny he would never have met her only for all this. He caught her hand and they walked along like two teenagers.

"Joe what happened out there I heard a siren and saw the ambulance arriving."

He explained about the accident, She gave a shudder.

"O the poor man, what about his family?"

"Your Uncle has sent some one to the house to break the news to them, its not a job I would like, come on we'll go out into the grounds you and I have nicer things to talk about."

She slipped her arm into his and they went out into the pale sunshine.

Detective Garda Sean Ryan was thinking that he should have kept his mouth shut. It was not a pleasant task to tell any family that someone had been killed. He drove to Garda HQ. Here he asked about a female Garda to accompany him. He was told that Mary O Keefe had just signed on for duty and he felt a surge of joy. At a recent dance he had met her and danced with her for most of the evening. Maybe he would end up with a date before this day was out. Finding her in the day room he made arrangements with her to come with him after he had something to eat. It was nearly three o'clock when they left to go to the victim's house. They found the address with little difficulty. It was typical council with a small front garden and a concrete path leading up to the door. A steel fence separated it from the one next door. Ryan rang the bell. Footsteps sounded and a figure was outlined against the glass. The door opened to reveal a pleasant looking woman of about forty with dark brown hair and rather plump. She looked curiously at Ryan and the uniform behind him. She spoke one word.

"Yes?"

Ryan showed her his warrant card.

"Mrs.O'Toole? Could we come in please."

She opened the door fully and stepped back.

"What is it, what's the matter?"

Her face had gone white she backed down the hall and into the sitting room. The girl moved forward and took her arm.

"Why don't you sit down Mrs O'Toole."

She gently led her to an armchair and sat her in it. Ryan took out his notebook. He cleared his throat this was the part he hated.

"Is your husband's name Michael?"

The woman nodded, she was twisting a ring on her finger. He went on.

"He was working at Ballyorney Castle this morning."

She again gave a nod.

"I'm afraid I have to tell you we have some bad news, there was an accident, your husband was killed, I'm very sorry."

The woman started to sob. Ryan looked on helplessly. Mary O Keefe put her arms around the woman and tried to comfort her. She asked Ryan.

"See if you can get one of her neighbours to come in to her."

He moved quickly, glad to be out of the room. Outside a man and two girls of about eight and ten were coming up the path. Both children were carrying shopping bags and the man had some parcels. The man looked at him curiously.

"What's happened, is there something wrong?"

Ryan told him.

"Yes' I'm afraid there is, Mrs. O'Toole's husband has had an accident, I'm afraid he's dead."

The man looked at him sharply and brushed by him into the house. Ryan heard him calling.

"May, May,"

The girls had pushed by him as well and he followed them in. Mary O Keefe was standing to one side looking on. As he entered the man turned.

"What the hell's going on, look at the state of her some one please explain what's happening."

The woman seemed to revive quickly. Suddenly she started to laugh. She stopped and gasped.

"O Mick. He said your were dead, killed in an accident, I didn't know what to think, he was going for one of the neighbours when you came in."

Ryan went suddenly cold. If this was Michael O'Toole, who the hell was the dead man? He turned to the man.

"I'm sorry about this, there appears to be some mistake here. There was an accident at Ballyorney Castle this morning and a man was killed. Your identity disc was found on his body, naturally we thought it was you, Mr.O'Toole can you explain how your disc was found on this man's body."

For reply the man reached into his pocket and produced his wallet, he opened it and handed a disc to Ryan.

"That's my disc there, I never let it out of my sight, I don't know where your man got that one but this is definitely mine."

Ryan was still looking at the pasteboard in his hand.

"Look, all I can say is there is some mix-up here, I apologise for any trouble I've caused you and your wife, I have to get back to the Castle now but if you don't mind I'll hang on to this for the moment. You will get it back as soon as possible."

May was wiping her face with a handkerchief.

"Sure that's all right Garda, you were only doing your job, thanks for being so kind, and you miss."

Ryan sat into the car and took of with a squeal of tyres. Mary O Keefe winced at the speed at which they were driving. Staring straight ahead he muttered between clenched teeth.

"Maguire is going to love this."

Looking at his watch.

"Its five thirty and I left him at one o clock to do this job, he's going to go through me, I've got to get out to the Castle as quickly as possible."

Fifteen minutes later they were pulling up at the door.

Ryan dashed into the hall. Maguire was talking to the Commissioner. The Inspector caught his eye and came over. As Ryan poured out his story frustration showed on Maguires face. The young detective apologised for not being back earlier. Maguire told him.

"Never mind that now, try and find out who our friend was, we must assume that he was the hit man or else one of a group, he may have planted something here or was going to hide and await his chance. See if you can get a check on his fingerprints, I'll have a word with the lads and see if we can find anything here."

Ryan hurried away and Maguire called his crew together and told them what had happened. John McQuillen met Joe Kearns by the stairs and gave him the story. By now the Castle was crowded with Ministers and their staffs. Small groups were forming to go through papers and discuss problems. The Taoiseach and his party had been in the conference room for the past hour. Dinner was being served at from seven thirty to eight thirty. Joe Kearns watched the hustle and bustle around him as Maguire's men tried discreetly as possible to carry out another search. He started to think about the man in the morgue. Now that he remembered there was something about the way he had been working on that switch in the conference room. Like a film replay Joe saw him crossing the passageway as he and Maguire approached and go into the conference room. There had been something about that. The man had come out of the dining room. It seemed as if he was going to walk towards them, then changed his mind and crossed to the conference room instead. The more Joe thought about it the more certain he became that he was right. He walked down to the door of the dining room and went in. Waiters were laying out the tables.

Joe sat down on a side seat under a painting of a stag being chased by hounds. He let his gaze wander around the room. Taking in everything. Nothing seemed amiss yet he seemed to feel a kind of fear. Walking up to the fireplace he stood looking at the logs. A voice from behind said.

"There's nothing there Joe, we've already looked."

McQuillen had come up behind him and was standing looking morose and cheerless. One of the waiters came up with a lighted taper and lit the log fire. The flames crackled merrily as if to say, look there's nothing here. McQuillen started to walk slowly towards the entrance to the kitchens. A waiter moving fast came through the door carrying a large tray of champagne glasses. McQuillen did his best to avoid him but the man cannoned into him and with an almighty crash the two men went down, glasses flying in all directions smashing into bits on the floor. Some even managed to land on the table. The two men picked themselves up and a couple of the others grabbed brushes from somewhere and started to clean up the mess. Joe watched in fascination as one complete glass landed on the floor and rolled under the table and came to rest near a leg. He got down on one knee and reached in for it and picked it up. Further in he saw another broken stem and crawled further under to get it also. Something glinted in the light as he raised the edge of the tablecloth. It was a slim red cylinder about nine inches long fixed to the table with a couple of spring clips. Some wires led away from it to another one some distance away. Joe went cold, this must be the gas. He gently backed out and stood up. McQuillen was brushing himself down. Joe caught his eye and nodded towards the table.

"I think you had better have a look under here John."

McQuillen moved over and looked. His face passive he addressed the staff.

"Okay. You fellows, just sweep up the rest and then get out of here, nobody is to enter here until we say so. Joe will you get the Inspector?"

He called one of the waiters.

"Better tell your boss the dinner is going to be a bit late, I'll see that the other Ministers are informed."

Joe found Maguire in his office. When he told him of his find Maguire was off like a shot. In a few minutes he had returned with a young

Army Officer and all three made for the dining room. After a quick examination the Officer gingerly disconnected the timer and removed the wires from the cylinders. The set up was one of the simplest he had ever seen. Whoever had put it there seemed to be almost certain it would not be discovered. He removed the cylinders from their clips and crawled out and laid them on the table.

"Inspector, these appear to be gas cylinders rather than bombs, these explosive charges were just put there to blow the nozzles off and release the gas, I'll take them over to the lab and get them checked out."

Maguire nodded and turned to Kearns and McQuillen.

"Well lads that's that problem solved, I suppose you can tell them to go ahead with dinner. Now we have more work to do."

Joe followed him out as McQuillen called the waiters back to go on with their preparations.

In his office The Inspector made several phone calls giving Instructions to various units. Then he called for his car and said to Kearns.

"I suppose you would like to be in at the finish of this operation Joe, seeing as how you were involved all along. McCall and his new Government are waiting in a room at the White Leprauchan on the quays. Its my guess our man who was killed today was to contact them by that radio he had when the gas had killed off the crowd at the castle, with a bit of luck we'll get them all in the next hour or so."

There was silence in the car as it sped towards the city, each man engrossed in his own thoughts. It was raining steadily now as they turned into a deserted side street a short distance from the public house. Although it was now early evening this part of the quays bore a deserted look. Half a mile further down the crowds moved up and down, O'Connell Street looking for Saturday night entertainment. There were a couple of black Transit vans parked at the kerb. Maguire got out and tapped on the rere door of one. Inside ten men armed with Uzi machine guns sat in two lines. Maguire told them.

"Right lads I want you to move out and cover the pub front and rear. Try and keep those guns out of sight, the public must not see anything, with a bit of luck we can take this lot with the minimum amount of fuss. Have you all got your caps."

The men all produced yellow baseball caps and put them on. The Inspector went on.

"Don't shoot unless it's absolutely necessary, now go, we go in at eight sharp."

The men moved out, Maguire put on a cap and handed one to Joe. They moved around the corner and met McQuillen.

"They're all in the upstairs room Chief, our lads are in the rooms each side of them and the rest are empty."

He fell in beside them and the three walked towards the pub. They passed the main doors and Joe could see a crowd drinking at the long bar and sitting at tables. Reaching the door they moved slowly up the narrow stairs. Joe followed, trying to move quietly. As they reached the landing a man wearing a baseball cap came out of a doorway and nodded. Steps sounded on the stairs behind them and they shrank back into the other doorways. A barman came in sight carrying a tray of drinks. McQuillen moved out and putting his fingers to his lips caught his arm and dragged him into a room. His face white with fear as he saw the weapons, he sat on a chair which Maguire pushed forward.

"Are those drinks for number six?"

He asked the startled man, who could only nod. Maguire told McQuillen.

"Right, knock on the door, they'll think it's our friend here, then straight in."

McQuillen moved out and Maguire and Joe lined up behind him. He knocked on the door and then entered. Maguire and Kearns were hard on his heels. Six startled faces looked at them. At the head of the table Michael McCall started to rise to his feet. Maguire's quiet voice stopped him halfway.

"Good evening gentlemen, I'm afraid the meeting is over, Mr. McCall, I would like you and these other men to come along with us please.

McCall sat down.

"This is preposterous, we were just having a few drinks and a chat, that's not against the law is it?"

Maguire moved further into the room and up to McCall. He picked

263

up the briefcase and opened it up. Taking out some papers he glanced through them.

"Come on gentlemen, we all know why we're here, now let's have no trouble or someone might get hurt, it's all over, the Government is safe, your man is dead. You are all under arrest under the offences against the State act, now come along please."

McCall's face was ashen with rage. He made a lunge at Joe, a string of obscenities flowed from his lips.

"You bastard Kearns, you are the cause of this."

McQuillen grabbed his arm and led him out with the others following meekly. They all moved out into the street where they were surrounded by the men in baseball caps and brought around the corner to the Transits. Maguire stood looking after them as they drove away while cramming tobacco into his pipe. He lit up with evident satisfaction. Turning to McQuillan and Joe he looked at his watch. It was eight-o clock.

"Come on lads, let's get back to the Castle."

The American Nuclear submarine Idaho had been travelling towards the Polar ice cap when it received a message from Washington Naval Headquarters reached it early on Saturday morning. It was to change course and find and follow a Russian factory ship off the Northwest coast of Ireland.

After driving at full speed for most of the day they found the ship pin pointing its position by satellite and took up station some two miles behind. The Russian radar operator found them immediately and reported their presence to the Captain and the fact that they were being followed. Earlier in the week he had been sure that the R.A.F. Nimrod they had spotted was keeping them under observation. Captain Igor Malenkov thought about this for a time before contacting the man who had issued his orders in the first place. Thus it was that Colonel Ivan Gudenuv received a message during Saturday evening, telling him that the ship was being shadowed, and, that they had sighted an American submarine. Another report reached him from an agent in Gibraltar that the American carrier Coral Sea and the battleship Maine, with attendant destroyers had passed through the Straight's into the Atlantic.

At eight o clock in Dublin when Maguire was leaving the back room of the White Leprechaun the President of the United States was reaching for the red telephone on his desk. A few moments later he was connected to the President of the Soviet Union in Moscow. The conversation lasted about fifteen minutes and when he put the phone down the President of the United States was smiling. He reached down and played with the dog's ears and it responded by licking his hand. Some time later Curley was on the phone to tell him of the arrests in Dublin. Gradually all over Europe tension eased as the night went on and armies were gradually stood down.

In Dublin at the Television and Radio studios that Saturday night, people arriving for the Late, Late show were puzzled by the number of uniformed Garda in evidence. A mini bus with ten young men in it was directed into a corner of the large car park between two buses. As it reversed into the shadows dark silent figures, their faces blackened converged on it and covered the van with rifles and sub machine guns. The occupants were ushered out and into one of the bus's which was then driven off. A man who was parking his car and saw the incident was told to go on in to the studio and forget what he had seen. All over the country Subversive elements waited for McCall's appearance on the small screen. At numerous locations Special Branch and Army units quietly seized arms and arrested people. At other venues Irish Freedom Army members sat by telephones awaiting orders which never came.

CHAPTER 28

In Moscow an enraged Dimitri Gagarin rang for his secretary Anatol Kirof.

"Summon a meeting of the Politburo for ten o clock to morrow morning Anatol and inform Colonel Gudenuv to be present. It's Ministers only, no secretaries, make that quite clear."

He stormed out leaving the little man looking after him. Kirof shook his head. Something had gone wrong. It had to be Gudenuv's crazy scheme to take over Ireland. Well he Kirov had said so all along. Too bad he liked Gudenuv, after all he had got his son out of trouble when he had drunk to much and had tried to climb a statue to Muscovite's killed in the war He went into his office and phoned the Colonel. Gudenuv received the news calmly. He had known from the reports filtering in during the day that the whole thing was coming apart. Kirov's description of the President's rage could mean only one thing. The Americans had been in touch. He sighed and sat looking around the apartment. In the sitting room his wife was watching television. He crossed to her and kissed the top of her head.

"I have to go out darling, I shouldn't be too long, about three hours probably."

He tried to sound casual. She was used to his coming and going and just raised her hand, besides the film was very good, she could enjoy it better on her own. The Colonel put on his cap and greatcoat and picked up the briefcase he had brought from his office. Closing the door gently behind him he walked across the hall and stepped into the lift. In the basement garage the K.G.B. man snapped to attention and Gudenuv bade him good night knowing that his departure would be noted along with the comings and goings of everybody else in the building. When he arrived at the airbase his plane was ready and waiting. The ground crew bustled around as he talked to the control tower giving his flight

266

details to East Berlin and getting weather reports. At o ten hours he lifted the Tubeluv off the runway and headed West.

He found Berlin. It was impossible to miss. The Western section was lit up like a giant Christmas tree. The Eastern section looked very dull by comparison. A movement on his right wing made him start. A Mig twenty-seven in East German markings was alongside him. When he looked another was on his left. The radio crackled and a German voice said in very good Russian.

"Good night Colonel, welcome to Berlin, we are your escort, if you will follow us we will guide you down."

Gudenuv acknowledged and the two Migs moved ahead and into a gentle curve to the right. If he followed them he would be moving away from the path he had chosen to land at Templehof on the Western side. He shoved the throttle forward and commenced a shallow dive towards the lights. The Migs were still flying away from him. He was about five miles from the airport now and could see the line of the river Spee, like a silver snake below. Only a few seconds more and he would be in West Berlin air space. He threw a look over his shoulder at the Migs. The pilots had strict orders to stop anyone trying to get to the West. Suddenly they were there on his left side so close he could see the pilot's faces. They were frantically waving at him to turn. He had switched off the radio. They must be thinking he had not under-stood their Russian. He acknowledged with another wave as they swept by expecting him to follow. Instead Gudenuv pushed the nose of the Tubeluv down towards the rooftops and swept across the river at about seven hundred miles per hour. Easing the throttle he lined up on one of Templehof's runways and to the horror of the crew of a Jumbo approaching runway four flew underneath it and landed in front of it turning on to the grass as the giant plane swept by. Two police Volkswagens raced to the scene and men spilled out, surrounding the Tubeluv. Gudenuv climbed down and was taken to the airport police station where he asked for the Americans. He knew he could make a deal with them for all the information he could supply. His briefcase full of papers would see to that. Since his first visit to America he had rather fancied the life style there.

Later back at the Castle, Maguire was busy co-ordinating the arrests and seizures of arms. When he got a chance Joe asked of him.

"What will happen to McCall and the others Inspector?"

Maguire sucked at his pipe before replying.

"I suppose that will be up to the Government Joe, they could be charged with treason but that sounds a bit foolish these days, there were no large amount of casualties, no great damage done. I really don't know what will happen to them. I must go now and report to the Taoiseach."

Joe found Jean and Val Nevin. Jean was in his arms and he gave her a long kiss.

"It's all over girls, McCall and the others have been arrested and everything is back to normal."

Jean's face was radiant.

"Great, then we can all go home, I'm dying to see Joanna and Mother, can we go now Joe?"

"Whoa, you had better ask your Uncle he's gone to report to the Taoiseach, you'll probably see him later, would you not settle for the morning?"

"Yes, I suppose you're right, but I'm so excited I know I won't sleep."

They all laughed. Val Nevin was looking a little put out and asked Joe tentatively if he had seen Harry Grant and seemed disappointed when he told her he had not. He was feeling a bit tired himself, so he bade them good night and went to his room. Sitting on the bed he took out his notebook and started to write up the day's events. This is going to be some story he mused. He wondered if he should give his old paper the first option. There was a knock on the door it was one of Maguire's men.

"Mr. Kearns, the Taoiseach would like to see you, will you come this way please."

Joe followed the man. Victor Fitzgibbon was sitting behind a desk, flanked by the Garda Commissioner and Inspector John Maguire. The Taoiseach rose and shook him warmly by the hand and indicated a chair.

"Joe, Mr. Kearns, thank you for coming. I want to express our appreciation of the role you played in saving this country from becoming a Soviet dominated state. Your help was invaluable, Help I might add which nearly cost you your life on a couple of occasions. Unfortunately there is no medal or decoration, which we can give you in recognition of your help. So all I can say is, thank you on behalf of the people of Ireland, Thank you."

The other two men nodded in agreement as the Taoiseach shook his hand again. Joe found himself rather embarrassed. He did not feel anything like a hero. He stood up.

"Taoiseach, gentlemen, thank you very much but I don't feel that I did anything out of the ordinary, anyone would have done the same, anyway its going to make a great story and I'll enjoy telling it, thank God it finished the way it did'

His voice trailed off as he saw the men look at each other. The Taoiseach cleared his throat and looked at the others before speaking.

"Joe I'm afraid that you will not be able to write this story after all, you see this all comes under the heading of Official Secret, The public must never know about this, do you understand?"

He picked up a typewritten sheet of paper from his desk and passed it over along with a pen.

"Please sign your name to that and we will witness it, unfortunately we are in your debt but we cannot pay off."

Joe took the pen and hesitated for a moment then signed. Maguire and the Commissioner signed and the Taoiseach carefully put the paper to one side.

"I will have to ask you Joe, for all your notes on the subject please."

Joe passed over his notebook. The Taoiseach stood up.

"Thank you Mr.Kearns and good night."

He was dismissed. Maguire came out with him into the hallway.

"Joe you realise that there was no alternative to what the Taoiseach has just done, I'm sorry about the story, but maybe you can tell it to your grandchildren. You will be receiving a check for expenses in the coming week, which will give you some compensation. You do realise that everybody concerned with this event will have to sign the Official Secrets form. So its not just you. Look after Jean, she's a nice girl."

Joe gave him a grin and shook his hand.

It was about ten days later. Things had settled down again. The Americans had gone home with an extra passenger in Val Nevin. Joe's old paper had asked him to return and work for them again on an all is forgiven basis and a larger salary. He was on his way to Galway when he heard the news flash.

A ship had blown up and sunk off the Norwegian coast. A British submarine in the area had picked up several bodies. One had been positively identified as Michael McCall, an Irish Member of Parliament, from papers in his possession. There were no survivors according to Captain Peter Pritchard. The ship was taking a party of Irish Socialists to Russia for a cultural tour of that country.

Joe pulled the car into the side of the road and on to the grass verge. He thought of Maguire saying that there was not much point in charging them with treason. Perhaps if he had refused to sign the official secrets document he might have been on that ship too. No doubt it was the same ship he had found the girls on. It certainly had solved the Taoiseach's problem. Then the funny thing about all this was that the Captain's name was Pritchard. Was that the same Pritchard that Joe had met aboard the Colombus. For a short time more he sat there. Behind the fence the placid cud chewing cattle watched. Then with a glance in the mirror he started the engine and rejoined the traffic.

GLOSSARY OF TERMS.

Irish Freedom Army. - Military wing of Irish Freedom Movement, dedicated to overthrow of British Rule in Northern Ireland and the formation of an all Ireland thirty two county nation.

Garda- Plural Gardai. Police force of the Irish Republic. Otherwise known as An Garda Siochana. English translation The Civic Guards.

An Taoiseach, - The Leader of the Irish Government.

T.D.- Teacta Dail – Member of the Irish Parliament.

R.U.C.- Northern Ireland Police Force. – Royal Ulster Constabulary.

MI5 British Counter intelligence Agency.

C.I.A American Central intelligence Agency.

K.G.B. Russian Intelligence Agency.

ISBN 1-41204068-X